Transformational Learning Experiences

A Conversation with Counselors about Their Personal and Professional Developmental Journeys

Edited by Michelle Kelley Shuler,
Elizabeth Keller-Dupree,
and Katrina Cook

Hamilton Books

An Imprint of
Rowman & Littlefield
Lanham • Boulder • New York • Toronto • Plymouth, UK

Copyright © 2017 by Hamilton Books
4501 Forbes Boulevard, Suite 200, Lanham, Maryland 20706
Hamilton Books Acquisitions Department (301) 459-3366

Unit A, Whitacre Mews, 26-34 Stannary Street,
London SE11 4AB, United Kingdom

Library of Congress Control Number: 2016940151
ISBN: 978-0-7618-6807-1 (pbk : alk. paper)—ISBN: 978-0-7618-6808-8 (electronic)

∞™ The paper used in this publication meets the minimum requirements of American
National Standard for Information Sciences Permanence of Paper for Printed Library
Materials, ANSI/NISO Z39.48-1992.

Contents

Preface

Me (EKD) to my counseling professor (and future mentor): "So, in theory, if there are over 6 billion people in the world, then there are really more than 6 billion different ways to counsel someone."

She (professor extraordinaire): "And, at the same time, we are all just people."

This simple, enlightening phrase created the framework for what I would later regard as my humanistic core. In one concise statement, my professor-turned-mentor captured the essence of my struggle. Prizing individual worth-while affixing the human connection.

Fundamentally, if we sit and think about it long enough, we all can likely identify that moment in life when *real* learning took place. Not just content learning, but real, applicable, feel-it-in-our-gut learning, that moved us to a deeper understanding of ourselves and others. These moments unearth our process, they profoundly impact us, and they shape who we are continually becoming. It is this type of learning that transforms our knowledge into deeply relevant experiences. It is in these moments that our personal self and our professional self intersect.

For many professionals, these transformational moments are the birth-place of our life's work. These moments awaken a curious posturing within ourselves of the innumerous ways that we can continue to learn and grow. Concomitantly, for many professionals, it also becomes the pivot-point by which we share our narratives. When we remember those moments of real learning, we care to share it with others. We recognize the fertility of process that occurred within ourselves and we seek to offer that as a gentle gift for others on their respective journeys.

These narratives are singular, individual, and unique. And at the same time, these shared reflections are our professionally unifying connection. They are separable reflections of growth; they are inseparable contributions to our field.

This book is our offering of shared transformational journeys. With contributions from novice and veteran students, counselors, trainers, and supervisors, this book presents an individual and collective conversation of growth-promoting experiences. Thematically, the catalog of lived experiences transitions between three movements—*transformation in life experiences, relational experiences (with self and others), and in training experiences*. We invite readers to experience the three overarching movements as both discrete and inextricably related conversations. Just as experiences that shape the personal self routinely impact the professional self, we acknowledge and celebrate that transformational experiences in life, relationships, and training often hold significant exchange. In fact, it is the symbiotic relationship between the parts that fully reflect the individuality—and shared humanity—of transformation.

Our hope for readers is that in reading this book, you experience the complexity and richness of transformational learning experiences that have taken place for others, and that in this understanding, you invite yourself to a deeper, more intimate, conversation about yours.

Section One:
Transformation in Life Experiences

Chapter One

Transformational Cultural, Religious, and Spiritual Experiences

Ria E. Baker

As I considered this topic of "transformation" in my journey in becoming a professional counselor and a counselor educator, I could not help but think of the word "metamorphosis." It is a word that is used to describe changes in an insect, like a caterpillar, as it gradually becomes an adult. Caterpillars are not the most attractive insects, but through biological changes, they eventually emerge as beautifully colored butterflies. As spiritual beings, we too move through phases of change. Lajoie and Shapiro (1992) describe transformative aspects of spirituality to entail experiences and practices that enable persons to develop transpersonally or toward "humanity's highest potential, and with the recognition, understanding, and realization of unitive, spiritual, and transcendent states of consciousness" (p. 91). I am in a phase of transformation and certainly far from reaching "enlightenment," but I look back now over the past 13 years, from the time that I began my studies in the counseling field to now as a counselor educator, and I recognize the transformative endeavors and encounters that have prepared me for my current work in academia and in community mental health.

My journey into the counseling field began with a serendipitous encounter at a hair salon with the department chair of the counseling program from which I eventually obtained my Master's degree in Counseling and Ph.D. in Counselor Education. I had been involved in Christian development ministries for over 20 years in South Africa and in the United States and had desired to obtain a terminal degree in counseling. This encounter is what I needed to propel me to take that daring step to apply to the counseling program. Little did I know that pursuing a counseling degree would not only lead to obtaining new qualifications, but most importantly would provide opportunities for personal growth and transformation.

When I met the department chair, I had been recognizing the need to obtain advanced training in the helping profession. This encounter coincided with a time in my life when I was sensing a need to change the direction of my career. Some differences in perspectives within the leadership of the church where I was employed, in terms of leadership style and lack of re-sponsiveness to members' concerns, eventually led my husband and me to resign from our positions. Toxic and hurtful experiences ensued after resign-ing from our positions which led us to reevaluate our involvement in this congregation and career direction. It was not an easy time to move away from what I had been involved with for close to 20 years, as my work and my relationships were all connected to one community. But after a few years of deliberation when we recognized that we were no longer in a place that was conducive to our spiritual growth, we left the congregation all together. We continued to provide spiritual support to a small group of individuals who also were "recovering" from their spiritual wounds.

I had meanwhile completed most of my academic work for the Master's in Counseling and it was apparent during the program that many of my fellow students were dealing with their own personal difficulties, such as divorce, loneliness, grief and loss, and some of these issues surfaced as class discussions allowed. A safe place to discuss spiritual or religious hurts and disappointments seemed lacking or it may be that I did not feel comfortable broaching the topic of religion in a "secular" setting. Years later, after obtain-ing a counselor education position at a theological school, I recognized that students who were dealing with toxic religious experiences or were wrestling with their faith, needed a place where they could feel safe discussing these issues. This counseling program in a theological school, that serves a multi-denominational and diverse student body, provided a platform that was con-ducive for students to process their religious or spiritual concerns, as they prepared to enter the counseling field.

The graduate counseling course work allowed me to gain new perspec-tives on life and the human experience and I learned the importance of providing healing spaces for persons of diverse backgrounds. The tedious endeavor of pursuing a master's degree and soon after a Ph.D. led me to new relationships and new communities. One of the communities I encountered was a community of resettled refugees. Unbeknownst to many, hundreds of individuals are resettled in our midst by state programs. I first encountered a group of Somali Bantu refugee women, who had newly arrived to our city. They had experienced displacement due to war and had fled to impoverished refugee camps in Kenya, where they remained for 12 years, while awaiting resettlement. Not only had they been marginalized in Somalia, but even in Kenyan refugee camps they had experienced persecution and discrimination due to their Bantu heritage and were driven to the outskirts of the camps. Having to set up make-shift shelters on the fringes of the camp, exposed them to even more danger and many men were murdered and women raped, as they tried to retrieve fire wood to prepare their daily meals. Now resettled in middle class America, these individuals had to adjust to American life and learn a new language and means to survive. Immersing myself in the community through service and eventually as part of my dissertation research, I gained a new perspective on my life and on the need to explore other cultures and religious traditions and to stop judging as right or wrong, but recognize the rituals, stories, music, ways of relating, that provide healing in other cultures. My dissertation research, which took a phenomenological approach, turned out to be a labor of love for me. After recognizing the gap in community-based social services that address the health and wellness needs of resettled refugees, I established a refugee center to address the psychosocial needs of resettled refugees that were being resettled in our community from all corners of the world. Refugees who are resettled in Texas by state programs, typically receive 6 to 8 months of case management services, after which they are expected to be self-sufficient. The resettled refugees that I encountered in our community were individuals from Africa, Asia, and the Middle East, needing assistance in adjusting to live in the U.S. as they faced linguistic, social, and economic barriers. It also became evident that the mental health needs of this population often go unaddressed and few have access to the resources necessary to address their daily adjustment needs. My interest in better understanding the Islamic religion, the main religious tradition of the Somali Bantu, also grew.

A six-month opportunity as a university counselor in Saudi Arabia, the seat of conservative Islam, gave me a much better understanding of this culture and religious tradition that I could not have achieved any other way than by spending time in that setting. I also obtained a better understanding of the culture shock that one experiences when transitioning from a predominantly Christian society to an Islamic society and vice versa.

A few years later, a mental health institute sponsored by the National Board of Certified Counselors (NBCC) grabbed my interest. My refugee center had been providing services for refugees from every corner of the world, including Bhutan. It fascinated me to think of visiting Bhutan and getting a glimpse of this mystical, isolated kingdom in the Eastern Himalayas. Bhutan had in recent years removed their self-imposed isolation from the international community and had opened up its borders to international visitors and proclaimed a democratic government. Going to Bhutan proved to be an excellent learning experience for me and gave me insight into what older and middle-aged refugees had left behind in the 1990s. It could perhaps give me an opportunity to advocate for them, but most of all, the adventurer in me was prompting me to apply to this opportunity to explore what some called the "last Shangri-La." During my three week visit, I encountered individuals who quietly shared that they had relatives who had been driven out of Bhutan and were now living in the United States as refugees. I learned that the displacement that took place in the early 1990s is not discussed openly in Bhutan. This reluctance, or perhaps fear, to openly discuss this mass removal of an ethnic minority group in Bhutan became apparent when a week later, after my first entrance into a school to provide consultation, a teacher approached me and confided in me that she had relatives in the United States who had been driven out of Bhutan and had spent 18 years in Nepali refugee camps before being resettled in the U.S. This teacher shared that she happened to not be in the South of Bhutan when the displacements took place during those years.

During my stay, more stories surfaced about family members who had been displaced. Buddhist religious practices were ubiquitous and similar to what I had seen in the Middle East in terms of the predominant religion Islam. Worship, prayers, rituals, and monasteries were an intricate part of the lives of the people. Experiencing this aspect the Bhutanese world reinforced in me that "…human beings are incurably religious. For wherever we find humanity—in widely different cultures geographically dispersed, and at all points from the dimmest moments of recorded history to the present—we also find religion" (Erickson, 2013, p. 4).

As an institute participant, I was tasked to introduce the counseling profession to my assigned site. I recognized once more that in order to engage in the practice of counseling, I would be required to gain a clear understanding of the religion, rituals, and indigenous healing practices of this people. Who were we as Westerners to go there and impose our worldviews and practices on these individuals who were immersed in their own unique ways of life and relied on their own indigenous healing practices? This experience, along with my stay in Saudi Arabia, was a realization for me to identify, embrace, and appreciate my own unique healing and coping practices and certainly not to be judgmental of those who have different values or belief systems than I. It was not that I had previously openly looked down on others who were not "one of us," and I had of course learned about having unconditional and positive regard towards clients during my graduate school years, but actually visiting these countries and taking the time to understand and appreciate diverse spiritual traditions and practices, opened up my capacity to have greater love and compassion for the "other."

As a counselor and as one who relishes food for the soul, I look forward to continuing to grow in my ability to better address the needs of my clients holistically. In Thomas Moore's *Care of the Soul* (1992), Moore reminds us of the Renaissance approach that did not separate psychology from religion or spirituality, and Carl Jung's (1973) view that every psychological problem is ultimately a matter of religion.

According to Moore, "a spiritual life of some kind is absolutely necessary for psychological "health"; at the same time, excessive or ungrounded spirituality can also be dangerous, leading to all kinds of compulsive and even violent behavior" (Moore, 1992, pp. xii—xiii). My work as a counselor and counselor educator provides me a wonderful opportunity to continue to explore psychological and theological foundations, allowing what I learn to continuously challenge me toward personal spiritual growth. As I work with clients and/or students of diverse cultural and spiritual traditions, it is important for me to continue to be open to understanding their worldview, beliefs, and values in order to better meet their need.

Transformation for me has come in the form of people and in immersion in diverse cultures and spiritual traditions. I am grateful for the individuals I have encountered along my journey as a professional counselor: professors, peers, clients, and current students, and I look forward to future learning opportunities and personal encounters that will lead to growth. I believe that I have expanded my worldview and grown in my respect for diverse traditions, and contrary to popular opinion, my role as a counselor is not one where I am the "teacher" and the client is the "student," but where the opposite is true. I am the student of the client and the client before me is the teacher or as in other words, as Richard Mollica pointed out in *Healing Invisible Wounds* (2006), when working with culturally and spiritually diverse populations, it is advisable to take on a phenomenological approach, abandoning our currently held assumptions, theories, prejudices, and biases, and "see" what is actually present in our clients, to best meet their need.

It has been an exhilarating journey thus far and as we prepare to meet clients who hope to experience personal transformation, it is imperative that as counselors we continuously seek opportunities for personal growth and change, in order to provide an authentic and accepting platform for client change.

REFERENCES

Erickson, M. J. (2013). *Christian Theology*. Grand Rapids, MI: Baker Academics.

Jung, C. G. (1973). *Memories, dreams, reflections*. New York, NY: Pantheon Books.

Lajoie, D. H., & Shapiro, S. I. (1992). Definitions of transpersonal psychology: The first twenty three-years. *Journal of Transpersonal Psychology, 24, 79-98.*

Mollica, R. F. (2009). *Healing invisible wounds: Paths to hope and recovery in a violent world.* Orlando, Fl.: Harcourt, Inc.

Moore, T. (1992). *Care of the soul.* New York, NY: HarperCollins Publishers, Inc.

Chapter Two

Perceptions of New Mothers and New Professors in Academia

Stories from the Front Lines

Laura Dawson-Fend and Leigh Green

The struggle of balancing motherhood with professional endeavors is well known. Men are expected to take the typical hunter/gatherer role, or in academia the intellectual provider, whereas women are to be nurturers (Acker, 1990). However, since Rosie the Riveter inspired women to join the workforce and then the surge of the feminist movement that led to more women seeking higher education, women often as mothers, have become a driving force in the workplace as well as in academia (Lundin, 2013). But these roles come at a cost for both men and women in the workplace and at home. This chapter will explore the experiences of two new professors in Counselor Education as they have navigated the role of being both professor and new mother. In addition, research discussing motherhood and gender roles in academia will also be explored to ground those experiences in theory.

Social construction helps counselors understand that clients experience situations based on their own worldview and perceptions (Mercadal, 2014). When discussing critical incidents as a mother in academia, and the experience of becoming a mother, the perceptions of mothers are important to the overall understanding and context of our journeys. Matheson and Rosen (2012) explain that in the struggle for work and life balance, the "women who described their current life as poorly balanced described a more insidious balance problem with which to cope" (p. 402). Some of the external indicators of work and personal life balance include family indicators, such as children's and partner happiness and success, and work indicators, such as spending too much or too little time at work. In addition to external, the internal indicators included "quality of their health, a sense of contentment with their balance, and the congruence between their personal values and their experience with their balance" (p. 403). The context of work and life balance, or integration, as well as the external and internal indicators for that balance/integration is highlighted in our personal narratives.

CAREER VS. MOTHERHOOD

Laura's Experience

I am the weird one among my friends because I did not get my doctorate to go into academia; I got my doctorate to change the world. I am also not the girl that found out I was pregnant and got all giddy inside. I love my daughter but when I found out I was pregnant I cried. I was in my last year of my doctorate degree and working full time and it had become evident early on that her father was not going to be involved. I am not a natural mother and to be honest I feel a little betrayed by all the women who came before me and made me feel that being a mother should have come naturally to me. I thought that I was going to travel and save the world and all of a sudden I felt that my life was over and that everything I had ever wanted to do was no longer possible. I had competing voices in my head. One voice was my mother who is feminist to the core, and the other voice was my southern grandmother. My mother would tell me that I can still do everything that I want to do even with a baby, but my grandmother would have told me that being a mom is a full time job and that anything else I may have wanted now had to be laid aside so that I could be "mom."

"Mom" seemed like an identity loss and to be honest I struggle most days with who I am beyond being a mother. My daughter is now 21 months and I have taken on several titles–mom, wife, military wife, counselor, and professor. I am daily trying to define who I am and how I can be the kind of mom that I want to be and still be the person that I was before my daughter was born. I am working to embrace the fact that she makes me want to fight harder for the things I believe in but also know that to do that I have to take time away from her. I am also amazingly blessed to have a husband who supports and understands my need to save the world.

Leigh's Experience

Going into academia was the dream for me. Becoming a mother, though, was also one of those dreams. But I knew that becoming a mother was secondary to my career. I became pregnant with our first child during the second semester and subsequently gave birth during my third semester. My husband and I were trying to get pregnant but it was still a shock when we did conceive.

This was the plan and having a baby was supposed to be the next logical progression in my life. We were excited and nervous and I thought that it would be easy, in typical Type A manner which for me means that it would go perfectly. Plenty of people in my department had children and were professors; if they could do it then I could do it. The day that she was born, a week early no less, we were in the middle of the semester and I was teaching three in-person classes and one online class. I remember having her and then thinking, I need to let my students know that she is here and I will not have their papers graded as quickly as usual as they expected. Hindsight being a reflective concept, I wish I would have taken more time to just be with her. I will not get those minutes and hours back to stare into her newborn eyes or watch her in her milk drunk sleeps. The guilt I felt during that time was palpable, as was a feeling of resentment and an overwhelming sense of panic that I could not get it all done as perfectly as I had envisioned. I felt guilt for not being fully with her and knowing that my students were being nice most of the time but they still needed me to do my job. In the difficult times, I would vacillate between thoughts such as 'why does she cry so much; doesn't she know I am working' to 'why do they need so much attention; don't they know that I just had a newborn'. Then in other instances, I would ask myself 'will she remember that I graded papers with my computer on the boopy and breastfed at the same time or that I hoped she would sleep for a few more minutes so that I could get another paper graded?' I am not sure about her but I will. I wish I could say that those were some of the best times of my life, holding my newborn and being an amazing professor, but I was just doing a sufficient job at both.

But, allowing the guilt to pass and time, it was what I felt that I needed to do to meet the needs of everyone involved in my life at the time. We tell our clients that they can only do the best they can with the resources that they are given and at that point I was pulling on that inner resource of strength to do my best in my situation. My students gave me the grace of time and compassion and I have since given myself the grace to be imperfect. Although this concept of imperfection is ideal, I must admit that it is still a work in progress. Ali, for her indelible sense of adventure, is a well-adjusted and outgoing child who, and I like to reframe our early experiences to reflect that because I was working, has learned to be independent. I managed to complete my classes with high evaluations from very kind students. As I mentioned before, both going into academia was a dream and so was being a mother. Both have been more difficult and also more rewarding than I could have thought by allowing a sense of pride in both my personal and professional life.

Chapter 2

DOCTOR MOMMY

Both of us have experiences with conflict between our professional lives and our lives as mothers. It would be safe to say that becoming a mother was a critical moment when our lives changed forever. However, becoming a professor and fulfilling a lifelong dream of obtaining our Ph.D.s was not only life changing but hard earned. Each of us made choices related to our daughters and our careers that impact how each role is currently navigated.

Women who want to and/or choose to be mothers continue to be torn between the desire of becoming a mother and the assumed pressures of being a career woman. The intensity of having a career while also becoming a mother has, for us, become one of the greatest challenges of our lives, as it does for most women, even the most influential. For example, Marissa Mayer, the CEO of Yahoo, accepted and began her new position with Yahoo right before the birth of her son Macallister. She publicly stated that she would work through her maternity leave and come back full time after only a few weeks (Grose, 2012). She was both praised and shamed for being a professional, particularly about the amount of time that people thought she was or was not being a mother to her newborn. It is this judgment from others that working mothers must struggle to navigate in their work and life integration.

Laura's Experience

Pregnancy, the birth of my daughter and being a single mother were critically important not only in my clinical work but in further shaping my passion to fight for human rights. I am passionate about the world that my daughter is going to grow up in. I was passionate before but now that I have a daughter in the world, I want her to see me fight for others. I want her to see me fight for her. I do not want my daughter to have to worry about so many of the things that I worried about growing up, that I worry about now. The women who came before me left a legacy of change and revolution but women and children about the world still need more powerful change. I want my daughter to have a mother that fought for women's rights to be educated, have clean water and not be raped, beaten and sold as property. I want her to know that I tried to help those in need and that I fought poverty and "isms." I believe in a world without slavery and gender inequality and I want my daughter to see that world in her lifetime.

Leigh's Experience

Becoming a mom and having a daughter, in particular allowed me to become a role model in a way that I could have never imagined. Marissa Mayer made a choice that resonates with me because I also went back to work after only two weeks of maternity leave, of which I worked most of it. I receive so much satisfaction from my career as a college professor that if I did not work I would not be living an authentic life. As she learns and grows, she imitates me and my husband by parroting our words (even the accidental 'bad' words) and gestures. She cannot pronounce her R's at this particular moment in time so I have to just tell everyone that she likes their shirt, instead of what it sounds like she said she liked. I hope that I sell it well enough to the world. So I definitely see the impact that my choices have on her life. Just as learning to spell and count are important, her perceptions and experiences of me pursuing and advancing my career while being a mother is important to me and will, thus, be important to her. My authenticity will be the model through which I hope she feels able to live her authentic life as well. In addition to the sense of accomplishment that my position as a professor provides, my mother always told me to 'not be dependent on a man' because she wanted me to be my own woman without the confines of financial dependency. I see each success in my career, and as a mother with my daughter, as a tribute to her. It is the best way I know to honor my mother and it is the best way I know to honor all mothers, especially those who did not have the choice and fought for the rights that I have as a career woman.

CAN I HAVE IT ALL . . . DO I EVEN WANT IT?

For professional women, especially those who lean towards a Type A personality, finding a balance between motherhood and professional competence can be difficult. Shaheen (2012) found that women who display characteristics of Type A personalities showed greater levels of role strain than did women who displayed characteristics of Type B personality. Women with a Type B personality tended to adjust to work life conflicts with lower levels or strain than did the Type A women. Type A women tended to be more aggressive, competitive and perfectionistic leading to increased stress in both roles as the women demonstrated the Type A behavior to both their careers and family lives. Shaheen (2012) indicated that one reason for this kind of strain is that humans only have a certain amount of energy in a given day and for women who have Type A personalities the task of using all of the energy in multiple roles with a high level of perfectionism is difficult to maintain long-term and may lead to increased conflicts in both their home and work lives. Both of us lean towards Type A as a preference and adjusting to motherhood has caused us to have to re-evaluate our priorities and find a way to make room for growing families and creating an upward trajectory in our careers.

Laura's Experience

I learn more about myself and the kind of world that I want to live in by watching my daughter learn about the world. She views the world as a magical safe place where she can explore, learn, sing and dance all day long. I want more than anything for that world to be a reality and I worry every day because I know she is more vulnerable to all that is ugly in this world just because she is a girl. My daughter's favorite movie right now is Mary Poppins and she believes that there will always be spoons full of sugar and time to stop and dance. She smiles and plays but she also notices the world around her and takes in more than I can ever imagine. What I want her to take in more than anything is the feeling that she is a strong, capable and kind girl and I understand that much of her belief in that will come from her father and me. I struggle daily with putting her in daycare instead of staying at home with her. I have to recognize my limitations and I know that I am a better parent, spouse and human being if I am working full time than when I stay home. I have a huge respect for my friends who are full time moms because that is the hardest job in the world but I also understand that I am not built that way. I need balance and more than anything I need to actively fight for what I believe in; for me and my family that means that I go to work. Yet, I must admit that I miss my daughter's laugh, her hugs and the light in her eyes all day when I am away from her. When I come home at night I know that my time and attention are hers. Being a working mom reminds me daily to be a fully present mom when I am with my daughter and that makes me a more present human being.

Leigh's Experience

My child is one of the most important aspects of my life but so is my career. The struggle to be a star in the workplace and be a star in my child's eyes is tangible. Sometimes I wish that I could be a stay at home mom but then I realize that I would not be very good at that and that I was made to be both a mother and a working professional. I have said multiple times that because of my job as a professor, I am better with Ali. But the appeal of doing just one is certainly present. My parents raised me to be independent, knowledgeable, and strong and in both motherhood and in my career, I can realize those hopes and dreams. I am raising my daughter the same way. I expect her to have her own thoughts and encourage that in her by asking her opinion and giving her choices. Granted those choices are do you want apple sauce or blueberries, but they are choices nevertheless. As she grows and experiences the world in her unique way, I also realize what an impact my actions have on her life. Based on my knowledge of child development, I know that even now she is making assumptions about the world based on how my husband

and I interact with each other and others. As mentioned, she imitates me often. When I am kind to the clerk at the bank she sees that being kind is a value that we hold in our family. So too when she sees me getting frustrated with a motorist she will perceive that as an acceptable value and action of our family. As I continue to reflect on the first weeks after her birth and how I was worried about my classes and students, I am proud of myself for managing to keep it all going and keep all the balls in the air. But I have some regrets and those have changed the way I interact with both my husband and my daughter. To be more present with them in the times that we have together is my promise to them. It is the act of disconnecting such as putting my phone, and therefore my email, away when I am at home with them or when I spend the entire day, again phone free, with them on Saturday and Sunday. I work when Ali takes naps during the day or after she goes to bed. In this primary way I can be relatively successful at this concept of balance between Ali, Wade, and being a professor.

SUMMARY OF OUR EXPERIENCES

The changes that mothers make in their lives and careers are critical to the success of each area. Mothers in academia make choices each day that affect the balance or integration of their work and life. In Matheson and Rosen (2012), "most of the women who were mothers described ways in which the context in which they came to understand their balance was impacted by having children" (p. 404). In fact, in the study one of the mothers noted that she was more balanced in her work and life because her family obligations kept her from overworking. Those areas that were considered balance enhancers included "flexibility at work, setting healthy boundaries, having a spiritual foundation, and positive feelings about their job worth and productivity" (Matheson & Rosen, 2012, p. 404). Another type of boundary setting was speaking up for one's self. On the other hand, balance reducers included bad habits such as procrastination, and situational events, such as the pursuit of tenure. Regardless of the changes that mother's made in their work and life, they still felt that the second shift (Hochschild, 1989) existed. The second shift is the concept that both women and men work the same outside the home but women are responsible for more of the home and childcare than men. Both of us experienced boundary enhancers and reducers in our first few years as professors.

Laura's Experience

I have learned many things from my daughter's birth. I have learned that trying to be a mom, a wife, a counselor educator, a colleague, a mentor and a friend is exhausting. I have learned that I have become one of those people who talk about my daughter all the time and that includes using her in countless examples in class. I have learned that being a mother does not come any more naturally to me than being a counselor educator does and that makes me feel a little lost sometimes. I continue to learn that I am not the one in control. I am also learning that the old saying about a village and a child is very true and as I prepare to leave my village I am a little scared that I may not find another one to help me raise my daughter. As I have become an adult I have learned that family is about much more than blood and my daughter has an amazing family, some who are related by blood and others through love and friendship. I have learned I know very little about being a mother and I need daily help, encouragement and grace. On the negative I have learned that I am very perfectionistic and critical of myself and I need to give myself grace. I am learning that my daughter is not a little adult and it is wrong for me to expect her to be. In the end my daughter will probably teach me more than I can ever teach her about the world and how to experience it. My daughter is teaching me daily how to live.

Leigh's Experience

Realizing how difficult it is to be a professional and a parent has given me much more perspective on what many of the students in our program go through on a regular basis. I am more understanding of life in my classes and have adjusted my syllabus accordingly. Quizzes are unlimited tries and due dates are more flexible than they once were to take into account that children get sick, or they just do not want to take a nap when a student had planned to work on a theories paper, or a student is just exhausted from being a mom/dad and professional and need a nap his or herself. I have given and received grace from places where it has been least expected but most appreciated. From the very beginning my students gave me the grace to grade their assignments at a slower pace during the semester. They did not have to do that at all, as they were paying their hard earned money to learn from me, but they did with such kindness and understanding. Our graduate coordinator, who coincidentally calls my daughter the star and with whom I share a few committees, has inserted his voice to make those meetings start a little bit later to give me time to get there with a sometimes unruly child. Through these brief examples, I started to live by the motto that we all need help every now and again and have begun to truly understand what it means when people say 'it takes a village'.

In addition to finally understanding my need for help from others, my husband and I have made specific changes to make motherhood manageable, and daresay even successful, on a household level. I have had to readjust the way I think about time. I am sometimes up early in the morning before my husband and daughter to answer e-mails and more frequently up late, after

Ali goes to bed, to answer emails, grade, and work on the 'other duties as assigned'. I have made a loose rule that I am completely present with Wade and Ali from the time that I get home until she goes to sleep. Then I respond to errant e-mails from students, texts that have arrived during family time, and tie up loose ends. I like to get things done, hence the Type A personality, where few things are more satisfying than marking an item off of a list and combined with being an overachiever, taking the time to respond to emails before and after gives me a sense of pride in a job well done on a professional level. Being torn between both my professional career and my personal career is most apparent when Ali does not go to school and I am caught, once again, trying to divide my time between being the best employee I can be and the best mother I can be for Ali. Being a mom does not stop and being a professor also does not stop, especially when I teach online. It can be frustrating to have a screaming child and to hear the ding of my email in the background. I know that each need the attention that they deserve and I am still trying to figure out how to balance each during those situations. Even with this small support, I continue to have responsibilities at home that cannot be overlooked such as the laundry, the dishes, and feeding the dogs, as the simple examples among others. I have started to include her in some of those tasks. She loves to pour the dog food in the bowl, as it gives her a sense of accomplishment in herself and it allows us to spend productive time together.

Is it hard to do all of it, yes, but is it worth it? The answer, for me, is almost always yes. The times when it is not yes, is when I am veering away from my goals to keep my promise to be present with Ali, Wade, and my work. I want to make my daughter proud of me, as much as possible, by being there for her but also setting an example that she can accomplish great goals in her life through her hard work and individualism.

WORK LIFE BALANCE

Laurijssen and Glorieux (2013) discuss alternate strategies for making the work-life balance less stressful for women. Their research found that women who continued to work full-time rather than move into a part-time position have more challenging jobs that allow for greater levels of autonomy and allow the women to manage the work-life stress more easily. Counseling and counselor education are extremely challenging fields that often allow for large amounts of autonomy. The daily challenges of working with clients and students allows us to become more empathetic and understanding professionals while the demands create a more efficient and organized professional. This is a journey that will have continued evolution with each stage of motherhood and career evolution presenting both challenges and chances for interpersonal and professional growth.

Laura's Experience

I have always believed that as counselors and educators we go on a journey with our clients and becoming a mother is no different. This is just a new chapter in my journey and with a toddler a very challenging chapter. I am learning that I need to work on my patience and my need for things to be controlled and perfect all the time. My journey with my daughter is full of twists and turns and new lessons daily. This is something I had forgotten a little not working directly with clients. I had forgotten what breakthrough felt like with a client that has been struggling with something for a long time. My daughter and being a mother has reminded me that like our clients are still trying to learn and master their lives I too must continue to learn and master my own life. I have to ask for help and trust others to know more than me. I am definitely not the expert and I am learning I do not want to be. Being a mother has brought me closer to many of my friends and further away from others. Being a mother reminds me that change is inevitable and we must all evolve into better people daily. I am so blessed to have Leigh along with me on this journey. We started out perhaps as unlikely friends but through school, families, teaching and now motherhood have become dear friends and confidants. This, along with the joy of watching our daughters grow, is perhaps one of the best gifts of motherhood and professional counseling. The gift of having someone who knows and sees you at your best and worst and accepts you at both, in the end, is that not what our students and clients need most.

REFERENCES

Aker, J. (1990). Hierarchies, jobs, bodies: A theory of gendered organizations. *Gender & Society, 4*, 139–158. doi: 10.1177/089124390004002002.

Grouse, J. (2012, October 18). *How relevant is Marissa Mayer's maternity leave? Not very.* Retrieved from http://www.bloomberg.com/bw/articles/201–210–18/how-relevant-is-marissa-mayers-maternity-leave-not-very.

Hochschild, A. (1989). *The second shift.* New York: Avon Books.

Laurijssen, I. & Glorieux, I. (2013) Career trajectories for women after childbirth: Job quality and work-family balance. *European Sociological Review 29*(3), 426–436. doi: 10.1093/esr/jcr082.

Lundin, L. L. (2013). Women in the workforce. *Salem Press Encyclopedia.*

Matheson, J. L. & Rosen, K. H. (2012). Marriage and family therapy faculty members' balance of work and personal life. *Journal of Marital & Family Therapy 38*(2), 394–416. doi: 10.1111/j.1752–0606.2009.00137.x.

Mercadal, T. (2014). Social constructionism. *Salem Press Encyclopedia.*

Shaheen, N. (2012). Type a behavior and work-family conflict in professional women. *Pakistan Journal of Social and Clinical Psychology, 9*(3), 70–74.

Chapter Three

Meaningful Turning Points

A Narrative Exploration of
How I Became a Counselor Educator

Tamara Hinojosa

As a counselor educator, my professional development has encompassed training in counseling, counseling supervision, and research. In the following pages I will discuss all of these areas, but because my career entails working both as a counselor and as a researcher, I am going to use a narrative theory, which also plays dual roles in our profession. Narrative theory is both a counseling theory and a research method that focuses on clients' or research participants' life stories to gain insight into who they are (Reissman & Speedy, 2007). In this chapter, I will use two components of narrative theory: storytelling and turning points. I will provide my professional development story while highlighting the turning points that prompted radical shifts in my life course (Reissman, 2003). My goal is that readers will gain awareness of the transformation I have endured to be the professional I am today and ultimately, that I will inspire others to recognize their true potential.

For my undergraduate degree, I was accepted to a great university, but there were many times that I thought about quitting and returning to my hometown. To provide context, no one in my family had ever moved away to attend college at such a young age. Although I was not far from my home-town, I felt like I was on a different planet- academically and culturally. While all of the other students seemed to earn A's so easily, I was behind in all of my classes. I could not make friends and I felt completely isolated. A part of me believed that I would never truly belong.

An important turning point occurred during a simple conversation with a friend from my hometown. He asked me if I wanted to quit college and I started crying. I knew that my loved ones would support me no matter what, but without hesitation I told him, "I do not care if I hate every single day here, I will graduate." He held me and wiped my tears away. I can still remember that day so clearly and all of the emotions of anguish and despair that I had within. Yet, even amidst this pain, I found the courage to persist toward my educational goals.

Eventually I began to adjust, but that does not mean things got easier. I worked and attended school, struggling to pay my bills, while meeting the demands of higher education. I did not have a reliable computer or internet so I spent many late nights in the 24-hour computer lab. But just as I told my friend, no matter what happened, I would earn my undergraduate degree and I did.

I was exhausted after enduring the challenges of my undergraduate program, but I felt like I had this internal force propelling me forward in higher education. So, I attended a presentation in which a panel of doctoral students from different disciplines discussed their academic experiences. They were brutally honest about the rigor of earning a doctorate. In fact, I became both intimidated and curious about earning my Ph.D. I decided to step even further outside my comfort zone and pursue graduate school out-of-state. However, I decided to apply to master's programs first because, honestly, I felt unsure if I had what it took to earn a doctorate.

I did not have a strong understanding of what counseling was all about, but when I began reading the course descriptions for a college counseling master's program, I became intrigued and applied. That decision represented a huge turning point that completely shifted the course of my life. When it was time for my first fall semester in graduate school to begin, I booked an overnight train to travel to what would be my new home for the next couple of years. My grandparents dropped me off at the train station at midnight and it felt so surreal. The city was eerily quiet, which intensified my feelings of doubt. Although I had willingly decided to leave Texas, I now realized the fear I had of being on my own in a completely new part of the country. My grandmother, who had very little money to give, tucked twenty dollars in my bag. I knew that she felt compelled to protect me, but because I had to go on this journey alone, she had no other way of alleviating her worries than to give me cash. I looked back at my family- yet again at a turning point. I knew that I did not have to go; my grandparents would happily take me back home. Instead, I took a deep breath and I walked toward the train station.

As I took a seat on the train, I reflected on the past. Growing up, I lived within ten minutes of all of my grandparents, aunts, uncles, and cousins. Even when I moved away for my undergraduate program, I would return home often to spend time with family. My world was communal and full of loved ones who supported me any time I needed help. Yet, the train I was in was pulling me further and further from that world. Moving forward in higher education, meant moving forward alone and this sparked sadness and guilt within. I had no idea what the next day held, but I did know that, for me, this journey symbolized letting go of the familiar and embracing the unknown — regardless of how scared I felt.

Adjusting to a new part of the country and the demands of grad school was difficult. However, it was not until the last semester of my counselor training that I endured one of the most significant turning points in my life. I was a graduate student conducting my internship at my university counseling center and working with a client who wanted help with anger issues. As our sessions progressed, I learned that she was in remission from cancer, which greatly shaped how she understood her anger. She explained that when first entering remission, nothing upset her. When the grocery store line was long or someone cut her off while driving, she did not mind. She was just so thankful to be alive. She described this time in her life as serene. But slowly, her peaceful attitude wore off and her anger emerged again. These sessions were intense because she felt like she was losing the person she really wanted to be and no matter how hard she tried, she could not get her back. As she discussed how she felt, I could hear the client, but I could not fully understand. Honestly, I felt completely unqualified to be working with such a complex client, but each session I pushed my insecurities aside and focused on being present with her.

Then, I learned that I was at risk of a terminal illness, but I had to wait three weeks for medical test results to know my prognosis. Numbness immediately sunk in. I could cognitively comprehend what I had been told, but initially I did not feel any emotions. This lack of an emotional response scared me. I wanted to feel something, but the news was too shocking. The next morning, however, I awoke with what felt like a ton of bricks resting on my heart and so began the wait.

During those weeks, the ambiguity of not knowing felt unbearable, but I did my best to maintain my daily responsibilities. One day I was walking to work and I looked up at the beautiful green hills ahead of me. The sky was a vibrant blue and the air was cool. It was a breathtaking instant in which I simultaneously realized my gratitude of this world, but also that I could easily lose it all. The first part of my realization was uplifting because my thoughts were focused on the beauty within that present moment. However, the second aspect of my realization was focused on future 'what ifs', which sparked fear. Suddenly I recognized that life experiences are neutral—we ascribe the meaning by the way we think about them.

Prior to this potential medical diagnosis, I was overwhelmed because my boyfriend had just dumped me and I was struggling to meet all the project deadlines required in my final semester before graduation. However, now the most powerful thought emerged; I could be complaining about my ex-boyfriend and graduate school, or I could be dead. Death was no longer an abstract, far off concept for me. I lived with it every day as I waited to know my prognosis. It was with me as I sat in class lectures. When I conversed and laughed with friends, I could still feel death lingering nearby.

With death seeping into every ounce of my life, I now realized that sadness from a break up meant that I was alive. Graduate school projects meant that I had the privilege of earning my master's degree. Being alive was not easy, but it gave me the gift of experiencing the spectrum of emotions. These were not just words; I genuinely felt appreciative for everything, even the things that I had previously viewed as stressful. The events in my life had not changed. The only thing that changed was how I thought about these events.

While I did feel appreciative of life, I still harbored intense pain during this time. When I heard people complaining about bills or work, I felt anger. Those were such petty problems! I wanted to turn to them and scream, "But you are alive!" I tried to engage in meetings at work, but I did not see the point. From my perspective, everything my co-workers were worrying about seemed so trivial.

Thinking of my own mortality also prompted me to do an internal examination of my life. As a first-generation, Mexican American college student, my family and I had sacrificed tremendously so that I could go to a strong counseling program out of state. Being far from home was extremely challenging, but I persisted because I wanted to use my degree to return home and give back to my community. Additionally, due to the unwavering support from my family, earning my master's degree was as much an accomplishment for them as it was for me. My pursuit of higher education was larger than myself and realizing this sparked a deep sense of purpose and meaning.

It was easy to think that with death so near, I would live impulsively, quit my master's program and just have fun. Yet, what I discovered was that more than anything, I wanted to know that I was truly living. For many years, I was always so hard on myself— worrying about what others thought of me and criticizing my mistakes. Yet as I reflected on my life, I saw that life is about releasing the things that hold us back and learning unconditional self-acceptance. That is when I knew that regardless of my medical prognosis, I would complete my master's degree—even if it meant it was the very last thing I ever did.

When my medical tests returned, I learned that I was not sick. I began sobbing and releasing all of my anxiety. It was an extraordinary moment that also marked a momentous turning point in my life. I still had papers to write and numerous other responsibilities, but none of that bothered me because I recognized my internal power: I was alive, I was healthy, and I was cultivating meaning in my life by earning a degree in counseling— something in which I truly believed.

Additionally, I could relate to the client I had been working with on a whole new level. Although she never knew what I had been through, I developed a stronger therapeutic relationship with her because my empathy for her was so profound.

In relation to my professional development, I had a new understanding of the psychological theories we used in practice. Before this incident, I had learned about a range of theoretical frameworks that suggest our beliefs impact our emotions. For example, an important tenant in Rational Emotive Behavioral Therapy (REBT) is that absolutist beliefs, such as demanding self-perfection, lead to self-defeating emotions and behaviors (Ellis, 1999). On a deeper level, Frankl (1984) noted, "When we are no longer able to change a situation.....we are challenged to change ourselves (p. 116)." This quote exemplifies how existentialism promotes reflection of self and the meaning we ascribe to our lives. However, I had dismissed these ideas because they seemed so complex. Although it took a traumatic event to completely shift my thoughts, I learned that if we are willing to reshape our thoughts, we can greatly enhance our lives. With this power, we can foster appreciation, even in the toughest of times; we can create a sense of freedom, regardless of any limitations that may surround us. In fact, I have spent my career in counselor education trying to better understand how to promote this type of growth in the clients we serve.

Before completing my master's program one of my professors pulled me aside after class and said, "You have to apply to doctoral programs and when you do, I will write you a recommendation letter." The intensity of her words took weeks to absorb. After earning my master's degree, I worked in the mental health profession and I tried to forget what my professor had told me. Yet, there was a small piece of me that thought if she, a successful faculty member believed in me, maybe I could earn my Ph.D. Although I did not yet see what she saw, I realized that the only obstacle holding me back was myself and if I really had been given a second chance, I was not going to waste it because I was scared. So, I began the journey of earning my doctorate in Counselor Education and Supervision.

The last step in earning a Ph.D. is to defend your dissertation research to a committee of faculty members in your field. Because my family had played such an integral role in my ability to persist in higher education, I invited them to my dissertation defense. At this point in my life I had earned three higher education degrees, but I had earned all of them while on scholarships for low-income and ethnic minority students. I was profoundly grateful for these scholarships, but I also believed that I had only made it this far because of my ethnicity. When I passed my dissertation defense and my professors called me Dr. Hinojosa for the first time, my parent's eyes swelled with tears and pride in their daughter. For the first time, I finally began taking ownership of my accomplishments as well. For so long, however, I had negated my own intelligence and worth until I was completing the last step of the doctoral program. I wondered what if I had realized this sooner. How would my academic experiences have been different?

At times this question still haunts me and I let self-doubt sink in. As a professor, I still attribute my career accomplishments to luck. I doubt my abilities and I feel like that young woman in undergrad just scrambling to get by. When I start thinking this way, I remind myself that falling into that pattern again will not help me and it will not help my students. Sometimes I have to remind myself of this several times in one day and by openly acknowledging this, I hope I can help others who relate to my story truly accept their own successes.

I tell my story and highlight the various turning points in my life to emphasize that although my higher education experiences were difficult, they have made me the professional I am today. As a professor of counseling, I strive to help my students see how gifted they are so they realize, at an earlier point in their education, the magnitude of their potential and move forward in their careers confidently.

Additionally, because I have fought to be where I am, I expect no less from my students. I expect that they are dedicated to learning course content, but also delving into exploration of their own conceptual frameworks of counseling (Teyber, 2007). When I am helping students develop their professional counseling identity, I ask, "What do you believe is your purpose as a counselor? What do you think it is about counseling that makes it beneficial for clients' mental health and well-being?" I ask these questions because I think, as counselors, we should be aware of the counseling frameworks that guide our work. Likewise, as a counselor educator, when I create a new course and introduce a new activity, I ask myself, "How will this assignment help my students be better counselors?" If I do not have a good answer, then I do not use that activity. I only want to utilize counseling training techniques that have a strong and effective impact on the professional development of my students.

I will end this chapter with something I tell my students all of the time: I am living my dream. I have returned to my hometown and I am a counseling professor and mentor to amazing students. My hopes are that my students will go out and do the same, far exceeding anything that I have ever done—as directors of counseling centers, as scholars, as world changers. This hope completely fuels my desire to persist in my career. I hope these questions and my story can motivate readers as they move forward in their professional development as well.

REFERENCES

Ellis, A. (1999). Early theories and practices of rational emotive behavior therapy and how they have been augmented and revised during the last three decades. *Journal of Rational-Emotive & Cognitive-Behavior Therapy, 17*(2), 69–93. doi: 10.1023/A:1023048830350.

Frankl, V. E. (1984). *Man's search for meaning: An introduction to logotherapy* (3ʳᵈ ed.). Simon and Schuster.

Reissman, C. K., & Speedy, J. (2007). Narrative inquiry in the psychotherapy professions. In D. J. Clandinin (Ed.), *Handbook of narrative inquiry: Mapping a methodology,* (426–456). Thousand Oaks, CA: Sage.

Reissman, C. K. (2003). Analysis of personal narratives. In J. A. Holstein & J. F. Gubrium (Eds.), *Inside interviewing: New lenses, new concerns* (pp. 695–710). Thousand Oaks, CA: Sage.

Teyber, E. (2007). *Interpersonal process in therapy: An integrative model* (5ᵗʰ ed.). Thomson Brooks/Cole.

Chapter Four

History Impacts Reality

How Parental Divorce Affected My Beliefs about
Committed Relationships,
and What I Decided to Do about It

Veronica I. Johnson

As a child, I was a hopeless romantic. I loved watching soap operas with my mom while imagining that I was one of the female heroines, swept away by the man of my dreams. My hopeless romanticism only grew in adolescence, as my diary filled with letters to crushes professing my undying, endless love.

My parents were divorced when I was 10 years old. I never saw them fight, or kiss, or play together. I remember my childhood in segments—I have lots of memories of my mom, and a few with my dad, and even fewer of the three of us together. When I think back, I always consider my mom a single parent, even though she was married for the majority of my first 18 years. As a child experiencing my parents' divorce, I remember feeling forced to choose a side, which was always my mom's, and not really having much regard for my dad, which I am certain was colored by my mom's influence, whether intentional or not. I learned to be independent, self-sufficient, and strong—qualities I continue to value. I have learned as an adult, however, that vulnerability, leaning on my partner, and making joint decisions only serves to strengthen a relationship, not make me less powerful or capable, as I was led to believe.

Observing the animosity that existed between my parents, and knowing first-hand how it impacted me as a developing adult, were the driving forces that led me to pursue an undergraduate degree in psychology, followed by graduate degrees in Counselor Education. I wanted to help couples mend

27

their relationships before they became irreparable, or to help them separate amicably so that their children would not have to experience what I did, and help them forgive. The fact remained that I was still a hopeless romantic, externally driven to help others, without considering how my experiences coupled with choosing this career path would impact my future relationship, and subsequently my outlook on the potential that exists in a committed relationship.

When I was 23, I met my current husband. We had worked together at a local restaurant for a couple of years but never really "knew" each other. One day, he came out of the kitchen into the servers' station and said "Who wants to go to the Caribbean with me?" I was taking a year off between my Bachelor's and Master's programs, and had just been through a breakup, was working two jobs, and felt a sense of freedom I had not experienced before. As a surprise to anyone who knows me, my response was "I'll go!" First, I never thought it would actually happen. Second, if it did, I was prepared to have a firm conversation with him about expectations and clear boundaries if we were to travel together. Finally, it did happen. I never had that conversation, and we fell madly in love in the proceeding three weeks before we went to Jamaica. My hopeless romantic was in full-bloom, and I was certain pretty quickly that this was the man I wanted to spend the rest of my life with.

A year and a half later, during a trip to Alaska, my current husband proposed. While I was surprised in the moment, I was not surprised by his question, as we had discussed marriage and spending our lives together. I was ecstatic. What surprised me was that in addition to the excitement and elation I felt was a profound fear and doubt about getting married that I had not anticipated. What would lead me to believe I could be successful in a marriage? I began wondering what it was like when my parents were engaged, and how it was possible that their love for each other had become so denigrated, resulting in bitterness and vengeance. Who was to say that same thing would not happen to me? I shared these fears with my partner, and his reaction also surprised me. He thought it was the most outrageous thing to even consider that our commitment to each other would not last. I came to realize as I listened to him that I was comparing our relationship to that of my parents, and he was comparing it to that of his parents, happily married for 30 years. He reassured me that we were different, and that just because my parents divorced did not mean that we would.

As I tell the story now, I realize that what we had going for us from the very start was openness and good communication. I expressed my fears; he responded. Responsiveness is one of the three key elements of lasting intimate relationships, alongside emotional accessibility and engagement (Johnson, 2008). My partner had these down. Despite my fears, I was still sure I wanted to marry this man.

Shortly after our wedding, I had the opportunity to return to school to pursue my doctoral degree in Counselor Education and Supervision. Part of this opportunity involved creating and teaching a course about intimate relationships. Another part, as you can probably guess, is writing the dissertation. Some of the best advice I ever received regarding research is that you have to pick a meaningful topic in order to maintain the perseverance to finish it. As I contemplated my topic, I wondered if others who had experienced their parents' divorce had similar fears and doubts about marriage as I did. I also wondered how those fears and doubts subsided, if they did, and what the chances were of achieving a successful marriage when one's role models were not relationship experts. I surveyed the literature on adult children of divorce (ACOD), and I found significant research demonstrating that ACOD in fact do have more negative attitudes towards marriage, and less optimism about their future relationships than adults from non-divorced homes (Gabardi & Rosen, 1991; Tasker, 1992). My question had already been answered. It was a relief to know that others shared in my apprehension and concern about my own potential success in marriage. However, knowing this did not change the fact that we (ACOD) still felt this way, and the research shows that "adults who experienced their parent's divorce may enact a sort of self-fulfilling prophesy, believing from the outset of their relationship that they will be unsuccessful, therefore putting little effort toward making the relationship work" (Johnson, 2011, p. 23).

An important piece of a counselor's professional identity is not just understanding why people suffer, but contributing to positive change. It was not enough for me to understand that other ACOD shared in my apprehension and doubt regarding my own marriage success. Now what could I do about it? As I mentioned previously, one of my doctoral responsibilities was developing and teaching an undergraduate intimate relationships course. My dissertation research examined how completing an intimate relationships course affected students' attitudes towards marriage and optimism about relationships, comparing outcomes for ACOD and non-ACOD (Johnson, 2011). While results were not significant in terms of change in scores from pretest to posttest, there were some remarkable results. On measures of optimism about relationships, ACOD demonstrated slight increases in scores at posttest assessment, whereas non-ACOD demonstrated decreased scores, perhaps reflecting more realistic optimism about relationships. The research also demonstrated that perceptions of family health influenced the way students thought about their potential for success in relationships and their attitudes towards marriage. Students who perceived their families of origin as healthy (regardless of parental divorce) scored lower on posttest measures of both relationship optimism and attitudes towards marriage, whereas students who perceived their families of origin as unhealthy (regardless of parental divorce) demonstrated slight increases in both relationship optimism and marital attitudes (Johnson, 2011). It turns out that relationship education can impact beliefs and attitudes about relationships and marriage, if only slightly—there was hope!

Hope is a powerful thing. Hope fueled my pursuit of a career in the helping professions. Hope drove me back to graduate school and gave me the passion I needed to create a course that could help ACOD, like me, change their "fate." Overwhelmingly, relationship research shows that ACOD are at higher risk for facing their own relationship difficulties throughout life as compared with their non-ACOD counterparts (Amato & DeBoer, 2001; Boyer-Pennington, Pennington, & Spink, 2001; Christensen & Brooks, 2001; Conway, Christensen, & Herlihy, 2003; Feng, Giarrusso, Bengtson & Frye, 1999; Franklin, Janoff-Bulman, & Roberts, 1990; Jacquet & Surra, 2001; Kahl et al., 2007; Kunz, 2000; Wallerstein, 1991; Yu & Adler-Baeder, 2007). What the research neglects to provide, however, are potential solutions to the growing divorce rate in our country. Couples counseling is underutilized, and often couples wait much too long to pursue counseling.

The call that I experienced was to effect change in a population that was ripe with possibility—young adults attending college as freshman or sophomores. Young adulthood could be considered a "critical period" of development—a chance to change or adjust beliefs and values instilled by parents, and develop an independent, informed set of beliefs that can function as resiliency factors. Through my own research about the risk factors of being an ACOD, to the teaching of the intimate relationships course, I became confident and hopeful that, despite my past experience of my parents' divorce, which I had no control over, I could control my behavior in my relationship. I could make better choices than my parents did about communication, expressing feelings, being vulnerable, and trusting my partner. I could put more faith in my ability to maintain a healthy committed relationship than I could in what my past had to say about my future.

I am happy to report two things: (1) I am happily married for 9 years at the time of this writing; and (2) the intimate relationships course is going strong, and has expanded to two sections of 60 students each, every semester. Hundreds of students have completed the course since I first taught it in 2008, and I hope that every one of them has changed in some small way as a result of taking the course.

When I teach about intimate relationships, I always share with students my passion for doing this work and my experience that led to my passion. I also share my hope for them. I believe that many students are drawn to take an intimate relationships course because of their personal experiences in their families of origin. There is a part of them, perhaps, that wonders if they can overcome some of the lessons that their parents never intended to teach them about intimate relationships. I do not believe that parents should stay together "for the kids," and that was reflected in my research findings regarding how perceptions of family health influenced relationship optimism and attitudes towards marriage regardless of parental divorce. I do believe, however, that children need good relationship role models to prepare them to effectively engage in their own relationships as adults. When relationship role models are not ideal, however, all is not lost. In addition to pursuing opportunities to learn and develop new skills, a good partner also really helps.

When I reflect on the person I was when I met my partner and the person I am now, I see some significant changes. Some are due to age and experience, of course, but many are due to my hope and confidence that I will be successful in this relationship, and I have a great partner by my side to help us succeed. My husband jokes with me that "we spend more time talking about our relationship than we spend having our relationship." He laughs as he says this, but the truth is that there is no substitute for good communication, and conversations about relationships are good for relationships! The most important thing I can do to maintain my relationship is to communicate with my partner about my feelings and keep the positivity alive in myself and in my relationship. John Gottman (2007) calls this building the emotional bank account. The more "money" I can invest in my relationship by expressing appreciation and gratitude, and responding to him when he needs me to, the better able we will be to face the challenges that life will bring to us, and to our relationship. I would not call myself a relationship expert. I know a lot about relationships—what makes them work, and what tears them apart—but I still have a lot to learn about how to behave in my own relationship. The fears and doubts, and dynamics that I learned as a child still exist within me, but I am much more aware of them now than I was 10 years ago. Now I know to pay attention to them and commit to making different decisions than what might come naturally.

Being a part of an intimate relationship is a universal desire. My hope is to help young adults develop and maintain healthy intimate relationships. My hope is not entirely altruistic, however. As part of this process I have learned a tremendous amount about myself, and how I can influence my own relationship success. I hope that as counseling students, professional counselors, and other helping professionals read this, that you look at your own histories to find the parts that influence you in various ways, and commit to learning experiences that not only promote change and growth in your clients' lives, but that bring about change and growth in your own.

REFERENCES

Amato, P. R., & DeBoer, D. D. (2001). The transmission of marital instability across generations: Relationship skills or commitment to marriage? *Journal of Marriage and Family, 63*, 1038–1051. doi: 10.1111/j.1741–3737.2001.01038.x.

Boyer-Pennington, M. E., Pennington, J. & Spink, C. (2001). Students' expectations and optimism toward marriage as a function of parental divorce. *Journal of Divorce and Remarriage, 34*(3/4), 71–87. doi: 10.1300/J087v34n03_05.

Christensen, T. M., & Brooks, M. C. (2001). Adult children of divorce and intimate relationships: A review of the literature. *The Family Journal, 9*(3), 289–294. doi:10.1177/1066480701093008.

Conway, M. B., Christensen, T. M. & Herlihy, B. (2003). Adult children of divorce and intimate relationships: Implications for counseling. *The Family Journal, 11*(4), 364–373. doi: 10.1177/1066480703255609.

Feng, D., Giarrusso, R., Bengston, V. L. & Frye, N. (1999). Intergenerational transmission of marital quality and marital instability. *Journal of Marriage and the Family, 61*, 451–463. doi: 10.2307/353761.

Franklin, K. M., Janoff-Bulman, R., & Roberts, J. E. (1990). Long-term impact of parental divorce on optimism and trust: Changes in general assumptions or narrow beliefs? *Journal of Personality and Social Psychology, 59*(4), 743–755. http://dx.doi.org/10.1037/0022-3514.59.4.743.

Gabardi, L., & Rosèn, L.A. (1991). Differences between college students from divorced and non-divorced families. *Journal of Divorce and Remarriage, 15*(3/4), 175–191. doi: 10.1300/J087v15n03_10.

Gottman, J. (2007). *Marital therapy: A research-based approach.* Seattle, WA: The Gottman Institute.

Jacquet, S. E., & Surra, C. A. (2001). Parental divorce and premarital couples: Commitment and other relationship characteristics. *Journal of Marriage and Family, 63*, 627–638. doi: 10.1111/j.1741-3737.2001.00627.x.

Johnson, S. (2008). *Hold me tight: Seven conversations for a lifetime of love.* New York: Little, Brown, and Company.

Johnson, V. I. (2011). Adult children of divorce and relationship education: Implications for counselors and counselor educators. *The Family Journal, 19*(1), 22–29. doi: 10.1177/1066480710387494.

Kahl, S. F., Steelman, L. C., Mulkey, L. M., Koch, P. R., Dougan, W. L. & Catsambis, S. (2007). Revisiting Reuben Hill's theory of familial response to stressors: The mediating role of mental outlook for offspring of divorce. *Family and Consumer Sciences Research Journal, 36*(1), 5–21. doi: 10.1177/1077727X07303494.

Kunz, J. (2000). The intergenerational transmission of divorce: A nine generation study. *Journal of Divorce and Remarriage, 34*(1/2), 169–175. doi: 10.1300/J087v34n01_11.

Tasker, F. L. (1992). Anti-marriage attitudes and motivations to marry amongst adolescents with divorced parents. *Journal of Divorce and Remarriage, 18*, 105–119. doi: 10.1300/J087v18n03_07.

Wallerstein, J. S. (1991). The long-term effects of divorce on children: A review. *Journal of the American Academy of Child and Adolescent Psychiatry, 30*(3), 349–360. doi: doi:10.1097/00004583-199105000-00001.

Yu, T., & Adler-Baeder, F. (2007). The intergenerational transmission of relationship quality: The effects of parental remarriage quality on young adults' relationships. *Journal of Divorce and Remarriage, 47*(3/4), 87–102. doi: 10.1300/J087v47n03_05.

Chapter Five

Life's BIG Decisions

Should I Start a Family
While Pursuing an Advanced Degree?

Angie Smith

Deciding upon when to start a family is a BIG consideration many young adults are grappling with during their 20s and 30s. Teaching and advising graduate students and within my own experience, the developmental stage of starting a family often collides with obtaining additional education and advanced degrees. The stress of pursuing a degree while being pregnant adds a whole other dimension to the experience. This chapter will offer the following structure as helping professionals contemplate the decision-making process:

• a few considerations regarding the balancing act,
• my story and background: having a baby while in graduate school and working full and part-time,
• activities and resources for reflection as helping professionals may be considering a BIG decision,
• tips and considerations before, during and after the decision-making process, and
• lastly, at the end of the chapter, I offer several reflective questions to ponder for future decision-making.

My hope is that by sharing my story, it may help counselors-in-training, new and "seasoned" counselors along their path to consider additional options or alternatives in making professional decisions.

As I describe my story, I will share and draw from my own experience in having two children while in graduate school. My first child was born about 2 years into my doctoral program while I was taking coursework and supervising master's-level students in their practicum experience. My second child was born a few weeks before I defended my dissertation in September, 2009. One disclaimer I want to highlight is that I am not promoting or endorsing the best approach in the decision-making process for this situation. It is my belief that each individual should consider all the options and personal circumstances before deciding whether or not to have children during graduate studies. I hope by sharing my journey, it will offer helping professionals some points to consider throughout this important decision-making process.

MY STORY: MOTHER, GRADUATE STUDENT, AND WORKER

Since I had my first child nine years ago, I continue to reflect on the overall experience and how it has shaped me as a counselor, educator, mother, mentor, partner, and human being. My level of awareness and compassion for others making similar decisions is more pronounced every passing year. The personal insight that came from having two of my three children while in graduate school has been more than I anticipated. As a faculty member, I never anticipated students coming to me for advice and suggestions around parenthood and beginning a family. Nor did I anticipate colleagues within the field noticing the way I juggle multiple roles and directing students to my office to discuss the manner in which I navigated in my graduate program the roles of mother, graduate student, and worker.

My first child came early on in my doctoral program and the arrival of my daughter was one of the most awe-inspiring events in my life. I remember vividly having Hannah in the summer (July 12, 2006) and preparing for the fall semester to teach and supervise three master's-level students. My whole world changed as well as how I organized my time and priorities. My identity was no longer wrapped up and associated with "Angie: the partner, employee, and student", but I remembered, at the time, the huge sense of responsibility I felt to another human life as I attempted to understand my new role as mother and caretaker. I found myself asking different types of questions that I had never considered before, such as, "how long is this meeting going to take, as I need to get home sooner than later to say goodnight to the baby before she goes to sleep?" and "will I have enough time to breastfeed the baby or pump between the supervision meetings, teaching class, and travel time back home?" Some of these types of questions and conversations may take the helping professional by surprise, but they are just a few questions to consider as individuals plan and prepare for parenthood. I have found that many of these topics and questions may not be on graduate students' radars as they make the decision to begin a family.

My story toward parenthood began well before I had my first child in 2006. Maybe others can relate...I am a planner. Thinking about being a mother, despite having limited control over many of the specific details, was a topic I thought about frequently. I truly believe I have been thinking about having children as early as I can remember, as I love kids and even as a middle-schooler have memories about talking to adults about how many kids I wanted to have in the future, the spacing of the children, their gender, etc. Of course, at this point in time, I was considering my fantasy future and had not even considered my future partner's perspective, desires, and needs, but nevertheless in this planning process, I always pictured children being a part of my life.

My partner and I married in 1999 and moved around the country a bit for various employment opportunities. We decided to settle down in the south in a region where there were a plethora of universities and colleges in the area. In moving to the state, a big draw to the area was my interest in attending graduate school at some point in the future and, luckily, there were lots of opportunities for graduate programs in the region. As part of this discussion with my partner to move to the south, we also spent time discussing the benefits of living in a state in the southeast as it related to our, at the time, "non-existent future children." Clearly, my decision-making prior to having children was directly impacted by my and my partner's career and academic pursuits and, potentially, for our future family. We charged ahead with our careers and made the move to the southeast for our respective career opportunities and possible academic studies.

Life was moving along as a working adult. I was working full-time at a private university career center and attending graduate school simultaneously. Overall, life was pretty good, but I could feel my biological clock teasing me and drawing me toward planning to start a family. My partner and I had discussed our readiness to start a family based on several factors, such as emotional, financial, and physical readiness. We felt like we were as ready as we could be as we embarked on the journey toward parenthood. We were not naïve about having children and had heard all the stories from friends, family, the media, and others who offered all kinds of advice from being mindful that we could get pregnant right away to the realization that we may not conceive quickly or at all for that matter. We tried to ready ourselves in the event that we could not have children during our planned time schedule. We heard from others to not be discouraged if we were not pregnant within the first year or two and that it could take time. Additionally, we were well aware and heard all about the possibility of not being able to conceive at all. This backdrop was on our minds, as we navigated this unchartered path, all the while remaining connected to one another as partners, employees, and for me, a graduate student.

In Fall 2005, my partner and I were overjoyed to find out that we were pregnant and would be expecting our first child in July, 2006. Being a graduate student and being pregnant at the same time had its advantages and challenges. One advantage was the almost automatic sense of responsibility and excitement toward completing the degree. In this short period of time, becoming a mother became the fuel that propelled me forward to complete and accomplish my goal, not only for me, but for my baby and family. During my first pregnancy, my hope was to finish the majority of my coursework before her arrival. I came very close to accomplishing this goal, but my plan of study and schedule changed due to some unexpected events within the department. I recalibrated and adjusted accordingly. My partner and I planned ahead to ensure we would have childcare for the baby while I was in class and counseling supervision sessions each week. Our partnership was and continues to be egalitarian in nature. Flexibility became our mantra. We figured we would make it work and take turns caring for the baby, as much as our work, school, and other factors would allow.

My partner and I were married for eight years before having Hannah. Intentionally, we waited to start trying to have a baby in order to settle down, establish ourselves in our working environments, and truly spend time together just the two of us before adding to our family. I think a lot of people thought we could not have children because we waited so long. Part of our decision also stemmed from our calculated decision for me to work full-time while obtaining my master's degree. Since we did not live near our families, we were concerned about having a baby, while moving to a new area of the country, balancing our finances, establishing ourselves in our jobs, and all that comes with starting a life together. Therefore, we waited until after I graduated with my master's degree in order to save up money, purchase a house, and feel more secure in our decision to bring another human into our family and care for a baby. In making our decision, we were very intentional and weighed the pros and cons of having a baby while working and attending graduate school versus waiting until after graduation. We also talked to friends, family members, mentors, and others who shared their perspectives with us. All the while, throughout a several year period, my partner and I remained in communication and stayed connected to one another, particularly as it related to our goals and ambitions for the future. It was important for us to check in with each other to ensure we were on the same page and our plan was congruent with regard to our careers, academic pursuits, and starting a family.

During the master's program, I applied for the doctoral program at the same university. I was delighted to be accepted into the program. At this point, my partner and I began to discuss what this would look like in terms of our future and children. I remember thinking that there were so many unknowns. Given my age at the time, we felt as if we did not want to wait until I graduated to start a family, as I knew I would have to work in some capacity, albeit full or part-time during my graduate studies. For us, we felt we would have more flexibility in our schedule when I was in school, since each class was once a week for three hour increments in the late afternoon and evenings. This schedule afforded me to work part-time on the days I had classes and only require part-time childcare. I worked part-time as a counselor and instructor at the same university I attended classes. I scheduled my appointments and time in the office on the same days I had school in the evening. The days I was not working and attending my own classes, I spent time with the baby, studied, wrote papers, and engaged in academic activities in the evenings and when the baby was asleep. The days were long, but the schedule was manageable.

As I reflect back, the schedule and configuration ended up working out for our family. However, in any situation there are pros and cons. In my mind, one of the advantages to having the baby while studying was that I knew if I would start a new job within the counseling profession, I would need to wait at least nine months or more until maternity leave would be available. With graduate school, I did not have this concern. However, I also did not have a scheduled maternity leave. The university does offer this benefit, but we decided not to use it and continue my studies as to not delay graduation. Additionally, depending upon the job and setting in which I was hired, I was not sure if my schedule in a counseling and/or academic position would initially offer flexibility in terms of hours at home to spend with the baby. I thought I may have more time at home with the baby as an infant with the class schedule and part-time hours. Admittedly, a drawback to attending graduate school and having a baby is that there is little free time and attempting to balance multiple roles was challenging some days. In my case, juggling the roles of mother, partner, student, and worker proved to be challenging when unexpected events occurred in the schedule. For example, one time, my daughter caught the stomach bug the same day I had to teach a class. I took care of her in the morning and my husband came home early from work to care for her while I taught my class. Most days, my partner and I could plan accordingly with daycare and caring for the baby, scheduling my appointments, teaching my classes, and other tasks. We were fortunate that my partner had a fairly flexible start and end time to his day and a generous amount of sick days. Therefore, if the baby was sick and I could not stay at home, my partner was able to do so.

During my first pregnancy, the reality set in that I was actually pregnant and my physical state (i.e. exhaustion) from carrying the baby, while working and studying full-time became tiring at times. The irony is that I was preaching self-care and even learning more about it in my coursework and at conferences. I had to be intentional and remind myself to carve out time for me, the growing life inside of me, and my partner. To keep focused, I planned out my schedule as best that I could to allow for time to experience and appreciate the pregnancy. During my lunch break at work, I would take a walk or spend time reflecting on becoming a mother either by myself or with colleagues. Sometimes I would invite others to join me, especially colleagues who had already walked the path of motherhood. I soaked up all their wisdom and experience as I listened to their stories. I highly recommend talking to other parents in general, especially parents who have experienced having a baby while in graduate school and/or working and asking them questions about their experience and anything that they would do differently. For example, I recommend being intentional about taking care of yourself and carving out time, even in small doses, to reflect on the experience of being pregnant. Thankfully, my first pregnancy did not have any major complications. I experienced morning sickness and feelings of being overwhelmingly tired, but for the most part, I was able to carry the baby, work full-time as a counselor and part-time student.

Our plan was to try to space out our children a bit, so that I would be completed with my dissertation before our second baby arrived. As you may have experienced in your own life, plans are malleable and can unexpectedly change. In December, 2008, my partner and I learned that we would be expecting our second child, Ella, in September 2009. We were very excited, but also anxious about the timing of the birth. I was diligently working on my dissertation and collecting data for my research study. I was developing an assessment instrument, which required multiple steps for completion. While pregnant with Ella, I would often say that she literally "pushed" me through my dissertation. Her little movements were a gentle reminder of our goals and propelled me to work even harder in order to be able to focus on her upon her arrival instead of my dissertation. She had other plans, but with perfect timing. Ironically, she decided to make her arrival only hours after my final draft was proofread and PowerPoint slides edited for my dissertation defense. I left my computer at midnight on September 26th with a sense of accomplishment for completing the paper and presentation materials and anxiously looking forward to some rest before Ella arrived. Little did I know at the time, but she had her own agenda and we prepared to welcome her into the world just two hours after the final edits.

Before having my babies, I was overwhelmed juggling my academic and career lives, but felt like it was somewhat manageable. I still had a little free time to spend with my partner, for friends, exercise, volunteering, community service, and the other parts of life that I loved and brought me fulfillment. After the baby, the feeling of being overwhelmed was an under-statement. The free time that I had appeared to be non-existent, as the multiple roles of partner, mother, graduate student, and employee became all-consuming. Navigating and integrating these roles proved to be a juggling act and a transition that I could only plan for to a certain extent. For example, I could plan for a paper that was due in a month, but could not anticipate or plan ahead for an unexpected ear infection that pops up or an unanticipated crisis with a student that would need to be handled after hours. In essence, my world had changed more than I had anticipated, despite all the well-intentioned warnings and preparation. Despite what felt like my constant state of exhaustion, reflecting back on my experiences, I believe it worked out for the best for me and my family. I believe I feel this way, because I was able to spend a lot of quality time with my children. Some days were awesome and I felt like "supermom", while other days I left either my home, school, and/or work in tears. Despite the rollercoaster of emotions, to this day, I believe my partner and I made the best decision for our situation and family. Our story and situation is not perfect, but we own it and both have grown tremendously from it. For me, I found a well of strength that I did not know I possessed. As I was going through the graduate program, I continuously reminded myself that I wanted to set a positive and healthy example for my girls and demonstrate to them that they have options and can make informed decisions about how they choose to configure their path to motherhood with the caveat that there will be bumps in the road. However, I will be there right by their side supporting, loving, and encouraging them every step of the way. Perhaps one day they will read this chapter. My hope is that it will give them, and others, hope and several ideas to consider about motherhood and academia.

I learned several valuable life lessons through the experience of having children during my graduate program. I found strength in several areas of my life: (1) my spiritual connection through prayer, (2) my partner, and (3) my family, friends, mentors, and colleagues support and encouragement. It became abundantly clear that some days were going to be harder than others, but I find this true whether you are a parent or not. Keeping my faith and praying each day in all situations helped to ground me and keep me focused. I found it extremely important for my relationship with my partner to be intentional about spending time and connecting with him, even when we both were exhausted. For example, taking the time to briefly touch base and recap our day or simply watching television in the evenings together once the children went to bed helped, and continue to help, us to remain connected. Family, friends, mentors, faculty, and colleagues, even if they did not realize it at the time, sustained me, especially in the moments when I needed to talk, an encouraging word, or validation about my experience as a mother, employee, and student. A few of my mentors also experienced graduate studies and motherhood simultaneously. I still remain in contact with the amazing women who shared their stories with me so many years ago. I am forever grateful for their honesty and the time spent with me to share their journey.

REFLECTIVE ACTIVITIES AND RESOURCES

As a career counselor, I draw from the literature and career counseling practice that drives my work with my students and clients. Since work-life balance often receives a lot of press and attention in terms of identifying ways of
integrating all of the roles we play, I offer a few resources and activities that
may serve as a guide for practice and reflection.

The first resource I offer is Crace and Brown's Life Value's Inventory
(Crace & Brown, 2007). The inventory is one that is offered for free online.
Regardless of your decision to have children, identifying and clarifying one's
values at this point in time, especially as a graduate student, is vitally important. The free value's inventory is one of several ways in which helping
professionals can begin to solidify the aspects of their life that are salient and
matter the most. I encourage helping professionals to think about how their
values may or may not shift before, during, and after having children and
throughout graduate studies.

A second activity may appear to be simplistic on the surface but can yield
powerful and tangible results. I have asked graduate students to create a
quadrant of squares (i.e. 4 total squares; two on the top and two on the
bottom) on a piece of paper. In the upper left quadrant, list the pros and/or
benefits of having a child during graduate school. The upper right quadrant,
list drawbacks or potential cons of having a child while in graduate school. In
the lower, left quadrant, share one's feelings, reactions, and considerations
about having a child during graduate studies and any limitations to this
choice. In the bottom, right quadrant, note the feelings, emotions, reactions,
and considerations about making the decision to wait to have a child until
after graduate studies and the limitations of the decision. The students' partner can complete the same exercise and a comparison and/or discussion can
transpire from the content. As the student thinks about the options and has
the opportunity to visually review their thoughts on paper, the student can
begin to identify their values related to the decision, begin a dialogue with
their partner around the bullet points, and comprehensively consider the pros
and cons of having a baby during graduate school and/or waiting until after
graduation. As a side note to this activity, I also have shared the harsh reality
with students that there is the possibility that they may make the decision to
have a child and it can take longer than anticipated or other unexpected
situations can arise. Preparing for the unexpected and creating a "plan B" can
be part of the conversation as well.

A value's card sort is another activity that can be helpful in sifting
through the values of each partner. The activity is to conduct a value's card
sort with the following contexts in mind: (1) as a graduate student, counselor-
in-training, or seasoned professional before having a baby, and (2) as a
graduate student, counselor-in-training, or seasoned professional after the

baby arrives. For the first round, the student can navigate the card sort and select the top three to five values before having a baby. Then, the student can imagine they have the baby and are in school simultaneously, then conduct the same value sort with this new context. Reflect and take note of any similarities and/or differences in the two value sort exercises. For example, highlight any responses that changed and explore the impact of the change(s) as well as identify how the student and partner will address the changes. Ideally, the student's partner would conduct the same exercise. Compare results and mutual and/or divergent values. It can be extremely valuable for the couple to discuss with their partner and other parents who have experienced both contextual factors to gain additional information, ask questions, and gain clarity about their lived experience based on their decision to have a baby or wait until after graduation. Hearing others experiences can provide insightful and useful information to think about in terms of one's own values and, ultimately, in making the decision of whether or not to pursue having a baby while in graduate school.

THE "BALANCING" ACT: WORK LIFE BALANCE

In the past few decades, the conversation about work-life balance and integration has been at the forefront of employment and business literature as well as within academia (Sandberg, 2013). The framework for the discussion often takes the slant of whether or not an individual, particularly women, can have it all. Graduate students are impacted by these same issues, particularly as graduate students are considering balancing work, school, and potential of the addition of family obligations. The decisions are critical and can be extremely stressful for both the graduate student and the partner, which can have a direct impact on academic performance and overall life satisfaction.

Work-life balance has been a hot topic with publications such as *Lean In* and others that focus on juggling the role of parent, specifically mothers, along with multiple other life roles (Sandberg, 2013). With the increase in technology usage and fast-paced nature in which we work, balancing multiple roles becomes the norm or standard routine. Whether an individual is employed in academia, a corporate environment, or any other work setting for that matter, the quest for finding and achieving balance is often a common topic of conversation. Professional development, training, and continuous improvement keep our classroom environments full with students who seek opportunities for growth and an even better future for themselves and their children, including current and future children. In my own story, the idea of achieving balance was always on the forefront of my mind. Currently, as a mother of three young children and full-time faculty member, I have arrived at the conclusion that the elusive idea and notion of *balance* is unrealistic and unobtainable. I prefer considering my story as *work-life integration*, whereby I aspire to navigate all my roles with ease and grace, rather than stress and strain. I find it overwhelming to attempt to reach an unrealistic societal bar or expectation for perfection at all times within all roles. Life is too short and there are truly not enough hours in the day to complete all tasks perfectly and with ease. Even within the research, models are being developed to highlight the notion of work-life integration versus the concept of balance (Sullivan & Mainiero, 2006).

Like in other professions, the counseling setting and environment in which one works can be a strong determinant for opportunities of work-life integration. For example, before joining a company, school, agency, or institution, identifying and inquiring about the work schedule, polices, and flexibility of the job and work environment are important factors. In my situation, I worked for a university and explored the Human Resource policies specific to family and medical leave, sick and vacation time leave, and maternity leave policies. In terms of work schedule, as a prospective employee, it is important to find out whether or not the company requires employees to be in the office from 9am to 5pm, offers work from home options, or other employee and family friendly configurations. Identifying the work culture can help a person to determine whether or not the environment and/or job are congruent with your values, life style, personality, family, and other factors. A suggestion is to explore policies through the Human Resource department and review the company guidelines and standards related to work-life balance. In researching the company, if you do not find policies such as maternity or paternity leave, ample vacation and sick time, etc., this would be a warning and red flag concerning the lack of work-life integration within the environment.

Some employers offer flexibility within the job. For example, an employer can offer an alternate work schedule, job share opportunities, and work-from-home options to support employees to integrate home and work life. One caution, from my own experience, is even if the company offers flexible options, set your boundaries between when you are working and clocked-in and differentiate this time, whenever possible, from family time. If possible, understand the expectations of the employer, plan and schedule your time early on in your job and revisit these boundaries frequently. Bringing a child into the academic and/or work scenario adds another layer of complexity to the situation.

TIPS, CONSIDERATIONS, AND REFLECTIVE QUESTIONS

As I explored my decision to have a child, I experienced many important questions that guided my process. Some of the following items may help others begin asking important questions to help guide their BIG decisions:

1. Prior to making a decision, connect and discuss with your partner the possibilities of having a baby during graduate studies or waiting until after obtaining the degree. Starting a family with a solid foundation and one in which both partners are on the same page is vitally important before moving forward. Explore and write down the advantages and drawbacks with each option.

2. What is your decision making style? What is your partner's decision making style? How have you made decisions in the past? For the decision, who do you want or plan to include in this decision-making process?

3. In making a "BIG" decision, I would recommend thinking about both partners' situation, preferences, work schedule, and other important factors. For example, before having a baby, what is your and your partner's schedule like? Do you and/or your partner anticipate or want to keep the same schedule after the arrival of the baby? If not, what needs to change? Currently, how do you "balance" your schedule? On a scale from 1-10, how willing are you to make a change in your lifestyle and schedule?

4. Do not forget the financial aspects of the decision. Plan ahead as much as you are able to in advance. For example, do you need to work while in school? In what ways can you plan ahead for the following scenarios:

   a. one parent staying home with the child,
   b. full or part-time childcare options (i.e. daycare),
   c. one parent working or attending school part-time versus full-time, while the other partner works part-time, full-time or another configuration,
   d. Consider other viable configures that work for your specific situation.

Plan your budget and discuss your realistic financial situation with your partner. What financial and logistical questions do you need to keep in mind as you make your decision (i.e. budget considerations)? For example, do you and/or your partner want or need to work to gain additional income for your family?

5. Talk with others in your graduate program of study, friends from high school/undergraduate studies, neighbors, current parents and others exploring this same decision who have pursued graduate school while having children. Ask specific questions about their experience, including pros and cons of their decision. For example, what did they learn and, if anything, what would they adapt or do differently if they could do it all over again?

6. Seek counseling and share your concerns, hopes, etc. with a trusted counselor, as needed.

7. Identify or find a mentor who you can touch base with periodically, especially before making the decision, during the pregnancy, and after the baby has arrived.

8. Share your values and goals (both immediate and future) with your partner.

9. Find out your partner's values, goals, immediate, and future goals. Note any discrepancies, strengths, issues, "red flags", etc.

10. Identify your support system while you are a graduate student. In the event that your plan does not occur the way you intended, calling upon your friends, family, and others can be vital to your sustained health and well-being. Who do you consider as part of your network and support structure? Do you want your support system to offer suggestions and/or support you and your partner prior to making your decision? If so, what would this look like?

11. Identify where you draw your strength. For example, when life becomes challenging, how do you tend to respond and where do you find hope? (i.e. through meditation, spiritual connection, exercise/physical activity).

12. Identify your strengths and areas of continuous improvement in multiple roles. For example, what strengths do you possess as a graduate student, counselor-in-training, or new professional?

13. If you decide to have a baby during graduate school, what childcare options are available for you and your partner to explore and consider?

14. How do you experience self-care? How can you incorporate self-care into your life before having a baby, during the pregnancy, during graduate school, and after the baby arrives?

15. What do you envision and anticipate parenthood to be like for you and your partner? For example, do both parents work, one parent work, while the other parent remains with the baby and attends classes, etc.?

16. If considering graduate studies, have you mapped out a tentative course schedule and 3-5 year plan related to your academic studies, including your intent to pursue full-time or part-time studies? Work options? Other considerations?

I felt compelled to write about my story, because this topic has been at the forefront of my mind as I continue to meet with graduate students who ask me poignant questions about how I managed having children while working and attending graduate school simultaneously. For this reason, I find this topic important. I believe many individuals are seeking answers and yearn for a deeper understanding for achieving work-life integration. These types of questions continue to be asked each and every semester by graduate students. The decision to pursue an advanced degree while starting a family is a critical question that should not be taken lightly. Several students who know my story and the fact that my partner and I started a family while working on my doctoral degree, ask me questions about the pros and cons of having a baby while maintaining a job and student status. I welcome these conversations and appreciate the opportunity to support students by helping (oftentimes women) consider the reality of the situation. My story is just one way or approach to the decision-making process. The decision was an intentional choice and may not be the best choice for everyone. I do hope that my story gives helping professionals additional information and aspects to think about as these BIG decisions are made.

As a counselor educator, I feel it is important for me to prepare, share, and engage with my students (i.e. counselors-in-training) about these "BIG" life decisions, particularly during the critical period of time when students are not only learning about the counseling field, theories, and practice, but also about themselves. Additionally, the "BIG" life decisions can significantly impact and even alter a student's academic pursuits. Both roles of becoming a student and parent are monumental decisions and investments in time, energy, and money.

As helping professionals begin to embark on their "BIG" decision, I offer advice. Be gentle with yourself and consider your unique story. Others may have walked this journey before you; listen to their stories, but create your own path filled with memories. Every individual and couple has their own exceptional history and authentic circumstance to sift through in making this monumental decision to bring another life into the world. Give yourself grace and no matter what decision you make, you and your partner should remain confident that you have reflected upon all your options and considered the decision from multiple angles before proceeding. I leave you with this quote to ponder from Elizabeth Stone, "Making the decision to have a child, it is momentous. It is to decide forever to have your heart go walking around outside your body." Wishing you all the best as you arrive at your own decision that makes sense for you and your family!

REFERENCES

Crace, R., & Brown, D. (2007). Life values inventory. In N. Salkind (Ed.), *Encyclopedia of measurement and statistics.* (pp. 533–534) Thousand Oaks, CA: SAGE Publications, Inc.

Goodreads. (2015, March 20). Elizabeth Stone quotation. Retrieved http://www.goodreads .com/quotes/14913-making-the-decision-to-have-a-child-it-is.

Sandberg, S. (2013). *Lean in: Women, work, and the will to lead* (First edition.). New York: Alfred A. Knopf.

Sullivan, S. E., & Mainiero, L. A. (2006). Kaleidoscope careers: Benchmarking ideas forfostering family-friendly workplaces. Organizational Dynamics, *36*, 45–62. doi: 10.1016/ j.orgdyn.2006.12.003.

Section Two:
Transformation in
Relational Experiences
(Self and Others)

Chapter Six

Critical Moments in Personal and Professional Development

Searching for a Sense of Belonging

Charles C. Edwards

In counselor education programs, courses on social justice and multicultural counseling serve the important purpose of educating students about various forms of oppression that impact different human groups. These courses also train students to become culturally-competent counselors (Ahmed et al, 2011; Bell & Griffin, 2007). In this chapter I will reflect on a critical incident that sparked my interest, as a nonWhite member of the counseling profession. After taking my third graduate course in multicultural counseling I came to the shocking conclusion that the required readings did not quite acknowledge my presence as a nonWhite student who aspired to become a counselor. Despite their good intentions, many courses on multicultural counseling have largely been geared at preparing White students to do counseling with nonWhite and other *diverse* clients (Das, 1995).

Consistent with the wider societal power structures, there seems to be an implicit rule regarding who will be counselor and counselee. In my courses there were no writings that supported nonWhite students to develop multicultural counseling skills needed to work with White clients. References to diversity have often excluded Whites, and instead focused on minorities and other oppressed groups. Whiteness is often presented as a *social norm* and therefore outside of the realm of what is referred to as diverse or multicultural (Guess, 2006). This realization took me on a path of exploring the intersection between my nonWhite or minority status and my personal and professional identity as a counselor. The complex intersection of race, ethnicity, nonWhite/minority status and gender produced personal and professional interactions that communicated in varying degrees that I was not expected to be a professional counselor or counselor educator (Hardiman & Jackson, 2007).

THE CRITICAL INCIDENT

With an intermingling of fear and excitement, I enrolled in a doctoral program in counselor education and supervision. I felt it was quite appropriate that multicultural counseling was one of the first courses to be offered by the program. This was my third course on the topic and I was looking forward to learning even more. At that time I was working as a school counselor in very diverse school setting and looked forward to improving my competence in this area. Somewhere towards the end of the course, as I sat in the class, I found myself trying to make sense of my role as a counselor and the hidden messages contained in the course. It then dawned on me that the texts we were using and by extension, the course itself, did not quite expect for me to be a student the class. I asked the professor why none of the required readings were geared at supporting nonWhite students to develop multicultural counseling skills for working with White clients or other nonWhite clients. It appeared as if the course and reading materials all were designed to support White students to do counseling with nonWhite clients. There was the implicit expectation that in the case of multicultural counseling, the clients would be nonWhite and the clinicians would be White. This was disturbing to me because the course did not address my presence and my need to develop multicultural counseling skills to also serve my White clients. The question was acknowledged respectfully, but I did not get a response.

AN EXPLANATION OF ITS IMPORTANCE

The incident was important to the extent that it led me on a journey of reflecting on my nonWhite or minority status within the counseling profession. It could have been a passing event, but there were deeper implications for my questions and concerns. I began to consider ways in which multicultural education and counseling reinforced the status quo that exists in the wider society. I recalled seeing sections in course textbooks dedicated to working with various nonWhite and oppressed groups but none that focused on working with White clients. The message implied by the content and structure of these curricula was that nonWhite persons were not expected to be in those classes or to practice as professional counselors. My interactions outside of the classroom produced more succinct messages that I did not belong or that it was not expected for someone like me, to practice as a counselor.

The incident also allowed me to explore my own identity as a minority person living in the United States. Prior to migrating, I had lived in a society where I enjoyed majority status and privilege. Coming to America to live, work and attend school required me to rethink my personal and professional identity. Prior to the incident there were experiences that caused emotional discomfort but I did not quite understand the reactions I was getting. I did not entirely understand why in many of my interactions, my educational and professional accomplishments were often unexpected and met with varying degrees of surprise. Somewhere in my interactions, the intersection of race, ethnicity, gender and my minority status seemed inconsistent with what I had accomplished or desired to accomplish.

PERSONAL AND PROFESSIONAL IDENTITY DEVELOPMENT: INSIGHTS

The incident and subsequent reflections began a process of coming to terms with my newly acquired minority status and my professional identity as a counselor, and later on, as a counselor educator. I developed an awareness of the various forms of micro aggression that were directed towards me (Wing Sue, 2010). It was always more likely for me to be mistaken for a student than a professor or a client than a counselor. On one occasion I was in the faculty computer room when a staff member challenged my right to be there. I felt my personal space being invaded; he got close to me and declared with certainty, "You are not a professor!" It seemed that nothing about me, neither age, height, gender, race, ethnicity or mere presence communicated to this person that I was in fact a professor. It was very common for me to be mistaken for a student instead of a professor and being required to show identification when my White colleagues were not asked. I came to the realization that the schemas and biases by which some individuals operated were in conflict with my desire to be a counselor or counselor educator. Not all of my interactions reinforced these ideas, however, those that did, caused varying degrees of emotional discomfort. The connection I make with these interactions and my experience in the doctoral course on multicultural counseling is that, at a very basic level, the message that they communicated were quite similar. I did not belong.

Black Male Identity

I also realized that the overt and subtle messages of not belonging in these professional and academic spaces had to do with the fact that I was now a Black male living in the United States. Prior to this, I was a male living in a predominantly Black society. Despite prior knowledge of gender and racial politics in United States, I had to learn new definitions and schemas related to being a Black male (Belton & Don, 1995; Wallace, 2002; Westwood, 1990). Many of my negative professional interactions were the result of conflict between who I was and the prevailing schemas of what a young Black male should be in America. In many of these interactions, educational and professional qualifications were no contest to prevailing stereotypes and biases. I was a trained teacher who had completed a graduate degree prior to migrating to the United States. I had pursued an additional graduate degree, received state certification as a school counselor and went on to complete a doctoral degree in counseling. It appeared that the facts related to who I was, and what I had achieved, had little relevance in these interactions. My mere presence in these professional spaces produced conflict, because it contradicted the prevailing racial and gender stereotypes.

My personal and professional identity has therefore been a complex interplay between, race, ethnicity, social class and gender. Throughout these professional experiences I have consistently received messages that I simply do not belong. One incident that brings this to light was when I attempted to secure a doctoral internship at a drug treatment facility. The clinical director proceeded to ask me which treatment facility was I a patient at before I could explain who I was and my purpose for being there. On another occasion, I was asked if I had insurance and if I had come to sign myself in for treatment. In none of these instances did I receive the opportunity (internship) I was seeking after sharing that I was a doctoral student. I was expected to be the client but not the clinician. The fact that actual demographic data supports the underrepresentation of minorities in counseling may serve to reinforce such beliefs and expectations (Atkinson, 1983; Haizlip, 2012).

Changing from Majority to Minority Status

I have long struggled with the term minority, even before I understood why the term was so troubling to me. I grew up in a society where the majority of the population was of African descent. I enjoyed numeric majority statuses. This status, its privilege and definition changed when I came to the United States. Having spent a significant portion of my life being in the majority I now recognize that I underwent a process of coming to terms with my minority status and the implications of living in the United States (Yakushko et al., 2010). One of the challenges I had with being a minority was the sense that the term came with many negative connotations that did not reinforce my own understanding and beliefs about myself. References to minorities, with few exceptions, were often in relation to inequities, disparities or problems to be solved. At a personal level, I had migrated to America to teach and to complete a doctoral degree; not a lot of what I learned about minorities reinforced my dreams and aspirations.

Professional and academic settings allowed me to learn more about what it meant to be a minority in America. In many of these settings, aggregated data that reflected the plight of minority communities were presented. While this was important in sensitizing individuals to harsh realities faced by minorities, they reinforced the narrative of minority as a problem. Throughout this experience, there was a process of making sense of who I was as an individual in relation to existing realities and conceptions of minorities in the United States.

Racial identity, ethnicity, gender and social class were all factors that I processed along with my newly ascribed minority status. I therefore learned about what it meant to be a Black male, and again this identity when presented in academic and professional settings was often saturated with problems. The awareness that I was often viewed as the 'other' in professional settings led me to later explore what parts of my identity supported a determination to succeed.

The Immigrant Identity

One aspect of my identity that remained solid throughout this process was the fact of being an immigrant. I was an immigrant person with dreams of being successful in America. Pursuing and achieving those dreams meant resisting societal definitions that were inconsistent with goal attainment. My experiences in the last ten years of migrating to the United States are littered with instances where I was a minority person who was not performing by the societal stereotypes. In one instance, I was a young 26 year old professional who enrolled in a six week professional development course for teachers. The course was taught in a predominantly White community. I was in the company of ten middle aged White women who struggled throughout the entire course to understand why I was there. It seemed nothing that they had learned about young Black males had prepared them to accept my presence in the professional development course. Their interactions with me were characterized by suspicious inquiries about who I was, what I had studied, and my qualifications as a teacher. Having reflected in this experience, it seems clear that the most enduring part of my complex identity was the fact that I was an immigrant. The immigrant identity has sustained me throughout the years; it provided insulation from the problem saturated identities that were ascribed to me, when I came to the United States (Deaux et al, 2007; Lee, 2005).

CONCLUSION

Das (1995) highlighted the need to expand the narrow definitions of multi-cultural counseling and practice to include nonWhite groups:

Because these definitions (multicultural counseling) are formulated in general terms, they do not tell much about the real world of multicultural counseling, which, given the demographics of the profession in the United States, primarily means White middle-class counselors working with minority group clients or with international students from developing and nondeveloped countries. Other examples of multicultural counseling should include (a) an ethnic minority counselor counseling a White client, (b) an ethnic minority counselor working with a client belonging to a different ethnic minority group, or (c) any other dyadic combination in which the client and the counselor come from markedly different cultural backgrounds, on the basis of social class, sexual orientation, or disability (p. 45).

Das's (1995) vision of a more inclusive approach to multicultural counseling remains relevant today. The intolerant reactions to my presence in academic and professional spaces collectively communicated messages of my status as 'the other', and therefore a person who did not belong. These messages varied in form, content, intensity, consequences and were often contextual (Hardiman & Jackson, 2007). Prior to that incident in the doctoral class, I had been experiencing far more than I was able to make sense of. In reflection, it was important for me to recognize and come to terms with the hidden and explicit messages that conflicted with my desired academic and career goals. I was going through a developmental process that involved, either adapting to, or resisting new schemas and stereotypes. Recognizing the pervasive nature of these messages, and being able to continuously find strategies to resist them were important aspects of the process. I continue to work in the areas of counseling and counselor education and therefore, this process is ongoing. The process is now characterized by insight, intentionality and continuous learning. The hope is that the discourse on multicultural counseling will make greater strides towards the inclusion of all individuals and groups, as both counselors and counselees.

REFERENCES

Atkinson, D., (1983), Ethnic minority representation in counselor education. *Counselor Ed & Supervision, 23*: 7–19. doi: 10.1002/j.1556–6978.1983.tb00583.x.

Bell, L. A., & Griffin, P. (2007). Designing social justice education courses. *Teaching for diversity and social justice*. In M. Adams, L. Bell, & P.Griffin (Eds.), Teaching diversity and social justice (67–87).New York, NY: Routledge.

Belton, Don, ed. (1995) Speak My Name: Black Men on Masculinity and the American Dream. Beacon Press Boston, MA.

Das, A. K. (1995), Rethinking Multicultural Counseling: Implications for Counselor Education. *Journal of Counseling & Development, 74*: 45–52. doi: 10.1002/j.1556–6676.1995.tb01 821.x.

Deaux, K., Bikmen, N., Gilkes, A., Ventuneac, A., Joseph, Y., Payne, Y. A., & Steele, C. M. (2007). Becoming American: Stereotype threat effects in Afro-Caribbean immigrant groups. *Social Psychology Quarterly, 70*(4), 384–404.

Guess, T. J. (2006). The social construction of whiteness: Racism by intent, racism by consequence. Critical Sociology, *32*(4), 649–673.

Haizlip, B. N. (2012). Addressing the underrepresentation of african-americans in counseling and psychology programs. *College Student Journal, 46*(1), 214–222.

Hardiman, R., Jackson, B., & Griffin, P. (2007). Conceptual foundations for social justice education. In M. Adams, L. Bell, & P.Griffin (Eds.), *Teaching diversity and social justice* (35–66). New York, NY: Routledge.

Lee, R. M. (2005). Resilience against discrimination: ethnic identity and other-group orientation as protective factors for Korean Americans. *Journal of Counseling Psychology, 52*(1), 36.

Wallace, M, (2002). *Constructing the Black Masculine: Identity and Ideality in African American Men's Literature and Culture, 1775–1995*. Duke University Press. Durham, NC.

Westwood, Sallie. "Racism, Black Masculinity and the Politics of Space." In Hearn, Jeff and David Morgan, eds. Men, Masculinities & Social Theory. London: Unwin Hyman, 1990.

Sue, D. W. (2010). Microaggressions in everyday life: Race, gender, and sexual orientation. John Wiley & Sons.

Yakushko, O., (2009). Xenophobia: Understanding the roots and consequences of negative attitudes toward immigrants. *The Counseling Psychologist, 37*(1), 36–66. doi:10.1177/0011000008316034.

Yakushko, O., Mack, T., Iwamoto, D., (2010) Minority Identity Development Model in *Encyclopedia of cross-cultural school psychology*, pp 627–629.

Chapter Seven

From the Inside Out

Dealing Effectively with Client Anger

Kevin A. Fall

Anger is an emotion that evokes a wide range of intra and interpersonal reactions. In my almost twenty years as a counselor and counselor educator, there are few other emotions that stir my students and clients as much as anger. Common responses from students, supervisees and colleagues when the topic of client anger comes up includes, "I don't do well with angry people", "Anger is scary because you never know what is going to happen", or "I get scared and defensive when people get angry with me". Much like these responses, I, too, was initially uncomfortable with the notion of having an angry client, but then I encountered Billy and I was given an opportunity to expand and change my perspective on anger. In this chapter, I would like to present a structure for understanding anger and provide a critical incident of my own learning that transformed my understanding of the dynamics of anger and my effectiveness in working with intense emotions.

So what is anger and why do clients and counselors alike seem to struggle with this emotion? Kassinove and Sukhodolsky (1995) define anger as, "a negative, phenomenological (or internal) feeling state associated with specific cognitive and perceptual distortions and deficiencies (e.g. misappraisals, errors, and attributions of blame, injustice, preventability, and/or intentionality), subjective labeling, physiological changes, and action tendencies to engage in socially constructed and reinforced organized behavioral scripts" (p.7). While that definition might seem overwhelming, the primary thrust is that anger arises from the subjective experience of each person and these perceptions impact and influence behavior. The focus on internal processes is vital, as it provides a signpost to help practitioners know where to start when processing anger. However, focusing on the phenomenology of the client only gives half of the story. To be effective in working with anger, mental health practitioners must be in tune with the client's world, while also understanding their own personal reaction to the client's anger. I first learned the difficulty of walking the tightrope of the intersection of client and counselor responses to anger from Bobby, an adolescent client.

Bobby was a 14-year-old boy who came to counseling due to issues related to school avoidance. Our first session together was fairly typical of first sessions with adolescents; he was guarded, and I was patient. Over the next few weeks we developed a comfortable rapport and he gradually opened up revealing his world. I learned that his home life was less than ideal, despite the façade of perfection that was shown to the public. His mother and father's relationship was falling apart, leading the father to avoid home and the mother to cling to Bobby. Bobby confessed he often felt scared for his mom and worried that she might be sad or lonely while he was at school. It seemed that his school avoidance coincided with his feelings of concern for his mother and would precipitate somatic complaints that would allow him to leave school and be at home, close to mom. As we worked through the dynamics of the mother-son relationship, I noticed Bobby was not as eager to talk about his dad. As time went on, the subject became the proverbial elephant in the room; the steps we had to take to maneuver around the obvious became almost ridiculous. Finally, I stated, "Bobby, we've done quite a bit of good work on the relationship between you and your mom, but we haven't really touched on how you feel about your dad. In fact, you seem to want to purposefully not talk about him." He replied with his usual deflection, "That's not true. There's nothing to talk about." I persisted and upped the ante, "Well, he is an important figure in your life, but I know he's not around much. I am guessing that his absence bothers you, but maybe you don't want to talk about it because you feel like there is nothing you can do about it." My simple interpretation was meant to push a little deeper, but I was not prepared for the well of emotion that was lurking underneath. "Fuck you!", Bobby exploded, "What do you know about him or me or anything?" I felt overwhelmed by his anger, which is something that I had not felt within our relationship up to that point. I immediately felt I had done something wrong and was aware of a pressing urge to both make it right and defend myself, but I took a deep breath and reflected, "You feel I don't understand the relationship." He replied, "You don't understand anything! You don't care about me." I was aware that I was fighting two urges within myself. One was the initial pull to defend myself and make the anger go away; the other was curious about the anger and wanted to know more of what was behind the intense emotion. My reply was a cautious intermediary between the two, "You feel angry because I don't understand and believe I am intruding on something important and perhaps painful to you." At that point he glared at me and threw the pencil he was holding. It went flying past my arm and broke against the wall behind me. I am sure the shock registered on my face and I believe it reflected his own reaction, but I quickly recovered and felt the need to set a limit. "Bobby, I am ok with you being angry at me, but throwing things at me is not acceptable." There was something in what I said that pierced him and he began to tear up and muttered, "I'm done. Coming here was a mistake. Bye." I followed him out the door and said I would see him next week. He did not reply as he shut the door behind him.

Once he left the office, I felt exhausted. My mind raced with all the layers of the events that had unfolded over a fairly brief 40 minute session. I have learned to rely on consultation when I have experienced a trying session, so I called a colleague to process the events. As I let the dialogue unfold, I realized that three levels were at work here. First, my own perception and reaction to anger, second, the client's use of anger, and lastly the consultant's interpretation of the events, which was interestingly enough, filtered through his own experience of anger.

In the consultation session, once my colleague heard about the client's anger, he said, "Before we go any further, tell me about your perspective on anger. How do you normally handle anger in your life?" While this question initially frustrated me because I wanted to talk about Bobby, not myself, I soon realized its importance to this process. One's internal responses to intense emotions are largely framed by one's experiences with those emotions. In my life, anger was not necessarily something to avoid. However, it usually triggered within me a personalization of the other person's anger, a feeling that I did something wrong and therefore, must "fix" the other person's anger. In processing this with my colleague, I was aware of the pull to feel responsible for Bobby's anger and that pull made me want to try to make him feel better. We were able to find examples of how I was responding to the client, not from the client's perspective, but my own interpretation of anger.

Personalizing the anger is not the only response. In fact, others may respond with their own anger (the fight fire with fire method), which escalates the conflict. In my experience, the most common response to anger is fear. As a counselor educator, in discussions about anger in supervision sessions, I am struck by how many counselors are terrified of their client's anger. This reaction tends to produce behaviors that steer away from all deep emotions, or explore only those that do not have the taint of anger or aggression. In these cases, counselors rob their clients of growth opportunities as they potentially cordon off fertile areas for change.

Regardless of a person's approach to anger, it is the responsibility of every counselor to do the introspective work necessary for understanding one's personal experience of anger. This self awareness will provide the insight needed to respond to the client's anger in a productive manner. In the case of Bobby, knowing that I would personalize the anger allowed me to

inwardly acknowledge that desire and take that perspective into consideration as I crafted my response. In so doing, I was able to consider what part of
the client's anger could be owned by me, but also gave me the balance to
consider that maybe it was coming from somewhere else.

That "somewhere else" is the client's own use of anger. As I mentioned,
the intensity was not characteristic of the work we had done and seemed to
erupt when I began to probe the depths of his relationship with his father. It
made sense that he would harbor some anger towards his father, considering
the distance between them, but why did he explode at me? I had my own
theories about this, but these ideas were clouded by my personalization of his
anger. Once the consultation helped me understand my own filter, the
client's use of anger became clearer. I asked my colleague, "Why me and
why now?" We explored the context of the incident and the possible answers
emerged. Why me and why now? One possibility was that I was a safe target
of his anger. His father was disengaged and not willing to have any authentic
contact with Billy, much less process anger appropriately. Our therapeutic
rapport was strong enough and the work had gone deep enough to bring the
issue to the forefront. Could it be that Billy was using the counseling relationship to safely experiment with his expression and working through of
anger? If so, responding to the anger in a constructive way was the most
important aspect of the work. This insight allowed me to analyze the session
from this hypothesis and identify the moments when I was able to provide a
safe container for his anger. I had some confusion about my boundary setting
when he threw the pencil at me. Did I reject him by setting this limit?
Perhaps, but limits can also be vital in the creation of safety. I did not want
Billy to think that my acceptance of anger had no limits, and personal safety
seemed an appropriate and genuine boundary to set. My colleague remarked
that the experience of the limit might be a good topic to discuss with Billy
during the next session.

The last layer to consider is the experience of anger that the consultant is
bringing to the conversation. If a counselor is going to go to the trouble of
accessing an outside perspective, it is good practice to know what filters the
person is using, especially in the case of processing anger. I had not thought
of the importance of the consultant's view until he asked me about my own
experience with anger. Once we finished discussing my foundation, I asked
him about his own view and it helped set the stage based on mutual awareness. If the consultant would have responded, "Oh I don't think about anger
that much" or "Yikes! I think anger is so destructive" then that would be a
cue to get another consultant for this issue. By exploring both the internal
(my own) and external (client and consultant), I felt a deeper level of understanding of what has transpired in that intense interchange, and I had many
avenues to explore should he return to counseling. He called me the next day
and apologized for his explosion. I told him he did not have to apologize for

his anger and that I actually saw it as a courageous act that he felt comfortable enough to share that part of himself with me. I added that I hoped he would come back the next week so we could continue our work together. When he did return the next week, I took the opportunity to explore what had happened and shared with him the awareness I had gained through consultation. Initially, he resisted talking about it saying, "It was nothing", but I persevered and he gradually began to explore with me. The outcome of this dialogue was what I believe he wanted in the first place: an authentic and safe place to process the anger inside him and to resolve some of it within a relationship.

In reflecting on this case, it had a deep impact on me in several ways. First and foremost, it provided me with an intense, here and now experience of the benefit of processing anger on multiple levels; that of the client, the counselor, and outside observer (consultant). Each view provided a deeper layer of the anger, its purpose and possible learning moments, not only for the client, but also for me. If the self is a valuable tool of the counselor, then processing anger in this way allows for the honing of that tool. There is a certain sense of comfort knowing that I have that tool (self) always available to me. As I have become more comfortable with the use of self in the processing of anger, I have found that my anxiety about client anger has greatly decreased and my need to "fix" it has also given way to a more productive and collaborative approach to the issue. In fact, I began to actively seek out clients who were struggling with intense manifestations of anger. My comfort level allowed me to create a safe place for them to express their anger and then move beyond the anger and into deeper issues. In my change process, I now see anger as an intense energy that should not be diminished, but instead, understood and channeled in a way that the energy can be used to motivate change.

As a result, in all of my work with clients and in teaching about counseling, I use this multi-level approach to help all gain a greater understanding of the current issues faced in the counseling session. When talking with students about anger, we do process ways of understanding the many possible phenomenological frames of the client's anger, but we also take time to introspect about each student-counselor's subjective reaction to that anger and explore how that reaction can impact the flow of the counseling. It also provides an opportunity to tie in the utility of consultation to provide another perspective on the experience.

REFERENCES

Kassinove, H., & Sukhodolsky, D.G. (1995). Anger disorders: Basic science and practice issues. In H. Kassinove (Ed.), *Anger disorders* (pp. 1-26). New York: Taylor and Francis.

Chapter Eight

Becoming a Puerto Rican Counselor

How My Twins Served as My Ethnic Mirrors

Anna Flores Locke

As a Latina doctoral student in counselor education at a predominately White academic institution, and as a married, middle-class mother of two-year-old twins living in a White suburb, I have experienced racialized critical moments that have served as transformative shifts in my development as a woman, mother, and counselor. This chapter will describe some of these critical incidents and explain how these events shifted my ethnic, personal, and professional development in transformative ways.

MY ETHNIC IDENTITY

My parents immigrated to the United States at a young age and were quite acculturated to the White-American culture, therefore, growing up, my parents spoke English at home, fed me baked potatoes, instead of rice and beans, and sent us to Catholic schools. My father taught us English, the value of hard work, individualism, and competition, which are typical White-American values (Katz, 1985) and made sure that we attended classical concerts, as a way of "getting culture", as if Puerto Rican culture was not "culture".

The one day of the year that I played the role of an *orgullo Puertoriqquena* (a proud Puerto Rican) was during the annual Chicago Puerto Rican parade. I donned my straw hat, Puerto Rican flag t-shirt, and yelled, "*Viva, Puerto Rico*". What was I doing? I was a White-American kid growing up in Chicago. I did not grow up hearing *Sabado Gigante* (Spanish talk show) in the background on the television; instead my mom watched soap operas, like

General Hospital. In every way, I was assimilated into the White-American culture. However, I was taught and upheld certain Latino cultural values, such as: (a) familismo, (b) personalismo, and (c) marianismo. For me, these contradictory messages, to be as White-American as possible, while upholding these Latino cultural values created a confusing situation.

It made me unsure of my ethnic identity and insecure in my sense of personal connection to either of the two ethnic identities. Growing up in this environment made me feel less grounded or rooted in a personal sense of ethnic identity and made me susceptible to external influences of what I should ethnically identify as—White or Puerto Rican.

I struggled with identifying as Puerto Rican and as White-American because I did not feel that I belonged to either. Learning about the Latino cultural values of familismo, personalismo, and marianismo made my lived experience as a White-American different from other White-Americans. I valued family, harmonious relationships, and self-sacrifice. For example, unlike most of my White-American peers who moved away from home for college, I did not. I could not leave my family and my father reinforced this belief and did not encourage me to move away for college. I found it hard to be assertive and to disappoint others. Still to this day, I sacrifice my needs for the sake of my children and family. These behaviors made me more Puerto Rican than White-American.

LATINO CULTURAL VALUES

Being Puerto Rican meant that I believed and valued familismo, personalismo, and marianismo, amongst other prominent Latino cultural values. Familismo refers to a preference to maintain a close connection to family, and emphasizes interdependence, cohesiveness, and cooperation amongst family members. Personalismo, or valuing and building interpersonal relationships where there is a great deal of emotional investment, is part of the collectivistic worldview of Latinos. Marianismo is the concept that suggests that girls must grow up to be pure, long-suffering, nurturing, pious, virtuous, and humble, like the Virgin Mary (Santiago-Rivera, Arredondo, & Gallardo-Cooper, 2002).

Familismo is a defining concept of the Latino culture, and has three components: (a) family obligations, (b) perceived support, and (c) that family members serve as role models (Miranda, Bilot, Peluso, Berman, & Van Meek, 2006). Here is a deep sense of family obligation that overshadows individual needs and maintains the family's harmony, which stems from a collectivist worldview (Guarnero & Flaskerud, 2008; Sager, Schlimmer, & Hellman, 2001; Santiago-Rivera, Arredondo, & Gallardo-Cooper, 2002). Family members may feel that they represent more than just themselves and desire to stay close to the family (Gloria & Castellanos, 2006; Lineros & Hinojosa, 2013). The family is the source of emotional and economic support, and is grounded with a sense of *orgullo* (pride), *dignidad* (dignity), *confianza* (trust and intimacy), and *respeto* (respect) (Falicov, 2010; Guarnero, 2007). Many times, I felt supported and loved by my family and nurtured. Other times I felt too overcome by the family's needs and my obligation to work at a young age to help support myself. As a highly acculturated Puerto Rican, I also received messages from the mainstream White-American culture to be independent from family and self-focused. Since I was bicultural, these conflicting messages coalesced into a more helpful one. I am both family-oriented and independent. I have learned to assert my needs and to maintain a healthy distance from family obligations, while retaining trust and respect from my family. I have done this by valuing my familial relationships.

Personalismo, or valuing and building interpersonal relationships where there is a great deal of emotional investment, is part of the collectivistic worldview of Latinos. Since lifelong relationships of mutual dependency and closeness are valued, positive interpersonal and social skills are valued (Santiago-Rivera, Arredondo, & Gallardo-Cooper, 2002). For example, the behavior of *simpatia*, or being charming and sociable, is a reinforced social behavior in Latino families; it may become less important when interacting with people from other cultures and more salient when interacting with other Latinos (Santiago-Rivera, Arredondo, & Gallardo-Cooper, 2002). For instance, I tend to smile often especially in situations that make me nervous. For some individuals, my smiling has been called into question and I have been asked why I smile so much and to "take that smirk off [my] face." For others, my smiling is well-received and adds to a sense of connection.

Females are taught to follow the concept of *marianismo*. This concept suggests that girls must grow up to be pure, long-suffering, nurturing, pious, virtuous, and humble, like the Virgin Mary. Following this concept, some mothers are seen as selfless, self-sacrificing, and nurturing individuals who provide the spiritual strength for the family (Santiago-Rivera, Arredondo, & Gallardo-Cooper, 2002). For me, being a Latina woman meant that I had to put the needs of my family before my needs, that I had to be obedient and selfless, and non-complaining. Even though I have a strong feminist spirit and reject oppressive gender roles, I had to comply in order to maintain the harmony of my family and receive the approval of my parents. As a young woman, I lacked self-confidence and self-esteem.

I felt ashamed to say that I was Puerto Rican because of the erroneous beliefs and viewpoints that I had accepted about Puerto Ricans. I did not want to be "that" loud and lazy Puerto Rican woman who was objectified for her beauty and subjected to oppressive gender roles. As someone who identified as a White-American, I wanted to be independent, successful, and educated, and assimilate into the White-American culture. I wanted to belong to the privileged racial group to avoid oppression. It was easier, or so I thought.

MY ETHNIC IDENTITY DEVELOPMENT

Three years ago, I entered a doctoral program as the only Latina in my cohort of 10 other students. During my first year of academic studies, I was fully immersed in the experience as a doctoral fellow and volunteer in professional organizations. During this first year, I was involved in leadership and was one of a few ethnic minority members on various committees. In many ways, I was the token minority (Flores Neimann, 1999) and sought to live up to the expectations that I must be the perfect student and ethnic enough to represent diversity in the classroom and on the committees. For this first year, that is exactly what I did; I lived up to expectations of being the token Latina in the graduate program. I was agreeable, friendly, accommodating, and academically successful. When necessary to demonstrate ethnic diversity, I self-identified as Puerto Rican, but racially White. According to Ruiz' (1990) model of Latino ethnic identity development, I was in the first stage of development, since I ignored my Puerto Rican heritage.

Ruiz (1990) posited five stages of Latino ethnic identity development. The first stage, causal stage, is a time when a Latino person is humiliated by dominant environment messages that ignore, negate, or denigrate Latino heritage. A person in this stage may experience traumatic relationships related to being Latino and may not identify as Latino. In stage two, the cognitive stage, this person incorporates erroneous belief systems related to being Latino. In the consequence stage, the fragmentation of ethnic identity intensifies and this person may reject his/her Latino heritage. During stage four, the working through phase, a person begins integrating a healthier Latino identity. This stage is characterized by an increase in ethnic consciousness and reclaiming, and reconnecting with a Latino identity and community. The last stage, successful resolution, occurs when a person has a greater acceptance of self, culture, and ethnicity. This person has improved self-esteem and believes that ethnic identity is positive and promotes success. Before entering the consequence stage of development, this person usually experiences a transformative event or encounter that triggers movement to the next stage (Ruiz, 1990). For me, that encounter occurred last summer at a picnic.

MY TRANSFORMATIVE PERSONAL EXPERIENCE

While attending my White husband's family picnic sponsored by his place of employment, I experienced my first overt racially-based experience that precipitated a major shift in my own thinking of who I am as a Puerto Rican woman, counselor, doctoral student in counselor education, and a mother of twins. This event served as my critical incident that propelled me into stage four, or the working through phase of my ethnic identity.

The event was as follows: I joined my husband at a picnic table with my twin son (who has olive skin, dark hair, and dark eyes) and daughter (who has fair skin, light hair, and light brown eyes), got introduced to his co-workers, and proceeded to share a meal with them. While making conversation, one of my husband's White co-workers asked me what my ethnicity was and if twins ran in my family; I replied that I am Puerto Rican and that my mother's cousins are twins. My husband and I conceived our twins via in-vitro fertilization (IVF), and therefore knew that we might have twins. She proceeded to ask me questions related to the IVF procedure, and if we had any frozen embryos that could be donated to other couples because "mixed race" embryos are in high demand.

MIXED RACE!!!! WHAT, DID SHE JUST SAY!!!!
MY KIDS ARE NOT "MIXED RACE."

I could not believe what I was hearing. At that moment, I was transformed. Before this event, I considered myself to be an English speaking White American person with Puerto Rican parents. Yes, I was ethnically Puerto Rican, but with olive skin, dark straight hair, and dark eyes. I was racially White, and highly acculturated into the White-American culture. In other words, I passed as White, yet somehow this person viewed me as non-White and of a different race than I had always identified.

To this White person, I was not White, and thus my offspring were not White either; they were "mixed race." It was earth shattering for me because although I knew that my kids would be perceived as different, based on their contrasting skin colors, no one had ever actually said it. Nor had my White identity been scrutinized and invalidated. To have such an experience at a family picnic was uncomfortable, shocking, yet transformative. This event served as a catalyst for my personal and professional identity development that before then had been stagnant.

MY PERSONAL AND PROFESSIONAL
DEVELOPMENTAL JOURNEYS

Before I entered stage four of my ethnic identity development, I had self-identified as White-American, had minimized my Latino heritage and incorporated erroneous beliefs about Latinos. For instance, I thought Latinos were lazy and uneducated. Since I was born in the United States, spoke English

fluently, and adopted White-American values, such as working hard for privileges and competing for wealth (Katz, 1985), I can be said to be highly
acculturated.

A person's level of acculturation can fall on a continuum from low to
high, and is a process of cultural learning that takes place when two or more
culturally distant groups come in contact (Guarnero & Flaskerud, 2008; Kohatsu, Concepcion, & Perez, 2010; Sager, Schlimmer, & Hellman, 2001). I
was not born in Puerto Rico, nor do I consider Spanish to be my first language (I learned how to speak Spanish as an adult), so to many "true" Puerto
Ricans (those from the island), I am not fully Puerto Rican, but a "gringa", or
White girl. Due to my high level of acculturation, I found myself without an
ethnic identity. I was not fully White-American, nor fully Puerto Rican.

I did not physically fit the dominant image of a White-American with
blond hair, blue eyes, and fair skin; nor did I fit the dominant image of a
Puerto Rican with dark curly hair, darker skin, and dark eyes. I have olive
skin, dark straight hair, and brown eyes. I also did not fully espouse the
White American cultural ways of life, since I upheld Puerto Rican cultural
values, as well. To White-Americans, I was not White and to Puerto Ricans, I
was not Puerto Rican. I was a combination or a mix of the two. I was
bicultural and lived in the borderlands. I lived in-between the two cultures,
straddling them both and utilizing strengths from both cultures to succeed
and navigate the differences between the cultures (Nguyen & Benet-Martinez, 2013).

For me, my twin children serve as *ethnic mirrors* through which I self-
reflect on what it means to be a Puerto Rican-American. These ethnic mirrors, my twins, through which I see both my Puertoricanness (in my son) and
my Whiteness (in my daughter), tells me that my olive skin, brown hair, and
brown eyes make me look more White than Black, yet to others, I am not
White, yet I am not Black. What am I as a Puerto Rican woman, counselor,
and mother?

As a Puerto Rican Woman

As a Puerto Rican woman, I am a mixture of three races—Spanish, African,
and Taino Indian. This mixture has influenced who I am ethnically and
racially. I am not White nor Black. I am a Latina with caramel colored skin. I
carry an ancestral spirit that propels me towards social justice, equity, and
action. I am a spiritual and optimistic person who honors the feminine spirit
and womanhood. I am connected to my homeland of Puerto Rico and demonstrate passion for all endeavors I engage in. I am strong and assertive, especially when I have to protect my family and speak up against injustices.

As a Bilingual Puerto Rican Counselor and Doctoral Student

For six years, I served as a bilingual (Spanish and English) mental health counselor for members of marginalized communities in Chicago and Paterson, New Jersey. Being bilingual and a Latina were both assets and sources of stress for me in my professional and academic career. For instance, I never had trouble finding a job since I was bilingual, yet I struggled with connecting with my profession. As a counselor, I belong to a predominately-White profession that upholds diversity, yet was founded on and continues to reinforce White-American worldviews and concepts that do not always align with my Latino cultural values. For example, while I believe in familismo, the psychodynamic training that I received encourages counselors to maintain appropriate boundaries and focus on individual and intrapsychic change. Here my ethnic and professional identities come in conflict and make me feel disconnected.

When I entered doctoral studies as the only Latina in my cohort, I continued to feel disconnected. I felt like the token minority who was obligated to serve as an ambassador for my culture. I was flattered to be asked to be on multiple diversity committees, and soon realized that I was serving as the token minority (Flores Niemann, 1999). During my first year of academic studies, I accepted this role as the token minority by excelling academically and accepting committee and leadership nominations. However, I felt undervalued and not supported in my research interests.

My advisor supports me as a student of color and the doctoral program values diversity and offers opportunities for multiculturalism. Since my research interest is on Latino professional counselor identity and no other faculty member is exploring this topic, I feel alone in my research. Since I value interpersonal relationships and collaboration, due to my Latino cultural beliefs of personalismo, I also find it challenging to engage in solitary research practices and to engage in an extensive dissertation project individually. As a Puerto Rican doctoral student in a predominately-White academic institution and profession, I struggle with being bicultural and often have to consider what cultural adaptations I will have to make to be successful, therefore making my academic experience complicated by race and culture.

As a Puerto Rican Mother

Upon returning to my doctoral studies, after being on leave for a year, and as a mother of twins, I had to negotiate new familial and academic responsibilities. My twins are now my priority, yet I had to complete my doctoral studies, and I had to excel at it, at the same time that I was excelling as a mother of twins. It is part of my self-identity that is reinforced by the Latino cultural beliefs of *familismo* and *marianismo*, to excel in academics and in my role as a mother. Education is highly valued in my family and my success in higher education is a gift and obligation to my family. Being a good mom is also highly valued in my family and culture. Yet, to satisfy both these demands is difficult, yet motivating.

As a Latina mom, I am responsible for the well-being and spiritual growth of my children. I am expected to stay home and care for them, and put their needs first. Trying to meet these obligations, while meeting my academic ones has proven to be a challenge. Also, as a Latina woman and mother, my cultural value of *mariansmo* makes it hard for me to ask for help and to put my needs first. I am expected to be selfless and self-sacrificing. However, since I am highly acculturated to the White-American culture, I have been able to learn to ask for help and to take time for my self-care. By harnessing the strengths of the White-American culture, I have been able to strike a balance between the two cultures that I identify with.

MY TRANSFORMATIONAL PROCESS

Who I Was Before

Before this transformative experience, I was a community mental health counselor who was trained in the psychodynamic tradition. As a new professional, I applied what I learned in my clinical training to my clinical practice as a counselor, which meant that I conceptualized and treated Latino and African-American clients from a psychodynamic perspective by focusing on the individual, while negating the family. I also applied cognitive-behavioral strategies to help them learn coping skills. I provided counseling in Spanish to those who requested it, and felt obligated to work in the Latino communities. In a way, I was doing what I thought I was supposed to be doing as a Latino counselor.

I learned Spanish as a way to strengthen my marketability as a counselor. I worked in Latino communities out of a sense of obligation to my ethnic community, even though I felt disconnected from it. As the years progressed and I got married to a White man, and moved to a White suburb in another state away from my family-of-origin, I began to wonder about what being Puerto Rican meant to me. When another person commented that I had "mixed race" children, and a babysitter asked me where my son got his skin color from, my ethnic identity development became even more important and urgent to me.

Who I Was After

After the transformative event, I began to answer the question, "What does being Puerto Rican mean to me"? By asking others this question, participating in a focus group addressing identity, and visiting Puerto Rico, I began to answer this question. Although this will be a life-long journey, I feel more confident in my ethnic identity development and have noticed changes. For example, I pronounce my name using the Spanish pronunciation, I speak Spanish with my twins and expose them to Spanish music, and I have changed my theoretical orientation to align with my ethnic identity.

My current theoretical orientation for counseling involves a multicultural, solution-focused, social justice perspective. This perspective aligns with my ethnic identity because it takes into account the cultural and social aspects of counseling concerns. Instead of applying a psychodynamic viewpoint to conceptualizing and treating clients, I now consider the multiple cultural and societal aspects that influence a person's life. Also, by knowing more about what Puerto Rican means to me, I feel proud to provide counseling in Spanish and working with Latino communities. I want to learn more about Latino studies, and I want to advocate for the fair and equitable treatment of all individuals, especially Latinos.

After my transformative moment when my twins were called "mixed race", I began to reclaim my Puerto Rican heritage. I understood why I smiled often, especially when interacting with authority figures, and why I played the mediator and peacemaker role in my family and social relationships. Instead of feeling ashamed of smiling and mediating, I now understand that I was enacting positive Latino cultural values of *simpatia* and *personalismo*. Also, by reclaiming my Puerto Rican heritage, I am solidifying my foundational ethnic identity that strengthens and motivates me to do what I do as a mother and as a counselor.

CONCLUSION

My personal and professional developmental journey has led me through an ethnic identity process that has shaped how I perceive myself and others. In this chapter, I shared my transformative event that propelled me into the next stage of ethnic identity development. I realized that I do not have to choose to be either White-American or Puerto Rican; I can be both.

Being in the immersion stage, I am actively seeking other Puerto Ricans, cultural events, and literature to enhance my understanding of what it means to be a Puerto Rican woman, mother, and counselor. From someone who was considered racially non-White, and in many ways not part of the White-American culture that I had adored and adopted, to someone who is proud to be Puerto Rican, I have grown into a more integrated person ethnically and professionally. Although, the process can be upsetting and unnerving, at times, I am grateful to my husband's co-worker who labeled my children "mixed race" because she helped me learn to embrace my biculturalism. My biculturalism is a source of strength, energy, passion, and perspective that is invaluable to my developing personal and professional identities.

REFERENCES

Flores Niemann, Y. (1999). The making on a token: A case study of stereotype threat, stigma, racism, and tokenism in academe. *Frontiers*, 111–134.

Gloria, A., & Castellanos, J. (2006). Sustaining Latina/o doctoral students: A psychosociocultural approach for faculty. In J. Castellanos, A. Gloria, & M. Kamimura, *The Latina/o Pathway to the Ph.D.* (pp. 169–187). Sterling, VA: Stylus.

Guarnero, P., & Flaskerud, J. (2008). Latino gay men and depression. *Issues in Mental Health Nursing, 29*, 667–670. doi: 10.1080/01612840802048949.

Katz, J. (1985). The sociopolitical nature of counseling. *The Counseling Psychologist, 13*(4), 615–624. doi: 10.1177/0011000085134005.

Kohatsu, E., Concepcion, W., & Perez, P. (2010). Incorporating levels of acculturation in counseling practice. In J. Ponterotto, J. Casas, L. Suzuki, & C. Alexander, *Handbook of Multicultural Counseling* (3rd ed., pp. 343–356). Los Angeles, CA: Sage.

Lineros, J. V., & Hinojosa, M. (2013). Hispanic Student Development in Higher Education. *FOCUS on Colleges, Universities, and Schools, 7*(1), 1–9.

Miranda, A., Bilot, J., Peluso, P., Berman, K., & Van Meek, L. (2006). Latino families: The relevance of the connection among acculturation, family dynamics, and health for family counseling research and practice. *The Family Journal: Counseling and Therapy for Couples and Families, 14*(3), 268–273. doi: 10.1177/1066480706287805.

Nguyen, A., & Benet-Martinez, V. (2013). Biculturalism and Adjustment: A Meta-Analysis. *Journal of Cross-Cultural Psychology, 44*(1), 122–159. doi:10.1177/0022022111435097.

Ruiz, A. (1990). Ethnic identity: Crisis and resolution. *Journal of Multicultural Counseling and Development, 18*, 29–40. doi: 10.1002/j.2161-1912.1990.tb00434.x.

Sager, J., Schlimmer, E., & Hellman, J. (2001). Latin American lesbian, gay, and bisexual clients: Implications for counseling. *Journal of Humanistic Counseling, Education and Development*, 21–34. doi: 10.1002/j.2164-490X.2001.tb00099.x.

Santiago-Rivera, A., Arredondo, P., & Gallardo-Cooper, M. (2002). *Counseling Latinos and La Familia: A Practical Guide.* Thousand Oaks, CA: Sage.

Chapter Nine

Confronting the Impostor

Addressing Anxiety and Self-Doubt as a Counselor

Shaywanna Harris

The most impactful moments of my career as a counselor have been my experiences with confronting the impostor syndrome. Anxiety is extremely common in counselor education and it is a construct that does not disappear after a set amount of education, experience or supervision. Instead, it changes to address concerns specific to the stage of development in which it occurs.

There are many counselors in training, professionals, counselor educators, and supervisors who have encountered the impostor syndrome at least once in their careers. The anxieties surrounding this experience have been noted and explored by many professionals in disciplines that vary from corporate business to academia and helping professionals. In her book, *The Secret Thoughts of Successful Women,* Valerie Young explores the impostor syndrome and potential ways to combat it. Young normalizes feelings of self-doubt and provides quotes from very successful women, such as Meryl Streep and Dr. Maya Angelou, who have experienced self-doubt and have felt like an impostor. As common as this phenomenon is, especially in women, it is startling that some counseling and counselor education programs do not overtly address it when training counselors.

In the beginning stages of my practicum experience in my master's program I was confronted by a fear of whether I had been properly trained to help the clients in front of me with their presenting concerns. Questions like "Am I good enough?", "Have I learned enough?", "Will my clients see how inexperienced I am?" and many others arose and caused my anxiety to skyrocket. I soon realized that I was not alone in my fears of being "found out" or discovered to be incompetent as a counselor; my classmates shared these sentiments. Through discussion of our experiences, we were able to find a sense of normality and confront our own inner impostors. This discussion and normalization of my experience helped me to feel better about the feelings I was having. I felt that my experience was not unique and that I was where I needed to be developmentally to be able to move into a position of growth. The biggest lesson I learned at this point in my life was that perfection was not expected and that growth comes from imperfection.

It was the first weeks in my PhD program that catapulted me into a position I had never been before. In all of my prior educational experiences, I was expected to sit in class, listen, and get good grades on tests. I soon realized that a PhD program is far different and that I would be expected to think critically and use my background and experiences to provide a different perspective in classroom discussions. I began my program with five other individuals in my cohort and immediately began to doubt my merit compared not only to the rest of my cohorts but compared to the rest of the students in my program. It seemed like everyone else had so much more experience and could offer so much that I could not. The familiar questions of "Am I good enough?", "Do I deserve to be here?", and others resurfaced. I struggled with these questions for a while, and since I was in a completely new environment surrounded by unfamiliar, yet supportive, peers and faculty members, I did not have a close group of people that I had known for a while to share my experiences with as I did in my master's practicum class. Overall, I felt overwhelmed, lost, and lonely. I felt that I had to deal with all of these feelings on my own for fear of exposing myself as "incompetent" or "unable to handle the PhD program" to my fellow students or faculty members. I had family and friends with whom I could talk about my feelings of inadequacy, and talking to people I was comfortable with who have known me for a while helped me to feel supported. However, I still felt alone as none of my family or friends could actually relate specifically to what I was going through in my program. Therefore, although I had a support system, I still felt lonely and isolated in my personal experience, which led to me not wanting to talk to my family because I felt they wouldn't understand.

Loneliness, isolation, and feelings of shame placed me in an uncomfortable situation. I am a firm believer in the notion that individuals grow as a result of uncomfortable situations. As such, this discomfort with feeling lonely, isolated, and ashamed led me to confront my anxieties on my own, reach out to those around me to normalize my feelings, and build a support system. In my efforts of reaching out, I was given very valuable advice from fellow students, recent graduates of my program, and faculty members. The most impactful advice I received from multiple individuals I came in contact with was to "Remember who you are and why you are in your program" and "You are here on your own merit; you are where you are because you are qualified to be here." These pieces of advice allowed me to reflect on my own accomplishments and come to the realization that I am competent and qualified to do my job as a counselor as well as a student.

As a woman of color, a challenge I faced was finding a mentor who I could relate to personally. I was extremely lucky to have other students and graduates of my program to reach out to and develop relationships with. I was also able to build a support system with other current students through the Holmes Scholars, an organization specifically aimed at providing mentorship and camaraderie for PhD students from backgrounds that are underrepresented in academia. Through this program I have built friendships with current and recently graduated students from universities across the nation. I have also made connections with current faculty members at universities that have provided insight into their personal experiences with feeling like an impostor. Learning that individuals I look up to and admire so much for all of their accomplishments still have the same feelings I have provided a sense of normality again and helped me to cope with my own impostor feelings.

Another challenge I faced when confronting my feelings of being an impostor was my personality. I consider myself to be an introvert, that is, when around a large group of people I tend to get exhausted and need time alone to regain my energy. I have never thought of my introversion as a challenge, however, when I realized how imperative it was for me to develop close mentoring relationships and a support system, I realized I would need to involve myself in more social activities. A vast majority of my feelings of not belonging or not being good enough disappeared when I developed new relationships with other students and individuals in academia. I realized how similar my experiences are with these other individuals and this knowledge helped again to normalize my feelings. This increase in socialization, of course, led to me needing a lot more time to take care of myself, which is important when considering the impostor syndrome. I find that it is easy to over-work myself in order to prove to others that I belong and that I am capable. However, self-care and self-compassion have been extremely important for me confronting my feelings of being an impostor.

Some of the ways I incorporate self-compassion and self-care as ways of coping with the impostor syndrome include learning how and when to say no, forgiving myself for being imperfect, and understanding that I'm not alone in my feelings of inadequacy or self-doubt. Feeling like an impostor makes me want to prove to others that I, in fact, deserve to be where I am and with this drive comes the desire to accept any and every opportunity that presents itself. In my first year as a doctoral student, I was asked to help with numerous projects and I accepted these invitations because I didn't want to make anyone think I couldn't handle the work. After taking on too many projects, and being advised that I needed to "say no sometime", I realized that in order to do my work well, I needed to not spread myself so thin.

Developing this ability to say no has been a struggle, however it has helped me to set boundaries for myself and regularly take care of me.

One of my cohorts introduced me to the concept of self-compassion, that is, giving oneself permission to be imperfect, and accepting oneself for who one is. After attending a workshop on self-compassion, I learned a lot about how harshly I treat myself and how that directly influences my feelings of inadequacy and self-doubt. The skills I learned from the self-compassion workshop have helped me to be less critical of myself and accept rather than be ashamed of my imperfections. Additionally, realizing that other individuals are having the same feelings as I am is very helpful in lessening my feelings of loneliness and isolation. Again, building relationships with my cohorts and other current students has helped solidify this sense of normalization and confirm that I am not alone in my struggles.

My experiences with confronting the impostor syndrome have provided me the opportunity to grow both personally and professionally so that I have become a more confident and effective counselor and student. The most important thing I have learned about the impostor syndrome is that it is something that returns with any new situation. I do not think it will ever be possible to erase uneasy feelings about being in a position where you feel like an impostor. I feel that recognizing this feeling and gaining the courage to reach out for support is essential in developing relationships which in turn will ease feelings of being an impostor.

REFERENCES

Young, V. (2011). *The Secret Thoughts of Successful Women: Why Capable People Suffer from the Impostor Syndrome and How to Thrive in Spite of It.* New York, NY: Crown Publishing.

Chapter Ten

In My Skin

Jacqueline S. Hodes

The skin is the largest organ in the body. The skin protects us from the elements and allows us to regulate our body temperature (WebMD, 2014). The skin is what we first see of each other and unfortunately judgments ensue. Our skin allows us to express our individuality. We show ourselves on our skin in the form of body art (e.g., tattoos and piercings), darkening or lightening and adornments in the form of clothing that we use to cover it up. We use the word skin to express ourselves in many ways—we have "skin in the game", it is "no skin off of our noses", we "jump out of our skin", we are "thick- or thin-skinned" and we all know that "beauty is only skin deep"!

My skin became the impetus of my transformational learning experience and the beginning of the development of my counselor identity. As a child I had very little awareness of my skin except for when it was damaged by falling on macadam at the playground, by the scorching rays of the sun, or by the annoying mosquitoes at dusk on a warm summer evening. To those who only knew my family on the surface, my childhood looked comfortable and easy, maybe even ideal. But make no mistake. It was not "The Brady Bunch", which premiered a few weeks after my tenth birthday. It was at ten that I can remember having the realization that what happened in my house was very different than what happened in my friends' homes. There were no television shows in 1969 that portrayed my life.

I was a smart, book-reading, Scrabble-playing, chubby, shy, Jewish girl. I imagine I could have been comfortable in my own skin had my mother been more comfortable in hers. My mother was often fun and always creative but she used shame and intimidation to control her children. I remember my mother berating me for being the fattest child in the third grade. When I look back on those pictures from third grade I see a normal, happy nine year old. I cannot see what my mother saw yet her voice lives in my head today. I was also a privileged child and did not know it. I lived in a nice, single-family house with three bathrooms and two phone lines, a cleaning woman who came twice per week even though my mother did not work, an 8-week overnight camp experience every summer, Girl Scouts, religious school, piano (and violin and flute and guitar) lessons, and wonderful birthdays and Christmas mornings (yes, we were Jewish and had a full secular Christmas, complete with a tree, stockings and Santa). I even had a grandfather who worked in the toy industry and I always had the latest game or toy on the market. And, I had clear skin.

The year I turned 10, my family had just moved from Long Island to the suburbs of central New Jersey. My parents' impending divorce was brewing, every day in every way. The violence and fighting in my home was unbearable and frightening for a young girl with two much younger sisters. I was apprehensive about being the new girl in school and very aware that I knew no one. I was doubtful that anyone would want to know me. We had moved away from family, friends and familiar places. For the first time in my young life I was aware that I was alone.

In an effort to fit in and to hide from the complications and embarrassment of my life and the dysfunction of my family, I found every way to develop a thick skin, an irony which is not lost on me now. I hid behind my thick skinned persona and marginalized others to avoid being ostracized by those I held (in error) in high esteem. My persona of an insensitive, gossipy, "go along with the crowd", mean girl helped me thoroughly mask the awkward, sensitive, insecure teenager within. At least I thought it did. In reflection, I had turned into someone who I did not know.

At 14 years old, my life changed suddenly in many ways when my mother announced her engagement to her second husband only 18 months after her divorce from my father. I did not think much about it at the time except that I hated her engagement ring. Within a week, my skin reflected my feelings of the impending marriage. My entire torso and limbs were covered with red patches and bumps. It took me days to tell my mother about the rash. I was unsure what was happening to my skin and knew that it could not be good. I was worried that I had done something to cause the rash and would be blamed for my own discomfort. Eventually my fear won out and I reached out to my mother in the hopes that she would have an answer and a solution. I was immediately taken to the dermatologist and diagnosed with psoriasis.

This diagnosis was not a surprise to my mother. She and my grandmother had struggled silently with the disease. Their skin had not been covered with the scaly patches, at least in my memory. If fact, until I had my outbreak I cannot recall my mother mentioning her skin at all. My mother was devastated though as she realized she had passed this "heartbreak" down to her oldest child. Psoriasis is a skin condition that is caused by rapidly growing skin cells producing red, flaky patches on the skin. It is an autoimmune disease with no known cure, just temporary relief from natural sunlight, artificial light sources, topical medicine and now biologic drugs (Healthwise Staff, 2014).

Following my outbreak of psoriasis I was desperate for a cure. Spring was on its way and I was terrified of letting go of the pants and long-sleeved shirts that hid my imperfect skin. I tried many topical treatments, including using Crisco shortening on my patches and wrapping my limbs in plastic wrap overnight. Much to my surprise, my mother announced that I would be going to Florida to stay with my paternal grandmother for three weeks in hopes to use the sun as a natural healer. According to John Updike (1989) in his essay *At War with My Skin*, "Only the sun, that living god, had real power over psoriasis..." I packed quickly. This time in the sun began my awareness and understanding of the power of empathy and compassion.

When I arrived at my grandmother's house in Miami, I was immediately homesick. I realized that I was alone and lonely. My grandmother was good company for watching *The Price is Right* but from my adolescent perspective she was too old to understand my life and my pain. There were no young people in her retirement community, just hundreds of transplanted, retired (i.e., old) New Yorkers.

When I entered the pool area in my bathing suit on the first day of my healing regime, I was surprisingly happy to be alone. I was very relieved that no other teenagers were near. My relief was temporary. I was surprised and then devastated to hear the whispers of the old women as they stared at my body. I overheard one woman remark that it looked as if my mother beat me or burned me with a cigarette. Their remarks and stares were cruel and hurtful. I wanted to escape back to the safety of my grandmother's apartment but I had no choice. I knew I had to sit in the sun and endure so I could heal and feel normal.

A few days into my routine of sunbathing and appearing nonchalant (which probably appeared rude to an adult) a very kind older man, a recent widower and friend of my late grandfather saw my alienation and took pity on me. He invited me to a game of tennis. After that first game he picked me up every morning at 7:00 and we walked to the tennis courts where he helped me perfect my tennis serve and game. On our walks he talked with me about his life and asked questions about mine. This was the first time I had ever talked with an adult who actually wanted to really listen to me. I looked forward to playing tennis but relished the attention and conversation. At the end of my visit he invited me to be his doubles partner in a tennis tournament held in the community. I do not remember his name or who won but I still, over 40 years later, have love in my heart for him. His compassion and kindness got beneath my skin and touched my soul.

The two hours per day of tennis were wonderful but I had many hours of time by myself at the pool. I was a voracious reader and although I had ninth grade homework to complete, I was consumed and distracted by my internal dialogue. I initially spent my time wavering between feeling sorry for myself and being angry at the world. I was terrified that I would be bullied and marginalized upon my return to high school. I was certain that my abnormal skin would be the object of ridicule. I was obsessed with worry that my friends and peers would use my marred skin as an excuse to not include me. My insecure adolescent voice told me that I was not good enough to be liked just for me.

It was a surprise to me when midway through my healing regime, my thinking and feelings transformed. In my quiet time at the pool I found myself in deep thought and reflection about life. I thought about why people discriminate against others and how perceptions are not always reality. I spent hours trying to understand why I had been given this burden to bear and slowly came to realize that my situation could be much worse. I reflected on the people I personally knew who had struggles worse than red, blotchy skin. I realized that right under my nose my grandmother was grieving the loss of the love of her life, my grandfather, who died as a result of a massive heart attack just months before I arrived. I thought about the people I did not know, their stories on the nightly news, who were suffering from poverty, illness, war, fear and loneliness.

And each day, I came to know more about my tennis teacher as we walked back and forth from the retirement community to the tennis courts. He talked with me about his life and accomplishments. He shared stories about his wife and family. I learned about the deep sadness he experienced from losing his wife and consequent loneliness during his retirement. He asked me about my life and he listened as if I were telling him the most exciting story. His attention to me and his willingness to share made me feel as if I was a very interesting person, a person worth knowing. He saw me for more than just my skin; he saw me for who I was and who I was becoming. My tennis teacher taught me more than tennis. He taught me the healing power of empathy.

It would have been easy for me to return to my life in New Jersey and pick up where I left off. But I did not. I returned to high school that spring with partially healed skin, a better tennis serve and a transformed sense of the vulnerability we each have within us, obvious or not. The sun had "healed" my psoriasis and I was left with tan skin and temporary loss of pigment where the red spots had been previously. The red spots had faded and so had my bravado and mean girl attitude. I imagine that there were times when I continued to serve my old persona but those times were few and far between. My "crisis" and subsequent reflection had given me the opportunity to transform. I was more empathic to others as I knew each person had their story to tell. I was kinder to myself. My life and my identity began to change.

I began to connect more deeply with others, sharing the secrets of my dysfunctional family and my own flaws, limitations, and difficulties. I took more risks and met new and different friends. I landed a job at a fast food restaurant. Although my school was integrated I rarely socialized with my classmates of color. The racial divide in the early 70's was significant. At my new job I formed friendships with people of all races. I was never more aware of the power of my white skin, even in its damaged state.

I was schooled in my privilege when my African-American friend invited me to his home for dinner. I was thrilled to join him at his home but was uncomfortably aware of his increased awkwardness as we got closer to the event. Once the day arrived I understood. He was living in poverty that I never knew existed. And he knew that I did not have any idea about his living conditions. He was "flipping burgers" to help support his family while I was doing the same to pay for college. I was humbled by his grace. At the time I knew very little then about the counseling profession and absolutely nothing about humanistic philosophy. In reflection, I was beginning to form my counselor identity as I explored my experiences and multicultural awareness coupled with my capacity for caring and empathy (Coll, Doumas, Trotter, & Freeman, 2013). My commitment to social justice work was sparked at that moment and continues to be an important part of my work today.

I allowed myself to explore more of who I was in the world. By sixteen, I knew I was a lesbian, another layer of skin to contend with at a young age. In 1976, the year of our country's bicentennial, high school students rarely "came out" without consequence. I stayed quiet and "red, white, and blue." This was a secret I could not tell. But I read everything I could get my hands on without my mother knowing. I longed to find others who were similar to me but did not risk the exploration. I counted the days until I could leave for college and begin my own life, out of the judgment of family and friends. As my skin continued to heal, my self-awareness deepened. Little did I know that these critical incidents were the beginning of my development as a counselor (Furr & Carroll, 2003).

I graduated from high school and enrolled in college. My psoriasis was dormant and my skin was surprisingly healthy and free from the unsightly red flaky spots. I was able to concentrate on my classes and my own internal personal journey. I explored my sexual orientation, my intellect, my relationships, my work ethic, my organizational skills required for balancing three part-time jobs and my new found but not easily obtained, autonomy. I enrolled in my first counseling class, a one-credit course designed to give undergraduate students an understanding of the helping relationship. I was selected to serve as a peer counselor in the counseling center. I served as a volunteer for the campus response group to victims of sexual assault. I entered into my own personal counseling relationship which helped me to gain even more self-awareness and integrity, an important critical incident to developing counselor identity (Furr & Carroll, 2003). I completed my under-graduate degree with the great desire to help others. I had found my passion.

I applied and was accepted to graduate school for a degree in college counseling and student personnel management. Developing a counselor pro-fessional identity takes time and requires the investment of strong mentors (Coppock, 2012). I was surrounded by like-minded mentors and had two years to concentrate on learning how to be a counselor. My professors' and supervisors' instruction and influence contributed to my understanding of my counselor professional identity (Calley & Hawley, 2008). For the first time since I was ten I felt at home in my own skin.

I entered my graduate program with a well-developed helper identity. I was known as a good listener, someone who could help others and a caring person on which others could rely. As a beginning counselor in a graduate program, my skills and my self-efficacy were challenged, an unpredictable surprise as a result of significant hubris. The lack of my ability to quickly master the skills and the anxiety of not performing to my expectation led to two significant consequences: (a) deep feelings of frustration similar to the feelings about my erratic skin and (b) erratic skin.

Psoriasis is a complicated disease. It can lie dormant for many years and then out of nowhere reappear. The lesions can recur and worsen for many reasons including injury to the skin such as nicks from shaving or pruning roses, infections of any kind and severe emotional stress (Brody, 1993). The lack of ability to predict and control the outbreak of the psoriasis requires great patience.

According to Levitt and Jacques (2005), embracing the role of ambiguity is a way to enhance counselor development and skills. Working through the stress of learning to be a counselor and living with unreliable skin has re-sulted in increased tolerance for ambiguity and uncertainty in my work and life. The ability to tolerate ambiguity is not my best work. I suffer through it and as a result I am a more effective, empathic counselor educator, support-ing students as they learn ambiguity tolerance.

Upon completion of my Master's degree I found work first in a non-profit agency implementing drug and alcohol education to elementary and middle school students. Soon after, my path took me back to higher education and into a position in student affairs where I served in various roles for 26 years. Throughout those years my counselor identity deepened and expanded as I worked as a counselor practitioner.

As I gained more personal and professional life experience, my profes-sional counselor identity coalesced (Auxier, Hughes, & Kline, 2003; Moss, Gibson, & Dollarhide, 2014). I was able to utilize my counseling skills in two distinct ways. At the "micro" level I used my counseling skills in my work with individual students, in advising student groups and in training and supervising paraprofessionals. At the "macro" level I found that my counseling skills served me well as a strategic and collaborative practitioner. During this extended time my psoriasis was present but kept at bay through various treatments. I had learned how to "control" the uncontrollable, a lesson that I learned over and over again in my work on a university campus.

My journey to my counselor identity continued to unfold and represented a synthesis of my experiences (Brott & Myers, 1999; Woodside, Oberman, Cole, & Carruth, 2007). I often struggled with self-doubt, a consistent theme in counselor identity development (Woodside, et al., 2007). I grappled with and balanced my own internal critical voice with the external pressures of new and more complex work. My awareness and appreciation of my skin and the "skin" of others informed my decisions about campus work, community involvement, and ultimately my career in a helping profession. During this time, I expanded our wellness model by incorporating an emphasis on diversity. I became a voice for LGBTQA students, faculty, staff, and alumni. I participated on two Boards of Directors—for a summer camp serving children infected and affected by HIV/AIDS and for the newly formed LGBT Chorale in the city where I lived. My capacity for empathy and building authentic relationships allowed me to work collaboratively to create true structural and institutional change in a variety of significant areas such as LGBTQA services, orientation and new student programs, and fundraising and development for student leadership programs.

I now find myself in the role of a counselor educator. I completed a doctorate while working full-time and was able to secure a full-time tenure track position at my home institution. I have the privilege to work with students in new and different ways, helping them on their journeys to becoming counselors and counselor practitioners. I have new "skin in the game" as I help students understand the human condition, the power of empathy, to create success from within (Chopra & Winfrey, 2015) and to serve with compassion.

As a current practicing counselor educator I am reminded daily that we each have our blemishes and imperfections and that "beauty" is only skin deep. We do need to take care of our skin as it is our greatest protector and it is the first part of us that others see. My psoriasis continues to be a teacher to me. Today I am less uncomfortable in public showing my less than perfect skin. I embrace the opportunity to be self-conscious—to be conscious of my thoughts, my feelings, my values and my intuition. This self-consciousness, the ability to be aware of one's self, is what I strive for as a counselor practitioner and educator. It is the lesson I teach to students. I am confident that as counselors and counselor educators we can help others get beneath the surface and under the skin to find the authentic self.

REFERENCES

Auxier, C. R., Hughes, F. R., & Kline, W. B. (2003). Identity development in counselors-in-Training. *Counselor Education & Supervision, 43,* 25-38. doi: 10.1002/j.1556-6978.2003.tb01827.x.

Brody, J. E. (1993, October 20). Personal health; Struggling for peace in the war against psoriasis. *The New York Times.* Retrieved from http://www.nytimes.com/1993/10/20/health/personal-health-struggling.

Brott, P. E., & Myers, J. E. (1999). Development of professional school counselor identity: A Grounded theory. *Professional School Counseling. 2*(5), 339. Retrieved from EBSCOhost on March 16, 2015.

Calley, N. G., & Hawley, L. D. (2008). The professional identity of counselor educators. *The Clinical Supervisor, 27*(1), 3-16. doi: 10.1080/07325220802221454.

Chopra, D. & Winfrey, O. (2015, March 16). Manifesting true success (Episode 1). Retrieved from https://chopracentermeditation.com.

Coll, K. M., Doumas, D. M., Trotter, A., & Freeman, B. J. (2013). Developing the counselor as a person and as a professional: Attitudinal changes in core counseling courses. *Journal of Humanistic Counseling, 52,* 54-66. doi: 10.1002/j.2161-1939.2013.00032.x.

Coppock, T. E. (2012). A closer look at developing counselor identity. *Counseling today,* 62-64. Retrieved from EBSCOhost on March 9, 2015.

Furr, S. R. & Carroll, J. J. (2003). Critical incidents in student counselor development. *Journal of Counseling & Development, 81,* 483-489. doi: 10.1002/j.1556-6678.2003.tb00275.x.

Gibson, D. M., Dooley, B. A., Kelchner, V.P., Moss, J. M., & Vacchio, C. B. (2012). From counselor-in-training to professional school counselor: Understanding professional identity development. *Journal of Professional Counseling: Practice, Theory, and Research, 39* (1), 17-25.

Healthwise Staff. (2014, March 12). *Psoriasis.* Retrieved from http://www.webmd.com/skin-problems-and-treatments/psoriasis/psoriasis.

Levitt, D. H., & Jacques, J. D. (2005). Promoting tolerance for ambiguity in counselor training programs. *Journal of Humanistic Counseling, Education and Development, 44,* 46-54. doi: 10.1002/j.2164-490X.2005.tb00055.x.

Moss, J. M., Gibson, D. M., & Dollarhide, C. T. (2014). Professional identity development: A grounded theory of transformational tasks of counselors. *Journal of Counseling & Development, 92,* 3-12. doi: 10.1002/j. 1556-6676.2014.00124.x.

Updike, J. (1989). *Self-Consciousness.* New York: Alfred A. Knopf.

WebMD. (2014). *Skin problems & treatments health center.* Retrieved from http://www.webmd.com/skin-problems-and-treatments/picture-of-the-skin.

Woodside, M., Oberman, A. H., Cole, K. G., & Carruth, E. K. (2007). Learning to be a counselor: A prepracticum point of view. *Counselor Education and Supervision, 47,* 14–28. doi: 10.1002/j.1556-6978.2007.tb00035.x.

Chapter Eleven

The Invitation of a Dying Man

Drew Krafcik

"The hope is in the simple fact that someone who dares to listen and to face life in its naked reality, will not run away but say with a word, a touch, a smile or a friendly silence 'I know you only had only one life to live, and it cannot be lived again, but I am here with you, and I care'" (Nouwen, 1976, p. 132).

Early in my professional counseling career, I worked in hospice with people who were actively dying. My average caseload at the time was about 50 families. The identified patient was certainly primary, but my scope of practice also included support for patient's partners, family members, and friends. Honestly, 50 families was a lot of people for me to process interpersonally, emotionally and practically. Case conceptualizations, treatment plans and progress notes were extensive and it took time to understand how to integrate paperwork into my daily routine.

Entering the field, I felt a mix of new emotions, accomplishment, and humility—like I had made it beyond internships and was able to be in the lives of others in meaningful and sustainable ways. Working in hospice had me out in the world each day responding to people who were experiencing incredibly difficult circumstances, often crises. I frequently had no idea what I was walking into, equipped with just basic demographic information like names, location and terminal diagnosis.

It took repetition, and calming practices, for me to acclimate to the feeling that I was routinely entering into the unknown. As I would get close to people's (patient's) homes, residences, or care facilities, for example, a common experience for me was to have butterflies and tingling in my stomach. I felt anticipation, sometimes fear and apprehension. I was also still adjusting to people's comments about how young I was to be working in hospice. I understood that behind their observations was a wondering if I could be of any help to them or their loved ones. I often wondered the same.

At times, I felt youth was of benefit in hospice, granting me access to spaces because I embodied a vitality that seemed to contrast people's diminishing capacities and ailing hopes. In these moments, I felt received with an impersonal but particular gratitude and welcoming which calmed the fearful, insecure parts of me. It was almost like I didn't even have to do anything, just show up. Other times, being in my 20's felt toxic to my emerging professional confidence and competence, as I was filled with persistent internal commentary about my inadequacies and insufficient life experiences.

Looking back, I would say that I identified with the Novice Professional Counselor Development Phase (Ronnestad & Skovholt, 2003). I felt engaged and out on my own, free from the formal constraints and evaluation of supervision (although I chose to stay in supervision with a wise mentor). Clinical work was intense, and I was constantly learning, reflecting, and reformulating. I felt I was growing personally and professionally, gaining familiarity with the various parts of my professional life and identity each day.

Personally, I felt that I was an old soul, and so being with other people in pain was familiar to me. I was also affirmed in my younger life for being "there" for friends and family. One of my vulnerabilities as a novice professional, in retrospect, was how much of my personal identity had been unconsciously formed by being helpful or supportive. I knew helping others met needs of my own, and I think I felt some shame about that.

In truth, the shame was most intense when I *first realized* how present my needs were in my personal and professional lives. It was humbling, too, having my needs seen by others sometimes before I recognized them. I preferred vulnerability on my own terms, and I felt exposed and raw. It's not that I would have made different clinical decisions, or even life choices; it was more a recognition that my emerging professional identity needed to be informed by these self discoveries. I was fortunate at the time to value learning as part of life, and so that assuaged some of the self-consciousness. I also *trusted* life, so from that perspective too I felt comforted that this process belonged as part of my unfolding professional journey.

I acknowledge and embrace my own needs now the best I can, and try and see them as clearly as possible, but then, I was less self-accepting. I knew cognitively, practically and literally that I could not save anyone, or support everyone, but deeper, older parts of me hoped that I could, and that I would be a meaningful presence in the lives of others who were hurting.

One spring afternoon, I arrived at a nursing facility that was unfamiliar to me. I had received an urgent text instructing me to please get there as soon as possible. Rushing had the effect of muting my usual pre-anxiety that day, which surprised me. I showed my credentials at the front desk, signed in, and walked down a long, sterile hallway. I approached the nurses' station and asked about the patient I was there to see. The nurse said nothing—only pointed over my shoulder to a room directly behind me. I thanked her, turned, and paused momentarily in the open doorway of this man's room. I did not know it at the time, but he literally had just been moved here from his home of 50 years with a very short time to live.

I recall the drab light that was filtering into his room, and the dull, dark, worn curtains that were fluttering aimlessly above the heater. The room felt sparse, used, and impersonal to me. Not a place I imagined that anyone would choose to be. He was alone, lying down staring intently at the ceiling. He nodded subtly for me to enter and I slowly approached his bed.

A visceral and perceivable feeling of intensity emanated from his whole body, what felt like a mix of heaviness and terror. I felt it in my bones—it was undeniable, and palpable. I paused to acknowledge the experience in me when he turned his head, looked at me with steely, pained eyes and then literally *screamed*, "YOU . . . have . . . NO-IDEA what-it-is-like to be . . . ME!" His gaze was paralyzing and unflinching, filled with desperation and rage. I was startled and my stomach tensed and stiffened, my body reflexively leaned away, and my eyes opened wide. "There is NOTHING you could possibly do to help me," he continued.

I felt energy flood my body and engulf me. I was inundated with helplessness and inadequacy as I witnessed myself register this moment as important. I experienced a temporary disconnection from my capacity to feel, like a vacant numbness, and noticed scripts frantically arising in my mind for what to do and say.

Professionally, I "knew" this could happen—that a person (patient) could, and would, feel and act intensely angry, and direct that energy *at me*. But, I could not believe that it was actually happening. In the moment, his words and energy were imbued with the grievous reality of his relationship to life, and the emerging realization of his dying. The moment was surreal in a way for me too, and things seemed to move in slow motion. My chest sunk inward, my shoulders bowed, and I experienced an unexpected, and yet probably predictable, descent into my own terrifying personal narrative. Fear arose that I think lived in conscious exile most of the time, but was always there, lurking. A fear that underneath my training, experience, naturalness, sense of self, I am actually nothing and of no value to others, and that someone will discover and expose the fraud and failure that I am. His intense expression of anger also triggered in me feelings of abandonment that I had experienced in my life when I upset people. I had spent a great deal of my life being what others wanted so that I would not fall out of their graces and "lose their love". In this moment with him, I felt stripped and exposed in a harsh, unsafe context - all done without my consent. The terrified parts inside seemed torn out of their ambient rest and shoved into what felt like their own death. I felt paralyzed, alone, disoriented, unresourced, and overwhelmed. I froze for what felt like an eternity.

Looking back, the moment his words and energy permeated me, I felt obliterated in a way, like I had no choice but to experience what was happening, and to be with it, as I was literally sitting there with him. I think I *endured* it because it felt like he was asking me to—to not move away from him—to not leave him alone in his anger, his pain, his fear, his dying. Experientially, it was as if I was being run over and deflated—I felt lost, ungrounded, adrift, disoriented, and dizzy—like I was forced to ingest the traumas of my life in a second, like my lifetime of hurt was captured in a single frame. I only realized later that maybe he was helping me to feel what he was feeling.

And then something happened that was insightful and ultimately transformative for me, and I cannot say that I *did* anything to make it happen. For some reason, I just *stayed there in the discomfort* while this internal inferno engulfed me, and luckily did not fight against it. The intensity faded slowly, and from within my body arose the re-emergence of my ability to feel, and from these feelings I sensed words come. The feelings and words were gentle, and tender, and I felt so connected to them and to him. I felt my fear and terror recede, and the words said, "You are so right," and I actually shared those literal words aloud with him. "You are so right." *I felt the truth of them inside me*. I continued, "I have no idea what it is like to be you. But I truly care, and I hear you are hurting, and would be so honored to listen to you. Maybe you can help me understand." He stared at me for what felt like a lifetime, and maybe it was. It seemed like he looked into my soul—vetting, discerning—and then his body softened subtly, and his eyes filled with tears. "I'm so . . . scared, and so . . . alone. My wife . . . and son . . . are gone too . . . and I have no one." I felt the gravity of his words, and my eyes filled with tears too.

Looking back, that moment of contact with myself first, and then with him, seemed like both a teacher and healer for me. I felt invited to sit with him in his experience and just be, offering who I was and what I could in the moment with honest limitation, sincere humility, and emerging self-acceptance. I experienced such freedom, presence, and availability, as I was not trying to be anything more than what and who I was in that moment. He was dying, scared, and grieving, and I had no answers for him, no fancy techniques, and nothing smart to say. But I was *there, with him*. We were there, *together*.

While the intensity of that transformative moment has faded, what remains for me is learning to *trust* moments of obliteration, helplessness, and disorientation. I do not have to fear them or fix them or even understand them in the moment. Instead, I can just *experience* them, and more often than not, they are teachers and doorways to openness and growth. And, I do not mean that we as professional counselors do *our* personal work with clients, but that at times we have no choice but to navigate our personal uncertainty in trying to remain in connection with ourselves and others.

For emerging and experienced counselors alike, self-work and self-awareness are essential components of ethical and effective practice (ACA Code of Ethics, 2014), and are cultivated, I believe, in a lifelong process of learning. I would offer that our personal and professional awareness work is not intended solely in *defense* of experiencing spontaneous moments of overwhelm, but in *service* of building ways to normalize and move through them consciously in relationship when they *do* occur. I believe that it is possible to both actively work on our triggers in our own personal and professional development, *and* also to learn to trust that we can tolerate, and even celebrate, the cycle of being lost in our clients stories, or enmeshed, and then recovering in the relationship, too.

Today, I might identify myself in the Experienced Professional Phase of Counselor Development (Ronnestad & Skovholt, 2003). What matters to me is applying my competence in an authentic way—bringing myself, seeing myself, and being able to relate to myself throughout all experiences personally and professionally. In this way, I feel present, available, and aware. I feel more grounded and clear in the unfolding understanding of my way of being in the world with others. I have experienced so often that the actual connection with another person is what matters, and that my theoretical orientation arises out of my own conscious naturalness, work with my habitual patterns, and the unique needs of each client. I tend to use techniques, methods, and tools with flexibility, creativity, and adaptability. I do not feel pressure to know the answers, and I do not know if I will even be of help.

I have also come to know and trust the space in my awareness from which intuition arises, and I have been through enough cycles of triggering to know that I do not have to be anxious, or afraid, about my body's reactivity, and fear. It has been my experience that there are no clear and easy answers, no adoptable frameworks or techniques that will protect me from the vulnerability of just being with someone else, as they are.

I embrace that I am affected by the lives of others, and that the cultivation of receptive spaciousness and potential in me requires attention, care, and kenosis. During client sessions, and in my life, I often feel embodied—in my body—trusting of the multiple ways of knowing that are possible, and resourcing them. I feel more and more like being a therapist is an extension of my conscious, natural life, that my personal and professional identities are resonant. Each is refined by practice and experience, honed by consistent self-awareness and reflection, and are nurtured by authentic connections with supportive peers and wise mentors.

More than ever, I feel both deep surrender and vital engagement in the lives of others. I wonder if the most important lesson this amazing, dying man taught me is that I am enough, as I am. That I am here, and I care. He had had this one life to live, and we shared his final moments, together.

REFERENCES

Ronnestad, N., & Skovholt, T. (2003). The journey of the counselor and therapist: Research findings and perspectives on professional development. *Journal of Career Development, 30*(1), 5-44. doi: 10.1177/089484530303000102.

ACTIVITY

An activity for emerging counselors is to pay more conscious attention to our naturally occurring difficult moments. Can we become increasingly curious and interested? Is it possible to become a bit more acclimated to being with our discomfort without trying to fix it or change it? How might we both take active steps in self-care within discomfort to reduce it and also balance allowing the process to unfold in its own way? What wisdom exists for us in the midst of our uncertainty and disorientation? How can we use these difficult moments to discover a deeper voice arising from within?

Chapter Twelve

Embracing the Dark

Laura Thompson

I have spent a lot of my life afraid of the dark (figuratively, not literally). For me, uncomfortable emotions, particularly anger or rage, were like the Big Bad Wolf – dark, scary, and to be avoided at all costs. This fear is one that started in my childhood, and although I was not conscious of it then, it has shaped much of who I am and how I have lived my life.

Many of those who know me would likely describe me as a sunny and bubbly person. Often smiling, I tend to be a "glass half-full" kind of gal, always looking for that silver lining. I am big on keeping my word and seeing projects through to the end. In fact, I am pretty sure I could be a contender for the gold medal in stick-to-itiveness. In many ways, these attributes have served me well in life. Friends and opportunities have come easily. I get along well with people, I am intentional about being kind, and I do my best to be a contributor instead of a taker. Most of the time, I finish what I start.

What I did not realize for many years, however, was that this modus operandi had some significant drawbacks. Unwittingly, it slowly took its toll. Sometimes being nice was not in my best interest. Sometimes looking for the bright side of an unhealthy dynamic or apologizing when I had not done anything wrong was *not* what I needed to do. And, sometimes staying in a painful dynamic and giving my all to make it work instead of walking away with grace was causing my spirit more harm than good. It was not until I met a very special teacher while living and working abroad in Switzerland that I finally began to understand this lesson.

After spending several years in a particularly challenging work situation and ignoring the multiple signs that were screaming at me to make change, I lost most of my hearing in my left ear. I visited several hearing specialists and the message was the same: "You will *never* regain the hearing in your ear." I was confused by what had happened, and frustrated by the inability of the doctors to point to the cause. It simply did not make sense.

While I would have loved to have met with a counselor for support, the only two English-speaking counselors in the community were both friends of mine, so this option was out. As an alternative, I began working with a woman who taught meditation. She was recommended highly by several friends, and at that point, I felt I had nothing to lose. Her name was Smadar, and I began meeting with her weekly. In our sessions together, we spent part of the time actually meditating, and the other part of the time discussing life, my experiences, frustrations, and perceptions of the situations I encountered. She became my teacher. She asked probing questions, listened intently, and provided new perspectives and intuitive wisdom that challenged me deeply in moments. Somehow, she always got to the core of what I was feeling.

Smadar was loving, supportive, and compassionate in many ways, but she did not "sugar coat" her messages. She told it like she saw it. Perhaps her biggest lesson for me was that I needed to stop wearing rose-colored glasses. She wanted me to face life head-on and to look at the things that were not working in my life, and instead of trying to run from them or put a shiny gloss over them, to embrace them. For these things were trying to tell me something. Instead of listening, I was ignoring the alarms.

My unwillingness to look at the dark, and to see the whole picture, instead of only the lovely parts, was what was holding me back and keeping me stuck in pain, according to Smadar. She was certain that if I could face the proverbial monsters that I was trying desperately to ignore, they would become less daunting and lose their powerful grip on my life. If I could be honest with myself by acknowledging the pain, frustration, anger, and sense of injustice I was experiencing as a result of the dynamics in my work life, I could choose a path that would bring me greater happiness. This, of course, would have required me to face emotions that I had been trying very hard to avoid, and at some level, I feared that once I allowed these emotions to surface, there would be no turning back. It would no longer be possible to tolerate the status quo, and I would have no choice other than to make a change. Smadar also told me that she believed I could get my hearing back if I started listening to myself. While I liked this notion, I was certainly skeptical given what the doctors had told me.

One day, several years after Smadar and I began working together, I was on a walk in the beautiful forest near where I lived. With each step, I pondered my current situation. The circumstances at work had become progressively worse, and it was hard for me to find light at the end of the tunnel. My soul was tired, and I felt like I had lost my sparkle. Suddenly, I was struck by what felt like a rare glimpse of clarity. In that moment, I *knew* that I had to make a change. A voice within told me I could anything else, but I could no longer continue to endure the pain of my circumstances. This time I listened. The next day, I turned in my resignation letter without any sort of safety net or plan apparent. It felt scary, yet I was absolutely clear it was the right thing to do.

As I think about that time in my life, I am reminded of the words to Alanis Morisette's Thank U (1998): *the moment I jumped off of it, was the moment I touched down.* Once I cleared out the parts of my life that were not working, new possibilities began to emerge, and things began to magically fall in place. I decided that it was finally time to pursue a Ph.D. While I had circled around this idea for years, the moment never felt exactly right before. I applied for a doctoral program in Counseling and was admitted.

Soon after, I moved back to the United States, and a new chapter of my life began. Following my arrival in the States, I sought out a new hearing specialist. After sending me to numerous specialists who performed a wide range of tests in order to rule out a brain tumor, multiple sclerosis, migraines, or a heart condition, the doctor concluded that while he could not find the cause of my hearing loss, I would not regain hearing in my left ear. Somehow, hearing this news for the third time did not feel any easier than it did the first two times. It felt more final. I was fitted for a hearing aid, and tried to accept this fate.

Throughout the past four years in my doctoral program, I have continued my meditation practice and have regularly reflected on the lessons and wisdom I gained from Smadar. They have served me well in my life and work with clients. I have also come to realize that while Smadar was not traditionally trained, her approach was aligned with some of the mindfulness-based approaches, such as Acceptance and Commitment Therapy (ACT), that I have learned about in recent years.

I think of Smadar daily. Because of her, my outlook on life is different and the quality of my life is better. Additionally, the lessons I learned from her helped me strengthen my skills as a clinician and have served as a guide in my work with clients. Today, I am better able to sit with someone in pain without feeling the need to be a rescuer or without feeling like I need to offer a positive spin on the situation. As a counselor, my overarching goals include helping clients to develop self-awareness and understanding, to love and accept themselves wholly (especially those parts that are vulnerable or imperfect), and to *listen* to themselves so they can make choices that support their wellness and growth. Using these as a guiding philosophy in my work, I have seen clients make tremendous strides in their lives.

Sadly, last summer, my extraordinary teacher died too young of cancer. Soon after her death, the hearing in my left ear returned.

REFERENCES

Morisette, A. & Ballard, G. (1998). Thank U. On *Supposed Former Infatuation Junkie* (CD). Maverick Records.

Chapter Thirteen

Crossing Borders

*Understanding the Muslim Experience
from a Non-Muslim Perspective*

Cheryl P. Wolf

As the world's fastest growing religion, Islam has grown in popularity with an estimated 6 to 8 million Muslims in North America (Rehman & Dziegie-lewski, 2003). Furthermore, 2010 estimates from the Pew Research Center reported that more than 5 percent of the U.S. population was comprised of individuals practicing Buddhism, Judaism, Islam, Hindu, and religions other than Christianity (Pew, 2014). For many individuals, their religious and cultural foundations are a crucial part of their lives. However, if their values and perspectives are different than the majority population, these aspects of an individual can draw criticism and discrimination from others who do not quite understand them. As counselors, it is our responsibility and ethical requirement to set aside our own religious and cultural values, respect the diversity of our clients, and provide unbiased services for them (ACA, 2014). Where the differences in values might cause potential harm or prejudice, counselors are encouraged to seek additional training.

Like a large percentage of the U.S. population that did not understand Islam or the Muslims who followed it, I felt it was important to better understand this group for my personal and professional development as a counselor. To over-come a prejudice that I had developed through personal experiences and mes-sages proliferated in the U.S. media, I devoted a semester to immersing myself in activities that expanded my knowledge and understanding of the religion and people who practiced it. I enrolled in two multicultural counseling classes, worked with a Muslim cultural guide, watched several documentary films, read journal articles, visited a Jumaa prayer at a local Mosque, conducted brief interviews with other practicing Muslims, and visited a Muslim country. This experience was an amazing growth opportunity for my cultural guide, my family, and me. It was helpful to gain a more culturally diverse perspective, ask questions or share concerns with my guide, and later share the ethnic, spiritual, and culturally diverse experience with others.

My misunderstandings about Muslims began while serving more than 11 years in the U.S. Navy during an earlier career. I spent many months visiting Muslim countries as I sailed across the globe on deployments to the Middle East. My understanding of the Muslim culture was one of oppression and subordination for Muslim women. I felt uncomfortable in the predominately Muslim countries that I visited like Bahrain, Oman, and Malaysia. I felt the stares and received offensive remarks during my visits; this increased my discomfort with the culture. Although I tried to understand the people, my mind was not open to a way of life that I did not understand. After September 11, 2001, the U.S. media proliferated the stereotypes and fear even more. Muslim men were considered suspect, even if they were long-standing American citizens. Muslim women who wore their head scarves, or Hijabs, were ostracized. This somewhat lessened my enthusiasm to learn more about that population.

However, in January 2007 I decided to proactively work on overcoming my prejudice. I was completing my master's degree in counseling and that semester I began taking two courses: multicultural counseling and spiritual issues in multicultural counseling. Around the same time, a classmate from India made the choice to begin wearing her head scarf on a regular basis. We had been friends for several months, but I never realized that she was Muslim. I asked about her decision to wear her scarf full-time and she expressed her desire to be more congruent with her life, religion, and research on being Muslim in America. Her openness to talk about her choice was helpful and I realized for the first time that many women were not forced to cover themselves. She shared that it was a common practice in their religion; however, it was a free choice for most of the Muslim women in America. This helped me realize how narrow and racist my views were regarding Muslims.

LEARNING FROM LITERATURE AND MEDIA

Enrolling in multicultural counseling courses was my first step in gaining more cultural awareness of a variety of cultural identities. In each class, I was encouraged to focus on a particular cultural issue; I chose to learn more about Islam and the Muslim culture because of my related limited preconceived notions. To gain additional insight, I immersed myself in readings, documentaries, and movies related to the Muslim culture. I talked with my friend regularly who served as a cultural guide for me. She shared that while the Koran, or Qur'an, served as a guide for living within the explicit rules, there is no governing body for the Islamic religion; each Muslim interprets the Koran individually. Similar to Christianity, Islam is comprised of a diversity of groups with different beliefs, practices, and traditions as well as varying degrees of fundamentalism and liberalism (Williams, 2005). Furthermore, my guide helped me realize that some of the rituals and traditions I had associated with the Islamic religion were actually *cultural* versus *religious* norms. I began to understand the differences of Muslims in Saudi Arabia versus Egypt or India. For example, many Muslim women in South Asia choose not to cover their heads, whereas most women in Arab countries wear a Hijab or burka, a more conservative garment covering their entire body (Kennedy, 2007). In addition to outward rites and rituals, a study of Muslim universal and mental health values showed that Muslim respondents valued benevolence and conformity and disvalued power, hedonism, and stimulation (Kelly & Aridi, 1996). Seeing the importance of collectivist values helped me better understand their traditions and behavior in relation to the U.S. individualistic expectations they face.

Documentaries about the Muslim experience in a variety of countries helped me to understand the religion from several perspectives across the U.S. and around the world. The documentaries showed that a majority of Muslims were typically passive and peaceful, even though many are por-trayed as terrorists and required to register with the U.S. government. The views presented in the documentaries were very different from the way the U.S. film industry portrayed Muslims. For example, films, even those based on true stories (e.g., Malcolm X, Savior), focused on the more violent and angry side of Muslims, helping to instill fear in the general public. Therefore, seeing the varying perspectives helped me better understand the ways the culture and religion are portrayed and how it has been misrepresented.

USING CULTURAL GUIDES

In addition to readings, documentaries, and movies, I was able to participate in real-world experiences with my cultural guide. Her willingness to share her way of life and listen to my limited perspective was the catalyst that motivated me to explore the Islamic religion and Muslim experience. She and I had very open and honest conversations about our experiences and perspectives which helped shatter my previously held beliefs on the religion and its followers. During this experience, she invited me to the Friday afternoon Jumaa prayer at her mosque. From a Christian perspective, this could be compared to a Christian Sunday morning church service. She prepared me for the visit and gave me some insight about the prayer, rituals, and dress. The women dressed conservatively and traditionally covered their heads and bodies to minimize the distraction to men. The women also sat on the balcony away from the men and used a separate entrance. Because I arrived with my cultural guide, I was prepared for the experience and accepted by the other women. However, I noticed two other non-Muslim young college women who appeared to be visiting on their own. They giggled, dressed inappropriately, and did not follow the rituals expected. However, a few of the Muslim women covered them with a head scarf and guided them in the rituals instead of asking them to leave. After I observed the afternoon prayer, my guide introduced me to other Muslim women at the mosque. I expected them to be docile and submissive, yet many greeted me with warm and welcoming smiles and even offered to answer my questions about their religion. Although I had believed them to be oppressed and forced to cover, I discovered that most of the women chose to cover for personal religious reasons. I even met one converted Muslim who was a previously practicing Morman. She was introduced to Islam through her former husband; however, she refused to convert to Islam or cover her head while she was married to him. Later, she said it was her decision to cover and convert after their marriage ended.

After a semester of immersion in my own city, my husband and I decided to visit a Muslim country. While Egypt is more than 90% Muslim, I was surprised to encounter a very Western and open attitude toward non-Muslim visitors. I went there prepared to respect their religious differences and brought scarves to cover my head. The first day, a Muslim woman who served as our tour guide to the pyramids put me at ease. She was also open to correcting some myths that I still held and shared with her. Many other cab drivers and guides professed their love for Americans and I came away from the experience with a better perspective and appreciation for religious and cultural diversity.

ARRIVING AT A NEW UNDERSTANDING IN MY PERSONAL AND PROFESSIONAL DEVELOPMENT

Several years after this experience, I noticed that media coverage and popular Western literature continued to portray Muslims as extremists who were violent and primitive. However, in my review of the journals, books, documentaries, personal conversations, and relationships, I found the opposite to be true. I discovered that Muslims are commonly peace-seeking people with a few rare extremists just like other religions. I also learned that not only do I need to open my mind to other cultures for personal growth, I need to understand what others are experiencing in relation to my culture as well. For example, the stressors that Muslims endure in the U.S. can negatively impact their mental well-being. Discrimination and threats against Muslims lead to feelings of alienation and fear when clothing, language, diet, daily rituals, and beliefs differ significantly from the majority of the population (Haque, 2004). Furthermore, religious profiling, threats, and hostility that many Muslims have encountered since September 11th has caused undo stress, segregation, and even incarceration to thousands of innocent Muslims. Seeing the registration of thousands of Muslim men showed how little progress the U.S. has made in the last 50 years, since they interred thousands of Japanese families during World War II (Foster, 2004).

I discovered different types of concerns Muslim men and women each experience in U.S. society. Men feel targeted as potential terrorists based on their skin color, language, or dress; even Middle Eastern men from other religions have been attacked because they appeared to be Muslim. Muslim women often face challenges when choosing to dress differently, especially when covering their heads. For example, a Muslim school teacher was afraid of being fired for wearing her hijab on the grounds that she could be perceived as promoting her religion in school (Rehman & Dziegielewski, 2003). While I did realize that women were treated differently when wearing a hijab, I had not considered the fear of losing their livelihoods or even their lives because of their religion. Religious discrimination can take a subtle, although illegal, form of prejudice during employment practices; it can also take a more overt form including threats of violence. In some of my work over the past year with international Muslim refugees from Africa, Afghanistan, and Iraq, refugees have expressed fears and concerns about feeling unaccepted in their new conservative rural town. Some experienced name-calling, threats, and even people spitting at them out a window of a moving car as they walked toward the mosque. I also recently found out that my cultural guide decided to stop wearing her hijab in public because of similar fears for herself and her family. Due to the consequences Muslims face when outwardly expressing their religion through dress, many feel pressured to conform to U.S. societal norms and minimize their external differences.

I also found that American and non-American born Muslim teenagers may also face an identity conflict when they are expected to act one way at school and with peers but another way at home with their families. Their need to fit into society often diverges from the cultural and religious expectations of their parents (Haque, 2004). Their desire to date and socialize is hindered by their rules against it. Prearranged marriages still exist in a few cases but marrying within their ethnic group is still standard practice. In addition, expectations for boys to seek lucrative careers can conflict with their desire to pursue a career they enjoy but may be accompanied by a lower salary (Kennedy, 2007).

Parents also struggle with challenges that their children face trying to fit into two worlds, especially if they recently relocated to the U.S. American-born children model new behaviors in schools, sports, and clubs and many of those behaviors are a departure from the accepted norms of their original culture. For example, children may talk back to a teacher, refuse to complete an assignment, or engage in risky or illegal activities. Although these behav-

iors may not be tolerated in their culture, parents notice their children adopt-
ing them and sometimes feel helpless to stop it. Consequently, conflicting
religious and cultural norms can create problems within the family and community systems.

THE TRANSFORMATIONAL VALUE OF THIS EXPERIENCE

In addition to becoming more aware of the culture and religious differences,
this experience sparked a professional interest in researching, publishing, and
presenting on multicultural spirituality. Understanding one culture and religion has helped open me to other cultures and religions. This experience had
important implications for my counseling practice and in my role as a counselor educator where I can help counselors-in-training address a prejudice
with this population or another.

Counselors should not only challenge their false assumptions in relation
to Islam and pay attention to sensitive issues when working with Muslim
clients, but challenge the stereotype that other non-Muslim clients hold as
well. Encouraging colleagues, clients, and students to become more open-
minded about other religious, spiritual, or cultural beliefs can help diminish
the stereotypes and discrimination that still exists in the U.S. today. Counselors must also be aware that Muslim beliefs often diverge from the traditional
Western views in which they were trained and that shaped modern counseling today (Kelly & Aridi, 1996). Muslims face typical human concerns as
well as a host of issues predicated on their ethnicity and religion. With the
awareness that many Muslims face strongly stereotypical images, counselors
can be better prepared to deal with the consequences of symptoms including
depression, anxiety, and PTSD that occur in the face of exclusion, isolation,
and fear. Better understanding their issues and how society reacts to them can
bring clarity into the counseling process. The discussions with clients must
meet the clients where they are and also be respectful of religious boundaries
like references to sexual issues, explicit language, revealing clothing, addictions in light of prohibited substance use, or eating disorders during fasting.

CONCLUSION

Learning about Islam or any new culture can be an eye-opening and myth-
shattering experience. Increasing the knowledge, understanding, and compassion for new religions or ways of life around the world can improve a
cross-cultural therapeutic exchange and broaden a narrowed perspective.
While anyone cannot be an expert on a culture of which they are not naturally a part, one can gain the basic rules necessary to effectively communicate
and understand a particular set of values, beliefs, and traditions. Being intro-

duced to a series of cultural readings, media, activities, and people can begin the process and make the journey much smoother.

As I took this cultural journey, a variety of questions sparked my interest and learning. The following questions may be helpful to another person's personal and professional growth as well:

- Is there a particular population about which I carry some prejudice or lack important knowledge? This may include religion, race, ethnicity, sexual orientation, age, disability, etc.
- How did I develop my limited perspective about this group? Was it proliferated in the media, by others, from personal experiences, or lack of knowledge about a group?
- In what ways can I expand my knowledge, perspectives, and experiences about this group? What resources and people are available to help guide me? Am I willing to get outside of my comfort zone to grow?
- By opening up to one population, how can that help me expand my understanding of other populations? What can I take from earlier experiences to help me better understand a new population, their challenges, and their perspectives?
- As I expand my understanding of a population, how can I help share this new knowledge with others to remove some of their limited thinking and prejudice? Are there ways that I can advocate for this group?

REFERENCES

A&E Television Networks (Producer). (2006). *Decoding the Past: Secrets of the Koran* [Documentary]. New York: Towers Productions, Inc.

American Counseling Association (2014). *Code of Ethics*. Alexandria, VA: Author.

Foster, Kathleen (Producer). (2004). *Point of Attack* [Documentary]. New York: Cinema Guild.

Grimm, William (Producer). (1992). *Mosque* [Documentary]. Maryknoll, N.Y.: Maryknoll World Video Library.

Haque, A. (2004). Religion and Mental Health: The Case of American Muslims. *Journal of Religion & Health, 43*, 45-58. Retrieved from http://www.jstor.org/stable/27511722.

Kelly, E. & Aridi, A. (1996). Muslims in the United States: An exploratory study of universal and mental health values. *Counseling & Values, 40*, 206. doi: 10.1002/j.2161-007X.1996.tb00853.x.

Kennedy, A. (2007). Teens leading double lives. *Counseling Today*, Apr, 18.

Pew Research Center (2014, April 4). *Global Religious Diversity*. Retrieved from http://www.pewforum.org/2014/04/04/global-religious-diversity.

Rehman, T. Sum F. & Dziegielewski, S. (2003). Women who choose Islam: Issues, changes, and challenges in providing ethnic-diverse practice. *International Journal of Mental Health, 32*, 31-49. Retrieved from http://www.jstor.org/stable/41345060.

Williams, V. (2005). Working with Muslims in counselling - Identifying sensitive issues and conflicting philosophy. *International Journal for the Advancement of Counselling, 27*, 125-130. doi:10.1007/s10447-005-2258.

Chapter Fourteen

Integrating the Dark with the Light

Learning from a Professional Sanction

Jane A. Warren

My home phone rang. I picked it up. "Would you like to go to the movie with me next weekend?" Wow, I thought, that would be wonderful. However, this was a person who had been a previous client of mine, a little less than a year before. I worked with this person for a few months; it seemed a short time. It appeared there were not serious or long term problems. "What do I do?" I called back a few days later and agreed to go. I had thought it would be a one day event and how nice it would be to share a time with a person for whom I had respect. The person mentioned how great life had been and thanked me. I appreciated the kind words. We seemed to have a lot in common. For the next few months, we dated. For numerous reasons, our relationship ended. Soon after, a two year malpractice event followed. I was mandated to attend ethics trainings. I had never been to an ethics training course as I had graduated more than ten years earlier before ethics education was even offered. My license was made probationary until I had completed one year of supervision and the ethics training. The licensing board would review my application in a year, to determine if I had met the requirements and could be fully licensed again, without a probationary status. I was humiliated, ashamed, doubtful, and wanted to die. What did I do? How did this happen?

To fast forward, I did my best to effectively respond to this ethical error, and was successful in meeting consequent requirements. However, I wanted to change my profession, disappear, or even die. Never in a million years had I ever imagined I would be subject to such scrutiny in my work. Even worse though, I never dreamed of inflicting potential harm on any living being. To me, my own death would have been easier. Nothing in my life would be the same again. This pain and embarrassment forever changed both my professional and personal identity, humbled my perfectionism, and taught me a new level of compassion, concern, and caution I had not before known.

INTENTIONS OF DOING GOOD

Most individuals enter the counseling profession with a desire to help others (Warren, Nunez, Weatherford, Zakaria, & Ahls, 2014). Even with a genuine desire to help and having the love for this work, a counselor is challenged with ethical issues (Flynn & Black, 2011; Ronnestad & Skovholt, 2003; Wheeler & Bertram, 2015). To deeply listen to the ethical needs of counselors is to be "people responsive" (Scholl, 2008, p. 3); to ascertain their personally identified challenges and needs may contribute to the improvement of counselor preparation and training. In addition, the practices of self-refection, self-awareness, and self-care are all identified as ways to enhance counselor development and reduce impairment (Griffith & Frieden, 2000; Guiffrida, 2005; La Torre, 2005; Lawson, 2007; Lawson, & Venart, 2005).

However, recognizing ethical quandaries and training needs takes courage because to admit challenges may be similar to admitting fault or weakness (Warren & Douglas, 2012). Goud (2005) identified courage as an energizing catalyst to face conditions of danger, fear, and risk: "Without courage, the individual or group remains stuck in existing patterns or immobilized in fear" (p. 103). Without debate, it is critical that counselors understand and value the experiences of clients; in fact, the counseling relationship has been found to be an important reason enabling clients to improve, as much as the method used (Lambert, & Barley, 2001; Norcross & Wampold, 2011). Similarly, what works with clients, may be what works with counselors. It is important that we as a counseling profession attentively listen to, recognize, empathize with, and acknowledge the ethical challenges faced by counselors and promote counselors' well-being as we would for a client. Perhaps the unconditional regard identified years ago by Rogers (1957; 1975) is a mantra we can use with ourselves:

> When the other person is hurting, confused, troubled, anxious, alienated, and terrified; or when he or she is doubtful of self-worth, uncertain as to identity, then understanding is called for. The gentle and sensitive companionship of an empathetic stance—accompanied of course by the other two attitudes [congruence and genuineness]—provides illumination and healing. In such situations deep understanding is, I believe, the most precious gift one can give to another (Rogers, 1975, p. 9).

I believe the majority of counselors-in-training and those in practice do not intend to commit ethical infractions. In fact, many counselors-in-training report they cannot even imagine getting close to making an error. In the real world there may be exceptions to the rule of practicing well and counselors do *intentionally disregard* or *carelessly disregard* (Wheeler & Bertram, 2015, p. 2–3) the rules and ethics of the counseling profession. Even so, most practitioners understand and carefully follow the legal and ethical expectations, "yet they still become involved in situations in which a client is harmed" (or alleges harm) (Wheeler & Bertram, 2015, p. 3).

Realistically in there is a slippery slope and in a second, a counselor can slip and fall. Counselors are ordinary humans living in ordinary settings. They have children, drive cars, pay bills, go to the grocery store, belong to the workout center, and are members of the school board. These daily commitments are part of life; similarly they can create unforeseen ethical challenges such as when your child befriends your child client, your loan officer is a member of your substance abuse treatment group, or you see your client at workout.

In training we learn to respond to the extraordinary circumstances like suicide and confidentiality, but we as counselors in practice may not learn how to professionally react to the daily events in our lives like our families, children, friends, and peers. These daily situations are not manifest destiny to the slippery slopes of ethical violations (Gottlieb & Younggren, 2009), but they can be beginning of cracks in our professional foundation.

Helping professionals do not plan to commit ethical infractions (Herlihy & Corey, 2014; Linton, 2012; Welfel, 2005). Ethical errors are diverse and can include such challenges as dual relationships, fraudulence, impairment, breaches of confidentiality, and practicing below a standard of care. In a national survey on counseling graduate students conducted by Trigg and Robinson (2013), numerous ethical violations were described including: (a) "practicing outside of the scope of one's training and experience and practicing while impaired due to substance use or mental health matters" (p. 28), (b) violations of professional boundaries (both nonsexual and sexual), and (c) breaches of confidentiality. Similarly Strom-Gottfried (2003) reviewed ethical complaints to the National Association of Social Workers (NASW) and reported ethical errors such as sexual activity, dual relationships, boundary violations, failure to seek supervision, a lack of using accepted practice skills, fraudulent behavior, premature termination records, informed consent, and referrals. Although a counselor can unwittingly make ethical errors (Linton, 2012; Welfel, 2005; Wheeler & Bertram, 2015), these are especially difficult when working with relationships. The therapeutic boundary is complex and can involve complicated situations and human interactions (Moleski & Kiselica, 2005; Pope & Keith-Spiegel, 2008; Trimberger, 2012; Younggren & Gottlieb, 2004). For example, boundary issues in counseling relationships are a common source of ethical complaints for psychologists. These occurrences may be in part due to the difficulties in navigating multiple relationships, with non-rational, poor reflective processes, internal conflicts, self-serving biases, and an absence of awareness (Rogerson, Gottlieb, Handelsman, Knapp, & Youngren, 2011). Regardless of the reasons, counselors make ethical errors and they are painful for everyone affected.

SHAME-BASED THINKING AND PROFESSIONAL SILENCE

Research suggests the actual numbers of misconducts are unknown (Wheeler & Bertram, 2015). In fact there may be more negative events than are reported (Gottlieb & Younggren, 2009). Similarly, counselors must also be careful to protect the identity of any client whether harmed or not, thus writing about any events is done with extreme caution and protection of identities (Sperry, 2010) and sometimes the writing is just not done. Even with unknown prevalence and considering confidentiality concerns, perhaps such fears like being judged, losing licensing, and being considered defective, drive counselors to silence. I have called this our professional silence (Warren & Douglas, 2012).

Realities of practice (Lawson, 2007; Lawson & Venart, 2005) suggest errors are made (Linton, 2012); however, the fear of disclosing errors remains (Warren & Douglas, 2012). Professional silence (not talking among ourselves) persists because we can so easily and unknowingly judge ourselves, form negative images of anyone who commits errors, and assume only persons with problems will make poor ethical judgments. Humans have a tendency to characterize and classify people; thus humans can hide personal experiences and stories, and "internalize and judge themselves" (Gladding, 2015, p. 348).

We assume those persons who make ethical errors must be defective. There is a stigma towards persons who are viewed as defective (Corrigan, Kerr, & Knudson, 2005; Corrigan & Penn, 1999; Livingston & Boyd, 2010). "Stigmas are negative and erroneous attitudes about these people [those with severe mental illness]. ... [a] stigma's impact on a person's life may be as harmful as the direct effects of the disease" (Corrigan & Penn, 1999, p. 765). Livingston and Boyd (2010) defined *self-stigma* as "the process of an individual accepting society's negative evaluation and incorporating it into his or her own personal value system and sense of self" (p. 2151). Similarly, Corrigan, Kerr, and Knudsen (2005) viewed "self-stigma [as] the loss of self-esteem and self-efficacy that occurs when people internalize the public stigma" (p. 179). Even with the fear of dialogue and the resulting stigmas, there are ethical guidelines and structures in place for counselors to use.

RULES AND STRUCTURE

Counselors follow ethical standards to ultimately promote the well-being of the profession and the clients (Ponton & Duba, 2009). There are many professional organizations and they provide comprehensive ethical guidelines to follow such as the American Association for Marriage and Family Therapy [AAMFT] (2012); American Counseling Association [ACA] (2014); American School Counselor Association [ASCA] (2010); American Psychological Association [APA] (2010); and the National Association of Social Workers [NASW] (2008). In addition to the ethical codes, there are federal, state, and licensing standards that professional counselors follow (Wheeler & Bertram, 2015). Although it may seem confusing to have so many bosses, so to speak, ultimately, practitioners who remain knowledgeable and mindful do avoid making ethical errors (Wheeler & Bertram, 2015).

PREVENTION STEPS: TALK, CONSULT, AND ACT

There are many reasons to talk about difficult incidents. For one, it is a critical part of our professional responsibility. For example, the standards of *ACA Code of Ethics* (ACA, 2014) specifically guide counselors to know the rules of the codes (Standard C.1.) and to supervise and consult with peers for any ethical challenges (Standard C.2.e). McGinty, Goldman, Pescosolido, and Barry (2015) demonstrated in their study that stigma was reduced when stories (vignettes) shared successes in treated patients. In essence they showed how public opinion can be improved and stigmas reduced through positive stories. Open and truthful dialogue is one powerful way to prevent ethical infractions.

There are steps counselors can take to avoid unethical decisions. For example, they can monitor their work, maintain wellness, stay current on procedures and interventions, use consultation and supervision, and apply an effective decision-making model (ACA, 2014). There are general interventions to help reduce the likelihood of making ethical errors found in risk management and education. Ethics education can reduce the challenges of making ethical errors (Warren et al., 2014; Warren, Zavaschi, Covello, & Zakaria, 2012); however there are not mandated or consistent training guidelines in ethics education for counselors-in-training (CIT) (Hill, 2004; Warren & Douglas, 2012). Even with solid educational structures, because of non-rational and emotional biases of counselors, "faculty should work to increase students' awareness of those occasions when their emotions might work in their favor" (Rogerson et al., 2011, p. 620). One way to address emotional reactivity is through use of a decision-making model.

DECISION MAKING MODELS

Decision-making models can promote self-awareness and slow down emotional reactivity. To use a decision-making model can provide a counselor with a strategic, analytical, and objective approach to making difficult decisions (i.e., client's needs, self-needs, emotional reactivity, competence, etc.) (Crowley & Gottlieb, 2012; Evans, Levitt, & Henning, 2012). Research suggests too, that effective ethical decision making requires well developed levels of ethical and legal knowledge (Lambie, Hagedorn, & Ieva, 2010).

There are many ethical codes and they each require counselors to use decision-making models to address ethical quandaries as well as they provide principles and best practices, and offer a structure to promote self-reflection and self-awareness (ACA, 2014; AMFT, 2012; APA, 2010; ASCA, 2010; Herlihy & Corey, 2014). Although there are diverse ethical decision-making models (Ametrano, 2014; Cottone & Claus, 2000; Rogerson et al., 2011), each is designed for a specific focus such as theory, practice, and specialized populations (Calley, 2009; Evans et al., 2012; Kocet & Herlihy, 2014).

Counselors may choose and/or create their own models (Evans et al., 2012); effective ethical practice employs a decision-making model (ACA, 2014; Herlihy & Corey, 2014). The model used for this article was adapted from the ethical decision-making model developed by Wheeler and Bertram (2015). *How* an ethical decision making model is used is as important as the model itself. It is important that practitioners at all levels integrate and summarize ethical issues.

One strategy to use to integrate ethical guidelines is through an ethical bookmark (Warren et al., 2012). A bookmark is a succinct way to summarize an ethical decision-making process and provides reminders such as consult, use the codes, document, and stay well. Using a bookmark can also provide a helpful structure to slow down automatic reactions. The book mark is like a safety seat or airbags in cars. The ultimate goal is to transform non-rational and biased reactions into time-enhanced, coping, protective, reflective, and effective responses (Crowley & Gottlieb, 2012).

TRANSFORMATION: DARK INTO LIGHT

Reflecting on the personal and professional changes that emerged from this event has allowed me to recognize that it was life altering and ultimately resulted in personal and professional growth. That is not to say however, that the event was easy or unimportant. The deep personal pain, the professional shame, the shock of committing an error, and the wonderment about my future, were all part of the process of understanding and integrating the gravity of my own lack of knowledge, blindness, impairment, and isolation.

Most humans make errors in judgments. Even so, this event permanently changed me. From this I will offer a reflective view on this experience.

I internalized negative attributions and I developed a self-stigma. I assumed I must be impaired, defective, and unable to be a counseling practitioner. I successfully applied to law school thinking maybe I would be a better lawyer than a counselor. I did not choose to attend law school, however. Mostly, I felt humiliated. How could I do this? No one else would ever make such an error. Although this event took place more than 20 years ago, today I feel as close to it as I did when it happened. The difference today is I talk about it, teach about it, and continually integrate it into a more aware, educated, and imperfect human counselor. There are few absolute rights or wrongs in decision making. This event permanently changed me and I share the primary following guidelines that I apply today in my teaching and counseling work. Every day I learn more and continue to update my guidelines.

1. Once a client, always a client.
2. Once a counselor, always a counselor.
3. Never assume you know. Maintain a not-knowing mind.
4. Ethics education is lifelong; neither one class nor one event is sufficient.
5. Embrace acceptance and compassion for each other. Any counselor can have a moment in time where an ethical error is made or about to be made.
6. Avoid imposing value judgments on professional peers.
7. Encourage dialogue. Avoid professional silence.
8. Eradicate professional isolation.
9. Develop counselor support networks.
10. Always have a supervisor, no matter how long you have practiced.
11. Never overlook ethical decision making.
12. Use a decision-making model that includes at least three peers. They can help you recognize outcomes not typically seen.
13. Maintain strong self-care and mindfulness.
14. Journal in whatever forms that help you to say what you need to say.
15. Realistic challenges and potential ethical conundrums happen and can enhance ethical decision making.

REFERENCES

American Association for Marriage and Family Therapy (2012).*Code of ethics.* Retrieved from http://www.aamft.org/.
American Counseling Association (2014). ACA *code of ethics and standards of practice.* Alexandria, VA: Author.
American Psychological Association (2010). *Ethical principles of psychologists and code of conduct.* Retrieved from http://www.apa.org/ethics/code.

American School Counselor Association (2010). *Ethical standards for school counselors*. Retrieved from http://www.asca@schoolcounselor.org.

Ametrano, I. M. (2014). Teaching ethical decision making: Helping students reconcile personal and professional values. *Journal of Counseling & Development, 92*, 154–161. doi:10.1002/1556–6676.2014.00143.x.

Calley, N. G. (2009). Promoting a contextual perspective in the application of the ACA Code of Ethics: The ethics into action map. *Journal of Counseling & Development, 87*, 476–482. doi: 10.1002/j.1556–6678.2009.tb00132.x.

Corrigan, P. W., Kerr, A., & Knudsen, L. (2005). The stigma of mental illness: Explanatory models and methods for change. *Applied and Preventive Psychology, 11*, 179–190. doi:10.1016/j.appsy.2005.07.001.

Corrigan, P. W., & Penn, D. L. (1999). Lessons from social psychology and discrediting psychiatric stigma. *American Psychologist, 54*, 765–776. doi:10.1037//0003–066X.54.9.765.

Cottone, R. R., & Claus, R. E. (2000). Ethical decision-making models: A review of the literature. *Journal of Counseling & Development, 78*, 275–283. doi:10.1002/j.1556–6676.2000.tb01908.x.

Crowley, J. D., & Gottlieb, M. C. (2012). Objects in the mirror are closer than they appear: Aprimary prevention model for ethical decision making. *Professional Psychology: Research and Practice, 43*, 65–72. doi.org/10.1037/a0026212.

Evans, A. M., Levitt, D. H., Henning, S. (2012). The application of ethical decision-making and self-awareness in the counselor education classroom. *Journal for Counselor Preparation and Supervision,4*, 41–52. doi.org/10.7729/42.0029.

Flynn, S. V., & Black, L. L. (2011). An emergent theory of altruism and self-interest. *Journal of Counseling & Development, 89*, 459–469. doi:10.1002/j.1556–6676.2011.tb02843.x.

Gladding, S. T. (2015). *Family therapy: History, theory, and practice* (6th ed.). Boston, MA: Pearson.

Gottlieb, M. C. & Younggren, J. N. (2009). Is there a slippery slope? Considerations regarding multiple relationships and risk management. *Professional Psychology, Research and Practice, 40*, 564–571. doi: 10.1037//a0017231.

Goud, N. H. (2005). Courage: Its nature and development. *Journal of Humanistic Counseling, Education and Development, 44*, 102–116. doi:10.1002/j.2164–490X.2005.tb00060.x.

Griffith, B. A., & Frieden, G. (2000). Facilitating reflective thinking in counselor education. *Counselor Education and Supervision, 40*, 82–93. doi: 10.1002/j.1556–6978.2000.tb01240.x.

Guiffrida, D.A. (2005). The emergence model: An alternative pedagogy for facilitating self-reflection and theoretical fit in counseling students. *Counselor Education & Supervision, 44*, 201–213. doi: 10.1002/j.1556–6978.2005.tb01747.x.

Herlihy, B., & Corey, G. (2014). *ACA ethical standards casebook* (7th ed.). Alexandria, VA: American Counseling Association.

Hill, A. L. (2004). Ethics education: Recommendations for an evolving discipline. *Counseling and Values, 48*, 183–203. doi:10.1002/j.2161–007X.2004.tb00245.x.

Kocet, M. M., & Herlihy, B. J. (2014). Addressing value-based conflicts within the counseling relationship: A decision-making model. *Journal of Counseling & Development, 92*, 180–186. doi:10.1002/j.1556–6676.2014.00146.x.

Lambert, M. J., & Barley, D. E. (2001). Research summary on the therapeutic relationship and psychotherapy outcome. *Psychotherapy, Theory, Research, Practice, Training 38*, 357–361. doi:10.1037//0033–3204.38.4.357.

Lambie, G. W., Hagedorn, W. B., & Ieva, K. P. (2010). Social-cognitive development, ethical and legal knowledge, and ethical decision-making of counselor education students. *Journal of Counselor Education and Supervision, 49*, 228–246. doi:10.1002/j.1556–6978.2010.tb00100.x.

La Torre, M. A. (2005). Self-reflection: An important process for the therapist. *Perspectives in Psychiatric Care, 41*, 85–87. doi:10.1002/j.1556–6678.2005.tb00574.x.

Lawson, G. (2007). Counselor wellness and impairment: A national survey. *Journal of Humanistic Counseling, Education and Development, 46,* 20–34. doi:10.1002/j.2161-1939.2007.tb00023.x.

Lawson, G., & Venart, B. (2005). Preventing counselor impairment: Vulnerability, wellness, and resilience. In G. R. Waltz & R. K. Yep (Eds.), *VISTAS 2005:* Compelling perspectives on counseling (pp. 243–246). Alexandria, VA: American Counseling Association.

Linton, J. M. (2012). Ethics and accreditation in addictions counselor training: Possible field placement issues for CACREP-accredited additions counseling programs. *Journal of Addictions and Offender Counseling, 33,* 48–61. doi: 10.1002/j.2161-1874.2012.00004.x.

Livingston, J. D., & Boyd, J. E. (2010). Correlates and consequences of internalized stigma for people living with mental illness: A systematic review. *Social Science & Medicine, 71,* 2150–2161. doi:10.1016/j.socscimed.2010.09.030.

McGinty, E. E., Goldman, H. H., Pescosolido, B., Barry, C. L. (2015). Portraying mental illness and drug addiction as treatable health conditions: Effects of a randomized experiment on stigma and discrimination. *Social Science and Medicine, 126,* 73–85. doi: 10.1016/j.socscimed.2014.12.010.

Moleski, S. M., & Kiselica, M. S. (2005). Dual relationships: A continuum ranging from the destructive to the therapeutic. *Journal of Counseling & Development, 83,* 3–11. doi:10.1002/j.1556-6678.2005.tb00574.x.

National Association of Social Workers. (2008). *Code of ethics of the national association of social workers.* Washington, DC. Retrieved from NASW website: http://www.naswdc.org/pubs/code/code.asp.

Norcross, J. C., & Wampold, B. E. (2011). Evidence-based therapy relationships: Research conclusions and clinical practices. *Psychotherapy, 48,* 98–102. doi:10:1037/a0022161.

Ponton, R. F., & Duba, J. D. (2009). The ACA Code of Ethics: Articulating counseling's professional covenant. *Journal of Counseling & Development, 87,* 117–121. doi: 10.1002/j.1556-6678.2009.tb00557.x.

Pope, K. S., & Keith-Spiegel, P. (2008). A practical approach to boundaries in psychotherapy: Making decisions, bypassing blunders, and mending fences. *Journal of Clinical Psychology, 64,* 638–652. doi:10.1002/jclp.20477.

Rogers, C. R. (1957). The necessary and sufficient conditions of therapeutic personality change. *Journal of Counseling Psychology, 21,* 95–103. doi:10.1037//0022-006X.60.6.827.

Rogers, C. R. (1975). Empathetic: An unappreciated way of being. *The Counseling Psychologist, 5,* 2–10. doi: 10.1177/001100007500500202.

Rogerson, M. D., Gottlieb, M. C., Handelsman, M. M., Knapp, S., & Youngren, J. (2011).Nonrational processes in ethical decision making. *American Psychologist, 66,* 614–623. doi: 10.1037/a0025215.

Rønnestad, M., H., & Skovholt, T. M. (2003). The journey of the counselor and therapist: Research findings and perspectives on professional development. *Journal of Career Development, 30,* 5–44.doi:10.1177/0894845303303000102he.

Scholl, M. B. (2008). Preparing manuscripts with a central and salient humanistic content. *Journal of Humanistic Counseling, Education and Development, 47,* 3–8. doi:10.1002/j.2161-1939.2008.tb00043.x.

Sperry, L. (2010). Writing about clients: Ethical considerations and options. *Counseling and Values, 54,* 88–102. doi: 10.1002/j.2161-007X.2010.tb00008.x.

Strom-Gottfried, K. (2003). Understanding adjudication: Origins, targets, and outcomes of ethics complaints. *Social Work, 48,* 85–94. doi:10.1093/sw/48.1.85.

Trigg, E. A., & Robinson, C. R. (2013). The impact of CACREP accreditation: A multiway frequency analysis of ethics violations and sanctions. *Journal of Counseling & Development, 91,* 26–34. doi:10.1002/j.1556-6676.2013.00067.x.

Trimberger, G. E. (2012). An exploration of the development of professional boundaries. *Journal of Social Work Values and Ethics, 9,* 68–75.

Warren, J., & Douglas, K. I. (2012). Falling from grace: Understanding an ethical sanctioning experience. *Counseling and Values, 57,* 131–146. doi:10.1002/j.2161-007X.2012.00013.x.

Warren, J., Nunez, J., Weatherford, J., Zakaria, N. S., & Ahls, C. (2014). Ethics issues and training needs of mental health practitioners in a rural setting. *Journal of Social Work Values and Ethics, 11,* 61–75. Professional Studies Department mini-grant.

Warren, J., Zavaschi, G., Covello, C., & Zakaria, N. S. (2012). The use of bookmarks in teaching counseling ethics. *Journal of Creativity in Mental Health, 7,* 2–15. doi: 10.1080/15401383.2012.685027.

Welfel, E. R. (2005). Accepting fallibility: A model for personal responsibility for nonegregious ethics infractions. *Counseling and Values, 49,* 120–131. doi:10.1002/j.2161–007X.2005.tb00258.x.

Wheeler, A. M., & Bertram, B. (2015). *The counselor and the law: A guide to legal and ethical practice* (7th. ed.). Alexandria, VA: American Counseling Association.

Younggren, J. N., & Gottlieb, M. C. (2004). Managing risk when contemplating multiple relationships. *Professional Psychology: Research and Practice, 35,* 255–260. doi:10.1037/0735–7028.35.3.255.

Section Three:
Transformation in
Training Experiences

Chapter Fifteen

The Laws of Aerodynamics Don't Pertain to Bumble Bees

Nicole Arcuri

Benjamin Franklin captured the essence of teaching when he wrote: *"Tell me and I forget. Teach me and I remember. Involve me and I learn"* (American History Central, 2015). Benjamin Franklin, a prominent author, political theorist, scientist, inventor, activist, and diplomat is "commonly accorded: the wisest American" and "a man of enlightenment" (Southgate, 2007, p. 14). Franklin suggested people most effectively learned when they are fully engaged in the process, more commonly known as experiential learning today (Wurdinger & Carlson, 2010). My goal as an aspiring counselor educator and supervisor [CES] is to provide my students with an environment that fosters openness and exploration while igniting in them a passion to learn. I agree with Franklin's stance which students learn best when formal learnings and past experiences are applied and reflected upon in order to form a personal, in-depth, and comprehensive understanding of the specific content.

Foremost, in order to most effectively guide counselors-in-training along their professional developmental journey, I believe it is imperative to understand both the intrinsic and extrinsic motivators for students to enter the professional field of counseling (Svinicki & McKeachie, 2011). Recognizing why students have applied to graduate school, why students have chosen the counseling field, and what their expectations are, can help guide counselor educators in planning effective lessons that empower students to become active participants in the developmental journeys. Additionally, counselor educators must act within a supervisory role in order to provide students an opportunity to gain a sense of confidence in the development of their professional counseling skills and to fully understand what their professional role as a counselor is (Friedlander, Siegel, & Brenock, 1989). However, when I first worked with counselors-in-training in the educator and supervisor role, I was unsure how I could provide a motivational spirit within the class as a whole. I was unsure how to apply Franklin's idea of involvement in a way that would correspond to all students' intrinsic and extrinsic motivators.

REACHING MY STUDENTS IN EACH PHASE OF DEVELOPMENT

When working with aspiring counselors-in-training as a counselor educator and supervisor intern, I was well aware that students learned developmentally. Skovholt and Ronnestad (2003) assert counselors-in-training progress through six developmental phases: the (a) lay helper, (b) beginning student, (c) advanced student, (d) novice professional, (e) experienced professional, and (f) senior professional. For my purposes of educating and supervising master level counselors-in-training, I was concerned with phases one through four. Throughout my supervision of students during their internship experience, I used examples and metaphors in order to increase their engagement, encourage their growth, and inspire their professional development across the developmental continuum. However, I had struggled to grasp an idea that would be applicable to all students when presented with faltering confidence and/or a sense of defeat throughout all phases of their development. This struggle continued until one of my internship supervisors, Dr. Alabama *(name has been changed in order to protect the person's identity)*, shared her bumble bees' story with me.

Dr. Alabama provided a great example of symbolism, which I have found myself continuously revisiting. Dr. Alabama gave me, as well as each of her counselors-in-training, a bumble bee pin and shared a short story, summarized as such:

> According to the laws of aerodynamics, bees are not capable of flight. However, no one ever told the bumble bees. Therefore, the bee kept flapping its wings, harder and harder, until the bees flew. Even though it is not possible by means of science, the bees never gave up. The bees were never self-defeated due to being told they were incapable. Therefore, they continued to try and attain flight. In turn, the bees were not labeled a non-flier. The bees flew because the bees gave it everything they had in regards to motivation, spirit, and desire. The bees eventually overcame their genetic obstacles and experienced flight.

As soon as Dr. Alabama began the story of the bees, I was instantly drawn in to each detail of the bees' experience. The crucial component that stuck with me was that no one ever told the bees that they could not fly. I literally sat there thinking of numerous students I taught and supervised as an intern and wondered who or what is telling them that they cannot be a successful counselor. I started to realize that many of them do not necessarily have an event or person deterring their confidence. The negativity was actually the students' own self-defeating cognitions.

As a counselor, I knew a self-defeating belief system can be detrimental to a person's developmental progress. Albert Ellis' Rational Emotive Behavior Therapy (REBT) highlights how irrational ideas lead to self-defeating behavior but also affirmed the possibility of having people replace their ineffective ways of thinking with effective and rational cognitions (Corey, 1996). Instantaneously I realized students who are aspiring to become a counselor, despite their intrinsic and extrinsic motivators, have the capability to foster self-defeating thoughts. However, all students have the capacity to change their thought processes while connecting to the basis of what led them to become a counseling student. This is the moment when I realized I found, what might be, the missing piece in establishing an environment that acknowledges weaknesses but fosters growth. The bees' story allows students to come to an understanding that their worst enemy, when it comes to not believing in themselves, is them. I knew that by providing students with an opportunity to understand how one can defy all odds, those students can reassess why they are in my course, what is blocking them in regards to progression, and understand that it is possible to do anything with effort. Additionally, I found a fundamental foundation for students to utilize when working with their clients. For example, many students had shared they felt incompetent when their clients were not progressing and would begin to question if they can be an effective counselor. The bees' story would allow for understanding of Albert Ellis' REBT in a symbolic manner and also provide background for why clients sometimes become stuck or experience resistance. The bees' story was the piece I knew I needed to incorporate into my supervision so that I could possibly ignite students' passion to learn.

I was literally overjoyed. I could not wait to start connecting with students utilizing the bees' story. I literally felt reenergized and had a new sense of confidence within my own ability to meet the needs of my students. This single event profoundly changed how I approached every student and how I encouraged students to approach current and future clients.

Prior to Dr. Alabama's story, I often found myself wondering what would reach the student who has been successful in their coursework but was struggling in the field, the student who has struggled the entire way, or even the student who has progressed with ease and will not admit when there is a time which promotes questioning of one's ability. I frequently pondered the question, "How do I provide an opportunity to reach all of my students?" The moment I heard the bees' story, I knew the symbolism would transform me as a counselor educator and supervisor intern and as an aspiring counselor educator and supervisor.

Before the bees' story, in order to explore possibilities which would moti-vate engagement among all students, I began to think of the counselor educa-tor and supervisor's introduction when meeting students for the first time. I knew having a teaching and supervision philosophy helps students under-stand the supervisor's viewpoints and also acts as a fundamental component of being a reflective and scholarly practitioner. When students are able to review their instructors' philosophies which relate to CES, students gain an understanding of how the educator views education as well as the course content while providing students with expectations of the objectives to be met (Brian, 2002). Personally, my teaching and supervision philosophy serves as an explanation of my professional and personal beliefs related to my general and core values, knowledge, and skills for academic and applied instruction in counselor education and supervision. Even as a CES intern, I specified the core concepts which guided my teaching, scholarship and ser-vice to my profession, its students, and clients. However, I felt presenting students with my educational philosophies still did not clearly establish an engaging learning community.

According to the Association for Counselor Education and Supervision [ACES] (1993), CESs have four primary roles: (a) assist supervisees by monitoring client welfare, (b) encourage student compliance with relevant legal, ethical, and professional standards for clinical practice, (c) oversee supervisee performance and professional development, and (d) evaluate and certify current and potential performance. Therefore, I understood finding motivation within my students and promoting progression is an ethical obli-gation of the CES. Additionally, I knew counselor educators have an ethical duty to communicate with their students to ensure a clear understanding of a course content and the expectations of the students' progress towards their professional growth. In summary, I was fully aware CESs must understand who their students are in order to best support them throughout their profes-sional growth experience while providing supervision and guidance. Yet exactly how I could draw all students under my guidance to a stronger belief in themselves was still a struggle, until the bees' story.

Phase One: The Lay Helper

The first stage, the lay helper phase, describes students with no prior training within the helping profession (McAuliffe & Eriksen, 2011). Such students need a lot of support. When information is new to students, they may feel lost and suffer from anxiety (Svinicki & McKeachie, 2011). There-fore, it was imperative I knew my students' intrinsic and extrinsic motivators to pursue a career in counseling in order to best meet the needs of my students to support them through the initial phase of development. A CES who can empower students to become invested and accountable for their learning to progress to the next phase of counselor development must consider students' purpose for aspiring to become a counselor in order to promote professional identity (Bernard & Goodyear, 2009). The bees' story promoted me to also discover students' self-defeating cognitions and behaviors that may be impacting their developmental growth as a counselor.

Phase Two: The Beginning Student

The second stage is when students begin to understand counseling is a dynamic approach where clients' well-being is their responsibility. As a result, students begin to self-focus. Content in practice is confusing for the students; students will often struggle with the same concept when applying it to different settings and situations. Counseling students at this point are more concerned with how to respond correctly to the client rather than what the client is saying and doing because they want to please the client (McAuliffe & Eriksen, 2011). As the CES intern, I had to find a way for students to believe in themselves and gain confidence in their knowledge and skills. Often, I had to help students find a way to restructure their thinking pattern concerning their skills. The bees' story afforded me with the additional approach to explore the students' thinking and behaviors pertaining to their counseling knowledge and skills. I knew the story would motivate students to self-reflect and identify their impairment.

Phase Three: The Advanced Student

During the third phase, counselors-in-training are orientated to counseling theory but are characterized by feelings of vulnerability, internal growth, the ability to handle ambiguity, boundary setting, disillusions of inadequate conceptual maps; students at this point in their training benefit from intensive supervision and training (McAuliffe & Eriksen, 2011). Once again, as the CES intern, I had to be there to support students when their confidence faltered. During this phase, students begin to act independently by being able to navigate the counseling relationship, but they still look for support to ensure that they are on the right path. The bees' story helped me as a CES intern understand the importance of exploring students' vulnerabilities in regards to their thought process as well as reflective behaviors.

Phase Four: The Novice Professional

Phase four is when the students are on their own walking down their own path with the skills necessary to counsel clients independently. Although, when new situations arise, students are advised to seek supervision in order to gain more confidence to continue to be most effective for their client. "Successful transitions and effective decision making require intentionality"

(Carlson, Portman, & Bartlett, 2006, p. 128). Therefore, at this point in time, I had to provide students with the confidence to navigate through new, ambiguous situations while asserting that new situations will continue to arise through their career and require reflective practice. The bees' story provided me with the additional support to encourage students about the importance of how they choose to approach novel situations.

APPLICATION OF THE BEES' STORY

During my CES doctoral internship phase, I had one student in particular where the bees' story became a blessing. The student was within her prepracticum course. She was truly a gifted, beginner level clinician, however, she was blind to her potential. In turn, she was rather critical of herself and had difficulty sharing positive aspects of herself. Prior to the bumble-bee's defying aerodynamic experience, I had supervised weekly one-on-one meetings with this student. We would discuss self-empowerment and the positives she possessed as a clinician but she failed to see. Additionally, I would provide her with motivational clips that highlighted nervousness as being a normal feeling while at the same time confirming she is knowledgeable and ready to go into the field.

Every once in a while, she would assert her knowledge, but mostly she would try to blend in with her classmates and not stand out. As a CES doctoral intern, I began to feel that I was failing my student. Just when I was becoming burned out trying to help the student gain confidence to move forward, the student bumble bee defied all odds and experienced flight.

I felt like the bees' story would be the wake-up call for all of my students in regards to why they are in my course and how they plan to grow professionally. I put a picture of the bumble bee on the projector screen. I asked all of the students to describe the bee independently. Then, I asked them to write down facts about the bumble bee. A few moments later, I had them draw a venn diagram, label one side as the "student's name" and the other the "bumble bees." I asked them to distinguish commonalities and differences they had with the bumble bees. Students at first had a great deal of confusion on their face and looked at me like I lost my mind. I encouraged them to just try their best and have fun with it. Their faces soon had smiles and they giggled as they took part in the activity. Next, I placed on the projector, the law of aerodynamics and how it relates to bumble bees. I asked them to read the passage independently and, without talking to others, create another venn diagram labeled one side them and the other side bumble bees. I asked that they now consider the law of aerodynamics while distinguishing similarities and differences they have with the bumble bee. The class grew silent and began to busily cover their pages with similarities.

For the rest of that class, the students actively took part in discussing the anxiety they were having in regards to going into the field. The students offered their peers support, thus, empowering their peers' motivation, spirit, and desire to persevere. Some of the students encouraged by telling her she was competent. Additionally, her peers in the course would encourage her. Her peers would assert that she has made it this far in the program because of her competence and the fact that her professors believed she is capable and ready. Also, the students reiterated to her that she is not alone, and they are together along this journey. Moreover, I was learning about students' extrinsic and intrinsic motivators for why they are in the program and what makes them overcome obstacles. I felt like I began to know my students in a whole new way. As the course progressed, and I heard self-defeating comments expressed or behavior displayed, I would challenge the individual and or class by asking them, "What do you think the bees would do?"

From that day forward, when I exchange corrective feedback with any of my students/supervisees, I provide an image of the bumble bee. In the past, it was something I have never considered doing for master level students. However, I now understand just how effective one image can be in providing encouragement and support for students to persevere and become empowered. The bumble bees' story supports Benjamin Franklin's idea of learning because the bees' story promotes self-reflection concerning why someone is becoming a counselor and how one's cognitions and behaviors either support or deter professional development. In turn, the symbol is meant to ignite a feeling of empowerment within the students/supervisees to find their motivation to pursue their career goals. The student therefore fully becomes involved in the learning process. The bumble bees' story has been a true inspiration to my teaching and supervision methodology. I hope it inspires you as well along your journey to become an effective professional counselor.

REFERENCES

American History Central. (2015). American History Central Encyclopedia of American History: Quotes By and About Benjamin Franklin. Retrieved from http:www.americanhistorycentral.com/entry.php?rec=469&view=quotes.

Association for Counselor Education and Supervision (1993). Ethical guidelines for counseling supervisors: Association for counselor education and supervision (ACES). Retrieved from http://files.acesonline.net/doc/ethical_guidelines.htm.

Bernard, J. M., & Goodyear, R. K. (2009). *Fundamentals of clinical supervision* (4th ed.). Upper Saddle River, NJ: Pearson.

Brian, P. C. (2002). Writing a statement of teaching philosophy: Fashioning a framework for your classroom. *Journal of College Science Teaching, 31*(7), 448-453. http://www.jstor.org/stable/42991436.

Carlson, L. A., Portman, T. A. A., & Bartlett, J. R. (2006). Self-management of career development: Intentionality for counselor educators in training. *The Journal of Humanistic Counseling, 45*(2), 126–137. doi: 10.1002/j.2161-1939.2006.tb00012.x.

Corey, G. (1996). *Theory and practice of counseling and psychotherapy* (5th ed.). Pacific Grove, CA: Brooks/Cole Publishing.

Friedlander, M. L., Siegel, S. M., & Brenock, K. (1989). Parallel processes in counseling and supervision: A case study. *Journal of Counseling Psychology, 36*(2), 149-157. doi: org/10.1037/0022-0167.36.2.149.

McAuliffe, G., & Eriksen, K. (2011). *Handbook of counselor preparation: Constructivist, developmental, and experiential approaches.* Thousand Oaks, CA: Sage.

Ronnestad, M. H. & Skovholt, T. M. (2003). The journey of the counselor and therapist: Research findings and perspectives on professional development. *Journal of Career Development, 3*(1), 5-44. doi: 10.1177/089484530303000102.

Southgate M. (2007). Benjamin Franklin. *Journal of the American Medical Association, 298*(1), 14.

Svinicki, M. D., & McKeachie, W. J. (2011). *McKeachie's teaching tips: Strategies, research, and theory for college and university teachers* (13th ed.). Belmont, CA: Wadsworth, Cengage Learning.

Wurdinger, D. D., & Carlson, J. A. (2010). *Teaching for experiential learning: Five approaches that work.* Lanham, MD: Rowman & Littlefield Education.

Chapter Sixteen

Planting Seeds, Blossoming Careers, and Birkenstocks

Angela Colistra

There are numerous experiences throughout my life and professional career that transformed me on my journey towards becoming a professional counselor and academic. This writing attempts to capture the potent parts of my career journey. Attending a career day at the age of 10 years old is one of the most influential events for my career. On that day a teacher scurried me into a classroom with a counseling psychologist who shared stories about helping others and how it was a noble and "cool" career choice. While wearing Birkenstock sandals and a suit, he shared about his profession, he held up his foot and pointed down to his shoes, and he mentioned that it was an added benefit that he could wear his sandals and socks to work. Birkenstock man now had my attention.

My 10-year-old self noticed that Birkenstock man loved his job and he got paid to help. From that moment forward, my college dream included earning the highest degree in counseling psychology and one day wearing sandals to work. That day, Birkenstock man planted a seed that would bloom over the next 22 years. Once in college, I immediately declared my undergraduate major in psychology.

PARAPROFESSIONAL YEARS

During my junior year in college, I attended a career fair and stopped at a table for a company named ResCare. The woman working informed me that wanting to help others was a job requirement and my Psychology major would help me be successful. Shortly following this meeting and application process, I was employed as a paraprofessional helper for ResCare in a group home for adults with severe mental health and cognitive impairments. The main goals included assisting the clients to reach independence by carrying out the treatment plans, attending team meetings, and assisting with daily living activities.

This job was not always easy but my main goal was to build relationships with these clients where some of them were nonverbal, cognitively delayed, and had been severely abused as children. Dealing with some of the clients' behaviors was challenging and at times my skill set did not meet the demands. During a night shift a client stripped down naked, went to the basement, and sat on the pool table singing all night long while drinking multiple gallons of milk. Since he was not harming himself or another, that behavior carried on until the sun came up, at which point, he promptly went upstairs to shower and start his daily routine. This is one example of the challenges in the work, but I was exposed to many challenges of the job and clientele and lacked the skill set and knowledge about how to respond. Learning about how to be present with clients and utilize contingency management systems was very valuable to my career and understanding principles of behaviorism.

I had pride in all aspects of the work and time ticked away at lightning speed when I was with clients. Reflecting on this, it is clear I was having a flow experience, which is defined as "a state in which people are so involved in an activity that nothing else seems to matter; the experience is so enjoyable that people will continue to do it even at great cost, for the sheer sake of doing it" (Cskikszentmihalyi, 1990, p. 4). This was evident on many occasions but one incident I remember was when my boss requested that I refrain from picking up extra shifts due to overtime costs. My response was that she did not need to pay me overtime which I considered as volunteering. Her look of disbelief after my response remains etched in my memory.

I invited the entire group home to my college graduation party and we sang karaoke, ate, and danced. This was prior to understanding ethics, professional boundaries, and dual relationships. A few years following this experience, after receiving my master's degree in counseling, I realized how unproductive and confusing this possibly was for the clients and created some ethical dilemmas that were beyond my scope of awareness at that time. Fast forward 12 years, after teaching courses on ethics and writing about burnout, these behaviors were not related to feelings of burnout but were more related to a lack of education about professional boundaries and ethics. This work experience is one that I have fond memories about and the flow experienced on the job is something I seek in my career experiences today.

A PSYCHOLOGY DEGREE . . . NOW WHAT?

After graduating college with an undergraduate degree in Psychology, I started working with a young boy who I will call Eric, and he was diagnosed with Asperger's. His real name has been changed to protect his confidentiality. It was 2002 and there was not a lot of information available about Asperger's syndrome. My job was to follow him around in school and help him contain his "disruptive" behavior in the classroom. With very few directions on how to do this job, I went forward with confidence in my ability to connect with Eric and fear related to my incompetence about how to help. I read a book by Temple Grandin (1995) where she shared her experiences of living with Autism, and her depictions were very similar to Eric's behaviors. I spent time listening and being with Eric and attending his individualized education plan (IEP) meetings.

Eric's behaviors appeared different in comparison to his peers and often evoked unfavorable responses from the teachers. For example, during lunch he sat in a chair directly behind the "cool kids" table, he stored his lunch food in his pockets, wore winter boots all year long, and sat in the front of every class. He would interrupt the teacher to make corrections, recite things verbatim that he read about the topic, pound his head, make loud noises, and do advanced math problems in his head. He was extremely imaginative, creative, caring, sensitive, and smart.

One time in class, Eric seemed distracted by fidgeting with his papers and books. The teacher had been talking for about 15 minutes and then said, "Eric, pay attention. I need you to focus and stop doing what you are doing!" Eric said, "I am paying attention" and the teacher inquired "Then what did I just say?" Eric started from the first words the teacher spoke that morning and politely began reciting the lecture. The teacher became frustrated and told Eric he needed to sit there and be quiet. Eric was distressed all day from this interaction; he did not understand the teacher's frustration because he believed he did what was asked of him. This was a defining moment for me.

I came to the conclusion that Eric was misunderstood by his teachers and classmates and he misunderstood them as well, so it was time to implement a system that would hopefully help. This consisted of stop signs created on cardboard (out of cereal boxes and markers) and on the front side was a picture of a stop sign and the back had a list of possible disruptive behaviors. For example, if he was in class pounding his head, I would drop the stop sign on his desk quietly. His task was to flip it over and point to the disruptive behavior (ex. head pounding) and then try to control it or replace it with a new behavior. There was a list of new behaviors on his trapper keeper (i.e. deep breathing, focusing on a picture in the classroom, or repeating a calming mantra or saying of the week in his head). If he could do this successfully and in a timely manner, he would earn points and during three times throughout the day (lunch, home room, and the end of the day) he could cash his points in for rewards. The contingency management system worked well for Eric.

I advocated for him in the IEP meetings by sharing the writings of Temple Grandin (1995) and requested that his teachers give him more advanced work. Also, Eric began sitting at the table with the "cool kids" and practicing his socialization skills. He was earning a lot of rewards daily, which mostly consisted of snacks that allowed him to stop taking food from the lunchroom. Soon after I started this position, the company offered me another job as a counselor in an at-risk youth camp working with adolescent girls. I was excited about the advancement and being given the opportunity to learn more about counseling, however, I was sad to leave Eric. He surprised me with a hug on my last day at work and then asked if he could have the rest of the reward bucket, which I promptly handed over.

In my new position as a therapist my caseload was 15 teenage girls and I was responsible for group, individual, and family counseling as well as completing treatment and discharge plans, taking clients on home visits, attending court, and communicating with probation, parole, and other involved parties. This camp operated using Rational Emotive Behavioral Therapy Techniques and Native American Rituals. I had no working knowledge of either approach. I remained open to learning the skills needed to be successful on the job. My clients were inner city youth and struggling socially, academically, and financially. Once again I relied on my ability to build a relationship with each client and followed the lead of my supervisor who was a Licensed Professional Counselor (LPC). I was satisfied with my job, but quickly realized the need for graduate school. l was accepted at East Carolina University in Rehabilitation Counseling and Substance Abuse and Community Counseling.

GRADUATE SCHOOL

During one of my first classes in graduate school, we reviewed the licensure process and it was overwhelming, but my determination did not fade. My work experiences allowed me to think more critically about my learning experiences in the classroom. My first practicum experience was in addiction counseling and I had a love-hate relationship for this specialty area. Over time I embraced all aspects of addiction counseling, especially the spiritual focus and intentional presence that this work required. I respected the clients' intimate journeys to reclaim their lives from addiction. Their journeys resonated with my own personal journey of having grown up within a drug plagued community with a parent addicted to gambling and grandmother suffering with a co-occurring disorder. This work allowed me to have the altruistic feeling of giving back to my community, my family, and friends who struggled.

Initially, I did not understand the 12-step focused treatment programs which were a major part of the job duties during my practicum placement. Through consultation with clinical supervisors, advisors, and mentors, I decided to seek out new experiences within the addiction treatment field by splitting my internship hours between a private practice and a hospital setting. It was at these two placements that I found treatment service opportunities that were individualized for clients and gained a perspective about different levels of care (i.e 12-step focused treatment versus process oriented treatment), when they are needed, and why they help clients at different stages of change.

My life was simpler during the graduate school years mostly because I was not married and did not have kids. At that time, I did not realize my life would get more hectic and harder to balance. My boyfriend, also a graduate student, understood my scholastic involvements. My prior work experience and personal connections facilitated my high academic performance and service as the president for the student association. Internship was a time commitment that required my presence and focus, but I also enjoyed my personal life, which included activities such as camping trips, karaoke, beach time, kayaking, spending time with my classmates, and yoga. This balance between school and home allowed me to be present academically and with myself during my off hours.

WORKING TOWARDS LICENSES

Following graduate school I took a job in Boone, North Carolina working in a medicated assisted treatment program with clients struggling with opiate addiction. At this time I also worked towards earning my license as a professional counselor (LPC), addiction certifications, and applying for Ph.D. programs. I was here for three years and it was here that I first experienced burnout. The paperwork demands, high caseload, and client demands were high and the low pay and added financial cost of paying for LPC supervision made my goals seem unreachable.

At one point, I had 115 clients on my caseload who needed to see me twice a month. Counselors operated on a first come first served basis and also served as a liaison for everything happening between nursing, medicine, and finance. It was a crisis-oriented, fast paced environment, which caused me to question my abilities to successfully complete all of the work. I experienced some successes and a lot of growth during this time. Initiating the development of a successful group treatment program was a huge success. It allowed the counselors to provide counseling to a large number of clients, making the requirement of seeing clients twice a month much more realistic. I learned how to deal with clients who were angry and to overcome my exhaustion from the work.

My feelings of burnout resulted in no energy for my personal life and experiences of anxiety before, during, and after work. My colleague recommended initiating intentional practices during my work day such as journal writing, visualization, and deep breathing exercises. This led to me completing a Yoga Teacher Training series outside of work and this combination of interventions allowed me to overcome these feelings of burnout and create more balance. Eventually, my attitude toward work began to change. For example, when a client expressed anger in a clinical session, I visualized myself with a shield and practiced deep breathing. I accepted that I could not be successful with all the tasks the job required and politely turned down opportunities for extra projects while prioritizing essential tasks (i.e. note taking). I stopped working late and started taking lunch breaks away from my desk. I regularly stepped outside to take deep breaths and sometimes cry before going back into my clinical space. Clinical supervision was utilized as a tool for my wellness, and slowly as these techniques worked, my energy returned.

BEYOND THE OFFICE AND INTO A DOCTORAL PROGRAM

During this same time, I met my mentor at a conference, the late David Powell, and traveled to Kathmandu, Nepal and Beijing, China to train addiction counselors and educate government officials about the importance of treatment. This opportunity was insightful for many reasons but mostly it provided me with understanding about the state of addiction treatment in Asia and helped me realize cultural impacts on addiction and treatment. I gained confidence in my abilities and skill set. To explore this new interest in training counselors and reach my goals I set at 10 years old, I began a doctoral program in Counselor Education and Supervision at the University of North Carolina - Charlotte. Once in school, I was not ready to leave my clinical work (professional counselor, providing clinical supervision, and trainings) and my financial responsibilities demanded I continue working. Between school, contract clinical work, and graduate assistantships, I worked 80-90 hours per week.

I had deep conversations with professors about work and life balance. I reflected on my burnout experience from my previous job and learned to say no to professors about publication requests, class coverage, or volunteer opportunities. I grieved the loss of my counseling identity and tried to adjust to the demands of being a doctoral student. I often disappointed professors by saying no to special requests and this was hard to acknowledge, creating an emotional journey which resulted in a miscarriage and caused me to revaluate my stressors. I cried often, relied on my support system, and struggled privately. I confided in a professor who understood my decisions to slow down and work from a more intentional space with the goals of completing my doctoral degree and working the minimum hours necessary for financial stability. I continued to have professors who did not understand my boundaries and inabilities to assume extra duties and this reflected poorly on me. But once again, I refocused my energy on surrounding myself with positive classmates and professors who understood my goals. Setting boundaries helped me focus on completing the Ph.D. program in four years while decreasing my stress. Shortly after this, I got pregnant and had my first son at the beginning of my fourth year of doctoral studies. I successfully defended my dissertation 6 months following his birth and graduated with a 4.0 grade point average.

DREAMING BIG AND BEYOND THE PH.D.

Two months before graduating with my Ph.D. in Counselor Education and Supervision I was having a conversation with a speaker I was hosting on campus, and he asked me "What are your dreams Angie?" I stumbled to answer this question because my dreams were coming true. I was graduating with my Ph.D. in Counselor Education and Supervision. I was an LPC and licensed addiction specialist. I shared that this had been my dream since I was 10 years old and acknowledged that I needed a new dream.

Following graduation, I gained a position as an adjunct professor and quickly moved into a full-time faculty and coordination position in clinical mental health counseling. I was challenged to oversee student advising, remediation, faculty hiring and evaluation, syllabi approval, and classroom management. I applied the skills learned while earning my Ph.D. and my clinical skills were advantageous during evaluation and remediation with students and faculty. I was overjoyed to teach students about the counseling profession and found a new connection to the profession due to their energy and eagerness to help others. Periodically, I feel lucky to have had all the experiences and drive that have guided me to my present moment. I realize that Birkenstock man sold me on the profession, my early experiences in the profession and work with clients confirmed my desires to help and motivated me to continue, and my determination and desire helped me succeed when challenged. Fast-forward 24 years, I have my Ph.D. in Counselor Education and Supervision and utilize my work experiences in the classroom routinely. I am still searching for my new career goals, but I look to my 10-year-old self for advice while remaining open to the unexpected.

Not long after my first job in academia, I was watching the President of my university give her commencement speech, and I was inspired. Afterwards, I thought that I wanted to be the president of a university one day. The little pessimist in my head said "Come back down to reality." Then, my 10-year-old self yelled "DREAM BIG!" Today, I am not certain about my future career goals or path, but I know the future is bright and filled with high hopes. As a Professional Counselor and Counselor Educator, I am constantly reminded that seeds do get planted and with care and time these seeds will blossom.

THE PRESENT MOMENT AND FUTURE

Currently, I am internally driven to develop professionally and personally. As a counselor educator I set and reach my own professional goals by writing, presenting, and researching topics that interest me on a deep level. These deep interests often wake me up and keep me up at night. I exercise and play with my children and husband every evening and strive to eat one meal with my family a day. I remind myself to be patient and chase my own dreams.

I recently took a new job in an undergraduate program at Drexel University in Behavioral Health Counseling. It was a challenging decision and transition to leave teaching in clinical mental health counseling graduate programs. However, my connection is that this is the undergraduate degree that I wish I had been exposed to during those early years in my clinical development. The position was a good fit for my career and for my family. It would bring me balance personally and professionally.

Currently, I am married and have two sons. My goals are to be a present mother who also has a focused, inventive, accomplished, and enjoyable career. My new position at Drexel University allows me the opportunity to be present with my students during such an important time in their lives. I acknowledge the beauty that comes from working with clients and students and the sacredness of being invited to join them on their journeys. I am exhilarated with my career in academia and often have that flow experience. I do not know when, how, or what seeds will be planted and eventually blossom in my future but I look forward to the journey ahead of me. My experiences remind me that people continuously evolve and make decisions that work for their life trajectories, and even though I do not wear my Birkenstocks to work anymore, I enjoy wearing my cowboy boots.

REFERENCES

Csikszentmihalyi, M. (1990). *Flow: The psychology of optimal experience.* New York, NY: Harper and Row.

Grandin. T. (1995). *Thinking in pictures.* New York, NY: Vintagebooks.

Chapter Seventeen

School Counselors and Illness-Related Trauma

Personal Reflections from an
African Outreach Experience

Eric Davis

As a former school counselor and counselor educator, I have a great dedication to my profession and students. It is imperative that I maintain an agenda of development to ensure that I am providing the best supervision and educational environments I can for counseling trainees. One of the more effective ways to accomplish this is through outreach into a variety of cultures and environments with the goal of sharing knowledge and collaborating to provide services for populations in need. For this particular endeavor, I will describe an outreach experience to southern Africa where I interacted and learned with teachers, counselors, administrators, and counselor educators. These experiences were influential and significant for my growth as a counselor educator, and more importantly, as a person.

Trauma and crisis issues related to interpersonal violence, human-made and natural disaster, death, and illness have become increasingly common within school communities. Yet, the professional development of school counselors in the areas of trauma and crisis, particularly relating to illness-related trauma, is lacking (Allen, Bunt, Bryan, Carter, Orsi, & Durkan, 2002; American School Counselors Association [ASCA], 2012). This fact can be of significance considering that 97% of school counselors reported working with students with chronic illness (Hamlet, Gergar, & Schaefer, 2011).

I experienced this first hand as a school counselor in training and as a professional school counselor. There were several experiences in which I worked with students who had a chronic illness or died. These situations were difficult for me because of my lack of training and experience related to illness-related trauma. While frightening, they did provide valuable opportunities to develop adaptive counseling styles and interventions as well as implementation of school wide programs to work with all school stakeholders in addressing students with chronic illness. For example, when two students in our school died from chronic illnesses, we found we were not prepared to deal with all of the effects of such a loss (i.e. announcing the death, providing counseling services to those affected by the loss, etc.) in an efficient and effective manner. Therefore, when this outreach experience to Africa presented itself, I was excited to continue my journey with clients impacted with illness-related trauma while also gaining a wider cultural lens related to chronic illness.

As a former professional school counselor and now as a counselor educator, I utilize a relational-cultural lens when focusing on school counselors' preparedness to work with children affected by illness-related trauma and crisis. Relational-cultural theory (RCT) emphasizes a culture-centered approach to interpersonal relationships as a mechanism for fostering resiliency, developing and making meaningful connections, addressing issues of power, privilege, stigmatism, as well as acceptance, and mutual empathy (Comstock, Hammer, Strartzsch, Cannon, Parsons, & Salazar, 2008; Jordan, 2010). This outreach experience exemplified the understanding and application of RCT because of the specific incidents of trauma experienced in southern Africa.

The first objective of the outreach program was to learn about the amount of preparation school counselors in South Africa and Botswana receive in the area of illness-related trauma with the goal of gaining a richer understanding of this issue from a broader cultural lens. The second objective was to learn about the actual interventions utilized by school counselors and counselor-trainees when working with students facing illness-related trauma. My final objective was to garner new perspectives on how to incorporate this new knowledge into my role as a counselor educator to aid counselor trainees in gaining culturally competent skills and knowledge for addressing illness-related trauma with a diverse array of students. Ultimately, my goal was to enhance my knowledge of possible interventions for illness-related trauma. I had been caught off guard too many times in my own experiences and did not want my students to face the same challenges and fear that I had.

One of the most devastating illnesses affecting the globe is HIV/AIDS. Almost 13.2 million children under the age of 15 have lost parents as a result of HIV/AIDS with this number expected to continue to increase. Africa is affected most severely by this epidemic due to the fact that 95% of HIV/AIDS orphans reside on the continent (Mbugua, 2004). Considering that in South Africa alone, adolescents aged 15–19 represent about 10% of the population (South Africa Census, 2011), there are significant issues that can arise in terms of receiving proper medical, reproductive, and counseling services (Otwambe, Dietrich, Laher, Hornschuh, Nkala, et al., 2015). Further, the difficulties faced by orphans of parents who died from HIV/AIDS (i.e. poor schooling outcomes, lack of enrollment, multiple moving, and becoming head of the household, etc.) result in significant areas of concern for school counselors (Case & Ardington, 2006; Evans & Miguel, 2007; Ford & Hosegood, 2005; Strydom & Rath, 2005). This information astounded me. I knew there was an issue in Africa with HIV/AIDS, but had no idea it was such an epidemic. It was at this time that I knew I was heading in the right direction for enhancing my own goals because there could be no better group of counselors to collaborate with to improve my counseling, teaching, and supervising skills.

PERSONAL NARRATIVE

While boarding the plane for South Africa, my thoughts and feelings ran the gamut of fear, excitement, doubt, and confusion. According to *The ASCA National Model: A framework for school counseling programs* (ASCA, 2012), it is the school counselor's duty to meet the immediate needs of students necessitated by life events, situations, or conditions with responsive services including individual, group, and classroom counseling as well as collaboration with parents, community members, and school personnel. Despite this statement, it is common for many school counselors to feel unprepared to deal with events like illness-related trauma and crisis due to issues such as lack of training and experience. This was absolutely the case for me.

Even though I had read several relevant articles, participated in trainings, and responded to a limited amount of illness-related trauma as a school counselor, it still seemed daunting that I would soon be in Southern Africa working with counselors who dealt with students facing such issues as HIV/AIDS on a daily basis. How would I handle such situations? Would I be prepared to discuss these issues with the counselors and students? I also questioned how I would be perceived by the counselors, staff, and students. Would they see me as another invader who just wanted to come into the school, snap a few pictures, say a few words, and leave—never to be seen again? Would I be accepted as a colleague? I pondered these issues as I walked onto the high school campus in Gabarone, Botswana. I took a deep breath and prepared myself for anything that might happen.

Fortunately, many of my trepidations melted away. Upon meeting the counselors at the school, their kindness and hospitality were overwhelming. The counselors were incredibly genuine with their welcomes and introductions. We even learned the traditional handshake greeting! They were truly curious about us, our backgrounds, and training as professional counselors as demonstrated through the insightful and respectful questions asked. They were also more than willing to share their experiences and knowledge with us. It was made clear to me that I was an honored guest and my presence was considered a gift because of the high level of respect and collegiality provided by our peers from across the globe. We were given the opportunity to tour the campus, meet several of the teachers and administrators, and provided with our own area in the counseling office as a workspace. The campus was open and spread out with lovely courtyards, allowing students to mingle during breaks. My team member and I were allowed to conduct an impromptu session with a classroom of eleventh graders. We simply conversed about ideas that they had about the United States and the ideas we had about Botswana. I was floored when hearing such questions as, "Do all of the teenagers act like Brittany Spears and Paris Hilton?" and "Are all schools in America really violent?" It was intriguing that my questions about HIV/AIDS were met with very little knowledge as most students did not mention that they had dealt with it personally. Overall, it reminded me so very much of my conversations with my own high school students. Students were mainly interested in learning about how to get to America, the best way to get into college, and what do I do for fun. It was so invigorating to converse with these young people from another continent!

The conversations with the counselors were even more enlightening. We began by meeting in their office with a cup of tea and some wonderful homemade bread prepared by the secretary. The counselors' office was small and served as the school infirmary as well. However, it was welcoming and strategically placed for easy access by students and staff. We began talking and, I must admit, there was a great amount of surprise on my behalf by what was said.

It was my expectation that the school counselors would be well prepared in handling illness-related trauma on a daily basis. I was incredibly mistaken. Not only did they not deal with many cases of illness-related trauma, but they also confided in me that, due to a lack of training and experience, they did not feel adequately prepared to face such situations if they arose. The literature confirms this notion stating that many counselors feel unprepared to deal with the issue of chronic illness (Kaffenberger, 2006; Senyonyi, Ochieng, & Sells, 2012). Despite this, school counselors are often expected to be aware of such issues as posttraumatic stress disorder (PTSD) and are often seen as the most qualified member of the school staff to recognize and provide recommendations for intervention (Marotta, 2000). Even with an awareness of this information, I was still quite unprepared to hear these statements. At this point, all of the preparation and reading came into light as my personal objectives for participating in this outreach experience became center stage and were thus highlighted in that moment. I realized I was not alone in my concerns in working with students facing illness-related trauma and chronic illness. I saw first hand that my colleagues whom I automatically thought would have all of the answers were struggling with some of the aspects of the problem just like me. The concept of universality that I had discussed with so many of my counseling students became abundantly clear. I was able to accept that we are all friends, colleagues, and professionals battling with lack of information, training, and confidence in addressing an ever-changing and incredibly emotional, painful, and frightening experience.

CULTURALLY-COMPETENT COUNSELING

The personal light bulb went off for me during our visit to a counseling facility for children and adolescents dealing with family illness, loss of loved ones to illness, and other trauma related issues. Again, my preconceived notions were inaccurate. I expected a very austere and bleak environment filled with despair and confusion on how to address such devastating matters. While the staff of teachers, administrators, and counselors admitted to having a need to gain more knowledge on effective skills and interventions, what was in place was astonishing. There was a great sense of hope, connection, creativity, and energy at the facility. The staff was dedicated to meeting the youth at levels that were culturally and developmentally appropriate. They used a variety of methods for dealing with such painful issues related to illness and loss. The use of music, dance, play, and story-telling were prominent in the facility. Once again, I found myself becoming more encouraged as I was able to take this experience and knowledge into my own perception of the counseling world and how I could be a more culturally competent counselor, supervisor, and educator. In particular, the five following examples were experienced and provided great insight for me:

1. Story-telling: Much of the counseling interventions involved story-telling. Clients and counselors both shared their issues within the context of culturally-relevant life stories. Woven into these stories were local and traditional aspects such as characters, lessons, and customs that could be used as tools for addressing the personal issues at hand. As a result, the youth were able to connect and process through their emotions, thoughts, and behaviors in a way that was familiar, relevant, and meaningful for their own personal stories.
2. Humor: Combined with these stories were the aspects of humor. It seemed therapeutic for the counselors and clients to weave jokes and laughter in with their stories and discussions. It was not uncommon to hear laughter during every conversation as the staff and youth connected and shared stories, jokes, and insights into what would typically be seen as not a laughing matters.

3. Art: Art was a common occurrence throughout my experience. Many of the clients utilized artistic aspects such as painting and sculpture not only in their counseling, but also in the classroom and community settings. As a result, there was a connection to the community as well as the facility. Family members were able to connect with the youth and the staff through these art projects that had been completed as a means of communicating their stories regarding the matters at hand.

4. Dance: It was not uncommon for every day to begin and end with a traditional cultural dance. These dances served to demonstrate the history and culture of these people as well as welcoming us into the group. It was also a way for the youth and staff to connect in a very physical manner. Through dance, the youth were able to express some of their emotions in a culturally accepted and encouraged way that did not require words.

5. Music: Along with the dancing, came song. One of the most common songs was entitled, "Never Give Up" providing an incredible view of the culture, resiliency, and beauty of the people. Further, the African counselors shared with us the children of the facility as they provided a spectacular musical performance using several of the traditional instruments and vocals.

These components are so vital due to the fact that psychotherapeutic interventions cannot exist separately from the society and culture of the people in providing culturally competent and effective services (Kohn-Wood & Hooper, 2014; Vontress & Naiker, 1995). After these personal experiences, it became very clear to me that several aspects of the school counseling profession and my role in it had to be pondered such as what aspects of training are missing and how can these gaps be filled for current school counselors and those in training.

RECOMMENDATIONS FOR TRAINING

One vital aspect of preparation for school counselor trainees involves dealing with cultural aspects of trauma response. Training programs must take into account current social, economic, and political realities while responding to the developmental needs of future counselors and students in rapidly changing multicultural societies (Arman & Scherer, 2002; Kohn-Wood & Hooper, 2014). This includes educating school counselors about their duties as advocates and agents for social change from a holistic, developmental, and systemic approach (ASCA, 2012; Evans & Miguel, 2007; Ford & Hosegood, 2005; Hamlet, Gergar, & Schaefer, 2011). As a result of this experience, this need became principal for me in my work as a counselor educator. The importance of addressing social justice issues in schools and society as a whole has become ingrained in all of my courses as a counselor educator through such activities as volunteering in schools and local agencies, collaborating with schools to provide services on campus, and discussing social justice aspects in all levels of training. Further, I also am very purposeful in discussing the trainee's role in this process as an active member of their internship site in social justice causes during the supervision portion of their educational training.

School counselor trainees must be made aware of challenges related to working with parents, such as locating adequate community resources, and dealing with possible bureaucratic red tape they might face in their roles as advocates (Hamlet, Gergar, & Schaefer, 2011; Musheno & Talbert, 2002). After this experience, I reviewed and adjusted my introductory and application courses for school counseling to provide more in-depth knowledge, experiences, and techniques for working with all school stakeholders including parents, administrators, and community members. Additionally, they need to be trained in ethical standards, ability to find and utilize resources, mediation/conflict resolution skills, knowledge of models and theories, ability to form partnerships and collaborate, and basic counselor skills such as communication, problem-solving, organization, and self-care (Jor'dan & Lee, 2014; Senyonyi, Ochieng, & Sells, 2012; Trust & Brown, 2005). An example of an assignment that I have included in one of my courses is that the students must collect five community-based resources for working with at-risk youth. They then all share them and we create a community-based resource list that the entire class can take and use in their future work in schools and other counseling settings. Ultimately, however, the most important piece that came out of my experience was the passion that was sparked in me to help our schools, school counselors, and students to have the most relevant training, experiences, and supervision so that they would not feel as lost, overwhelmed, and angry as I had when working with grieving families, confused teachers, and chronically ill students.

An additional component involves training in known and effective methods for dealing with illness-related trauma and crisis. Play techniques such as bibliotherapy, art, and puppet play can be strong methods for counseling children affected by trauma and crisis in a culturally competent manner (Davis & Pereira, 2014; Mbugua, 2004; Nicholson & Pearson, 2003). When selecting courses, it is imperative that counselors-in-training select classes that will provide training and learning in understanding and utilizing such techniques as well as advocating for them if they do not exist. In my role as a counselor educator, I have become much more clear and purposeful in my advising to explore students' areas of strength, limits, and interest to ensure I am directing them to the proper courses, experiences, and internship sites to properly prepare them for working with their desired populations.

This does not end with training, however. Of particular interest are the potential relationships that can occur between school systems and universities. This collaboration can result in valuable resources, service learning opportunities, and insight into needs for both populations (Musheno & Talber, 2002). I have worked diligently to develop and maintain relationships with not only our school systems, but all mental health providers in the surrounding areas to have meaningful conversations to share ideas, concerns, and knowledge regarding the best courses of action for providing the most effective training for our counseling students. For example, we have a quality relationship established with one of the local Native American tribes who allow us to collaborate and share knowledge to understand how we can best serve this underserved population in our local community. Our students are an integral part of this experience and gain a great deal of knowledge about advocacy and alternative counseling interventions as a result. As such, I am constantly looking for collaborative opportunities for myself and my students to work with local, national, and global partners to enhance the profession through training, research, and pedagogy that will best educate and prepare our counselors-in-training to work with the terminal ill populations that exist in our schools and communities throughout the world.

CONCLUSION

Illness-related trauma and crisis is an area full of questions and doubt, but also full of hope and potential. Through outreach experiences such as the one I encountered in southern Africa, students, counselors, and educators can gain incredible insight. This includes becoming aware of differing cultures and how new and different aspects can open a person's mind and consciousness. They can also provide insight into the needs of counselor training programs, school counselor interventions, school system development and training procedures, and personal perspectives, thus allowing for progress and ultimately change. However, it is up to everyone as counselors, educators, supervisors, and other adults in the lives of children to take risks to allow for exploration and growth. As I reflect back on this experience and where I am today as a counselor educator and human being, I am pleased that I have made great progress in achieving the three objectives discussed earlier. I look forward to continuing to enhance myself in these areas because counselor education, like life, is in a constant state of ebb and flow and we must always be open to the process and experience to ebb and flow with it.

REFERENCES

Allen, M., Bunt, K., Bryan, E., Carter, D., Orsi, R., & Durkan, L. (2002). School counselors' preparation for and participation in crisis intervention. *Professional School Counseling, 6,* 96–102. http://www.jstor.org/stable/42732398.

American School Counselor Association (2012). *The ASCA national model: A framework for school counseling programs.* Alexandria, VA: Author.

Arman, J. F., & Scherer, D. (2002). Service learning in school counselor preparation: A qualitative analysis. *Journal of Humanistic Counseling, Education, and Development, 4,* 69–86. doi:10.1002/j.2164–490X.2002.tb00131.x.

Case, A., & Ardington, C. (2006). The impact of parental death on school outcomes: Longitudinal evidence from South Africa. *Demography, 43,* 401–420. doi:10.1353/dem.2006.0022.

Comstock, D. L., Duffey, T., & George, H. S. (2002). The relational-cultural model: A framework for group process. *Journal for Specialists in Group Work, 27,* 254–272. oi:10.1177/0193392202027003002.

Comstock, D. L., Hammer, T. R., Strartzsch, J., Cannon, K., Parsons, J., & Salazar, G. (2008). Relational-cultural theory: A framework for bridging relational, multicultural, and social justice competencies. *Journal of Counseling and Development, 86,* 279–287. doi:10.1002/j.1556–6678.2008.tb00510.x.

Davis, E. S., & Pereira, J. K. (2014). Child-centered play therapy: A creative approach to culturally competent counseling. *Journal of Creativity in Mental Health, 9,* 262–274. doi:10.1080/15401383.2014.892863.

Evans, D. K., & Miguel, E. (2007). Orphans and schooling in Africa: A longitudinal analysis. *Demography, 44,* 35–57. doi:10.1353/dem.2007.0002.

Ford, K., & Hosegood, V. (2005). HIV/AIDS mortality and the mobility of children in Kwazulu Natal, South Africa. *Demography, 42,* 757–768.

Hamlet, H. S., Gergar, P. G., & Schaefer, B. A. (2011). Students living with chronic illness: The school counselor's role. *Professional School Counseling, 14,* 202–210. doi.org/10.5330/PSC.n.2011–14.202.

Jordan, J. V. (2010). *Relational-cultural therapy.* Washington, D. C.: American Psychological Association.

Jor'dan, J. R., & Lee, R. M. (2014) The Children's Place Association: Supporting families impacted by HIV/AIDS. *Young Children, 9,* 50–53.

Kaffenberger, C. J. (2006). School reentry for students with a chronic illness: A role for professional school counselors. *Professional School Counseling, 9,* 223–230. doi:10.5330/prsc.9.3.xr27748161346325.

Kohn-Wood, L., & Harper, L. M. (2014). Cultural competency, culturally tailored care, and the primary care setting: Possible solutions to reduce racial/ethnic discrepancies in mental health care. *Journal of Mental Health Counseling, 36,* 173–188. doi: 10.17744/mehc.36.2.d73h217l81tg6uv3.

Marotta, S. A. (2000). Best practices for counselors who treat posttraumatic stress disorder. *Journal of Counseling and Development, 78,* 492–495. doi:10.1002/j.1556–6676.2000.tb01933.x.

Mbugua, T. (2004). Responding to the special needs of children: HIV/AIDS orphans in Kenya.*Childhood Education, 80,* 304–309. doi:10.1080/00094056.2004.10521276.

Musheno, S, & Talber, M. (2002). The transformed school counselor in action. *Theory Into Practice, 41,* 186–191. doi:10.1207/s15430421tip4103_7.

Nicholson, J. I., & Pearson, Q. M. (2003). Helping children cope with fears: Using children's literature in classroom guidance. *Professional School Counseling, 7,* 15–19.

Otwombe, K., Dietrich, J., Laher, F., Hornschuh, S., & Nkala, B. (2015). Health-seeking behaviours by gender among adolescents in Soweto, South Africa. *Global Health Action, 8,* 51–59. doi:10.3402/gha.v8.25670.

Snyonyi, R. M., Ochieng, L. A., & Sells, J. (2012). The development of professional counseling in Uganda: Current status and future trends. *Journal of Counseling and Development, 90,* 500–504. doi:10.1002/j.1556–6676.2012.00062.x.

Statistics of South Africa. Census 2011 municiple report Gauten. 2012. Retrieved from www.statssa.gov.za/Census2011/Products/GP_Municiple_Report.pdf.

Strydom, H., & Raath, H. (2005). The psychological needs of adolescents affected by HIV/ AIDS: A South African study. *International Social Work, 48*, 569–580. doi:10.1177/ 0020872805055321.

Trust, J., & Brown, D. (2005). Advocacy competencies for professional school counselors. *Professional School Counseling, 8*, 259–265.

Vontress, C. E., & Naiker, K. S. (1995). Counseling in South Africa: Yesterday, today, and tomorrow. *Journal of Multicultural Counseling and Development, 23*, 149–157. doi:10.1002/j.2161–1912.1995.tb00270.x.

Chapter Eighteen

Creative Arts in Clinical Supervision

Kelly Dunbar Davison

Using creative approaches in clinical supervision has the potential to enrich the overall experience for both the supervisor and the supervisees. Although using creative approaches may seem intimidating, they can be successfully implemented with a little practice and a willingness to try something new. This chapter covers the use of a creative art activity, the mandala, in triadic clinical supervision. The mandala was introduced into the supervision sessions as a way to help the supervisees gain a deeper understanding of their thoughts and feelings about their work with clients. As the supervisor, I was critically impacted by the way the supervisees related to the art materials and how we were able to immediately go deeper in our discussions of the counselor/client relationship. Additionally, I was both impacted and surprised by the way the creation of the mandala strengthened the supervisory relationship. Finally, details for creating and introducing mandalas in supervision are outlined.

During my doctoral training, I had the opportunity to facilitate triadic supervision (CACREP, 2015) with several master's students who were in their last semester of internship. One of the many topics in supervision that semester was the supervisees' ability to gauge his or her level of rapport with clients. In fact, it was common to hear the supervisees describe feelings of inadequacy and insecurity in their counseling sessions. Knowing that these feelings are common for supervisees in the beginning stages of counselor development (Stoltenberg, McNeil, & Delworth, 1998), I wanted to help them gain a better understanding of their relationships with their clients. It was at this point that I began seeking an appropriate intervention to use in our triadic supervision sessions and ultimately, I decided to introduce the mandala.

I went to the literature for resources on mandalas and developed a plan to incorporate them into supervision (Allen, 2005; Jackson, Muro, Yueh-Ting,

& DeOrnellas, 2008; Lahad, 2000). Supervisees were instructed to draw a mandala focusing on line, shape, and color. They were also told that they could draw any images that they felt were significant. They began to draw and I watched how the room became quiet as they were intently focused on their drawings. It appeared to me that this intervention was guiding them to focus in on feelings and thoughts in a different way. They seemed to examine their feelings and thoughts from new perspectives; they had to think about their experiences in images instead of words. In these moments, I became eager to discuss their images and their thought processes behind making the images. In other words, I wanted to discuss the process and the product in the creation of their mandalas.

Once their drawings were complete I asked them to describe each aspect of their mandalas. As they discussed the meanings of the pictures, colors, shapes, lines, etc., they also shared with each other that they had experienced similar thoughts and feelings with their own clients. However, they were not able to put those feelings into words in previous supervision sessions. For example, in looking at each other's mandalas in triadic supervision, they were able to project upon and relate to one another through images. These images provided a means for supervisees to see their relationships with clients. It also seemed to offer a unique way to externalize the issues they were having which allowed them to take a more objective view of their situations. Finally, the normalization of feelings and thoughts described by the supervisees was an added bonus potentially due to the triadic format of the supervision session (Bernard & Goodyear, 2014; Dunbar, 2011; Lawson, Hein, & Stuart, 2009).

It was during those supervision sessions that I was critically impacted. I realized that I had potentially found an intervention that could enrich our supervision and I was excited! I had formally studied art therapy and had used creative approaches in counseling but this was the first time that I experienced the significance of using creative approaches in the supervision. I was amazed at the way the supervisees related to the art materials, how they engaged in the creation of their mandalas, and how we were able to immediately go deeper in our discussions of the counselor/client relationship. I was thankful that they had enough trust in the supervision process that they jumped right in to this intervention. Additionally, I was surprised by the way the creation of the mandala seemed to have strengthened the supervisory relationship and the overall working alliance. While using Bordin's (1983) working alliance model which focused on the goals, tasks, and bond in supervision, I thought the bond was foundational to a successful supervisory relationship. Therefore, I was thrilled to have potentially found a way to have a direct influence on the supervisory working alliance (Bordin, 1979; 1983). The prospect of being able to effectively use creative arts interventions specifically, the mandala, in supervision was exciting! Equally as exciting was the way the supervisees related to one another through their mandalas. I thought that having an intervention with potential to assist the supervisees in developing a bond in triadic supervision could be a tremendous tool. Furthermore, as they shared the experience of mandala making and explored the meanings of the images created, they displayed trust, sharing, and understanding.

I remember a supervisee in a triadic session talking about her feelings of fear and apprehensiveness about her work with clients and the evaluative nature of the supervisory relationship. As the supervisee shared, the second supervisee expressed that she had very similar feelings. I was thankful for this opportunity for us to work through these feelings in our supervision. I was also glad that the supervisees were able to connect with one another and strengthen the bond in our supervision.

In another example, I recall a supervisee's mandala that included an image of her client that was drawn disproportionally smaller than the other images. The client was also blocked into a corner by a large triangular shape. After reflecting upon her mandala using words to describe her images, the supervisee realized that she may need to try a new approach to further engage the often quiet and timid client in the counseling process.

After seeing the outcomes of the supervisees creating mandalas in our supervision sessions, I decided to make a mandala that would represent my perspective of our relationship. It included images of my thoughts and feelings about our supervisory relationship and how I saw each supervisee at that point in their development. Just like the supervisees, I was able to put into images what I had not been able to put into words during our previous supervision sessions.

Personally, I realized that I could connect in a significant way with supervisees by creating my own mandala based on my perspective of the supervisory relationship. As I shared my mandalas with the supervisees, I felt a deepening of the alliance occur. I described in words the significance of each image, color, line, shape, etc., the supervisees listened intently. They seemed genuinely thankful for the added insight and encouragement that came from this unique exchange. Having created mandalas themselves, they understood my process in creating the images. They knew first hand that I had taken the time to examine our relationship from different perspectives to create my images. I also deepened my understanding of the supervisees. Through creating my mandalas, I was able to gain clarity in their perspectives.

I have included an example of a mandala that I created for a final triadic supervision session (see Figure 1). I used oil pastels and black construction paper to create the mandala.

Figure 1. My mandala drawing using oil pastel on black construction paper. *Note.*
The original mandala that I made was in color. It was reproduced in black and
white for publication purposes.

The image of the dove (on the left side) represented the supervisees
development in the areas of freedom and independence, growth in understanding of self and clients, and my overall sense of peace about the process.
When I was creating the dove I visualized releasing the dove into the air and
seeing it fly away. It was a way to say goodbye to the time we had spent
together while recognizing the professional growth we had all experienced.
The image of the door (on the right side) symbolized our stepping into new
roles and moving beyond our supervisory relationship. The window in the
door was filled with bright light to convey happiness and an optimistic path
ahead. The dark shape (near the top and center) represented the unknown and
the wonder about what the future might hold for all of us. The circular
patterns and organic shapes in and around the mandala represented connectedness, happiness, and sense of pride that I felt in our work together during
supervision. As I made these patterns and shapes, specific conversations
about clients came to mind and I reflected upon the challenges that we were
able to overcome and some that were still a work in progress. The colors I
used to signify my feelings in this mandala included orange for excitement,
purple for pride, green for peacefulness, red for hopefulness, black for wonder, and blue for confidence.

As a counselor educator and clinical supervisor I have the opportunity to
teach counselors-in-training (CITs) various supervision techniques and models. I greatly enjoy teaching the use of creative arts approaches in clinical
supervision. With each new supervisory relationship, I continue to learn

more about myself and I have a front row seat to the professional development and growth of CITs. I also see how creative arts, specifically, the mandala, helps counselors of all levels to communicate beyond words and to go deeper in the understanding of ourselves and others. I hope that the experiences I have shared in this chapter inspires others to try using creative arts in supervision.

Here, I have included a basic overview of the way that I introduce and implement mandalas in supervision sessions. First, I instruct supervisees to get in a comfortable position and try to remove any potential distractions. Sometimes, we will start with deep breathing or guided imagery exercises to help clear and focus our thoughts if needed. Next, we select the art materials to create our mandalas. The art materials can vary widely but it is helpful to offer a few choices to supervisees. For example, you may offer crayons, oil or chalk pastels, colored pencils, markers, paints, and white or colored paper. The list of materials is up to your imagination however, I have found that I limit the materials to those that are less messy given the location and professional attire of supervisees. The next steps are listed in the order that I typically follow. They can be modified to best meet the needs of supervisees.

1. Start with making a circle on your paper that is large enough to fill the space.
2. Using lines, shapes, colors, images, or symbols, create an image that represents your focus in the supervision session. Note that the focus can include any topic addressed in supervision including but not limited to client rapport, seeking intervention strategies, feeling stuck with a client, parallel process issues, countertransference, self-care, etc.
3. Remember that creating your mandala is about the process and not the product. In other words, do not worry about your artistic ability. The focus is on you processing your experience.
4. Once your mandala is complete, begin to assign meaning to what you have created. You can talk it out or write it down. You may find it beneficial to record what each color used represents to you. Identify themes or common colors, shapes, patterns, etc, and discuss their significance.
5. Allow yourself to be free to explore your mandalas. Using the same skills as in talking through supervision sessions, you can explore the images in your mandalas.

REFERENCES

Allen, P. B. (1995). *Art is a way of knowing: A guide to self-knowledge and spiritualfulfillment through creativity*. Boston: Shambhala.

Bernard, J. M., & Goodyear, R. K. (2014). *Fundamentals of clinical supervision* (5ᵗʰ ed.). Upper Saddle River, NJ: Pearson.

Bordin, E. S. (1979). The generalizability of the psychoanalytic concept of the working alliance. *Psychotherapy: Theory, Research, and Practice, 16*, 252-260. doi.org/10.1037h0085885.

Bordin, E. S. (1983). A working alliance based model of supervision. *The Counseling Psychologist*, 11, 35-42. doi: 10.1177/0011000083111007.

Council for Accreditation of Counseling and Related Educational Programs (2015). *CACREP 2009 standards*. Retrieved on March 29, 2015 from: http://www.cacrep.org/wp- content/uploads/2013/12/2009-Standards.pdf.

Dunbar, K. A. (2011). Creativity in triadic supervision: Using mandalas to impact the working alliance (Doctoral dissertation). Retrieved from ProQuest. (UMI No. 3474240).

Jackson, S. A., Muro, J., Yueh-Ting, L., DeOrnellas, K. (2008) The sacred circle: usingmandalas in counselor supervision. *Journal of Creativity in Mental Health, 3*, 201-211. doi:10.1080/15401380802369164.

Koltz, R. L. (2008). Integrating creativity into supervision using Bernard' s Discrimination Model. *Journal of Creativity in Mental Health, 3*, 416-427. doi:10.1080/15401380802530054.

Lahad, M. (2000). *Creative supervision: The use of expressive arts methods in supervision and self-supervision.* London: Jessica Kingsley Publishers.

Lawson, G., Hein, S. F., Stuart, C. L. (2009). A qualitative investigation of a supervisees' experiences of triadic supervision. *Journal of Counseling and Development, 87*, 449-457. doi:10.1002/j.1556-6678.2009.tb00129.x.

Stoltenberg, C. D., McNeil, B. W., & Delworth, U. (1998). *IDM: An integrated* developmental model for supervising counselors and therapists. San Francisco: Jossey-Bass Publishers.

Chapter Nineteen

Research Mentoring

An Empowering Process for the Protégé and Mentor

Jessica Headley and
Varunee Faii Sangganjanavanich

Mentoring is a bi-directional, relational process between a protégé and mentor that primarily focuses on promoting the personal and professional development of the individual with less experience, the protégé. To this end, and specific to the research context, mentors provide a number of functions that aim to foster a protégé's research and writing efficacy and skills such as assigning challenging research related tasks, role modeling desirable research behaviors, and providing personal support. Mentors, too, accrue a number of benefits such as feelings of generativity and new personal and professional learnings. In acknowledgement of these potential benefits for both parties, we (Jessica and Faii) looked back and reflected on the impact our first research mentoring experience as part of our larger mentoring relationship that has continued to flourish over the last several years. At the time of this particular experience, one of us was a second-year counselor education doctoral student (Jessica) and the other was an assistant professor in the counseling department (Faii). The excerpts to this narrative are written in a turn-taking fashion to reflect our personal insights and learnings that emerged during various phases of the research mentoring experience to include the invitation to write, the writing process, and writing outcomes. Following these excerpts, we conclude this contribution with general takeaways that we hope will promote quality mentoring relationships in our profession.

THE INVITATION TO WRITE

An invitation conveys two messages. First and foremost, that you are special! And, second, that you have an opportunity for a new experience. There are many invitations that we have both received across our lifetimes that have been meaningful such as being invited to share a meal with a loved one, join a social group, and attend a celebratory event. The ones that stick out to us the most are those that have changed our relationship with self and others for the better—or as the title of the text speaks to, those that are *transformative* in nature. The invitation to co-author a manuscript for publication (from Faii) and the acceptance (from Jessica) was just that: it was transformative on both the personal and relational level.

Faii's Experience

I have been fortunate to have wonderful mentors who are not only interested in helping me grow professionally, but also are invested in building supportive relationships with me which facilitate my personal growth. During my doctoral training, I experienced self-doubt regarding my research and writing ability. I felt ambivalent about what and how much I knew and could accomplish. Conducting studies or writing for publications seem far-fetched. However, my mentors included me in their research and writing projects and taught me everything about it. As cliché as it is, I told myself at that time that when I became a counselor educator, I would need to pay this forward.

One of my roles as a counselor educator is to facilitate professional development among students in the area of scholarship. Research and writing have become a focus of a doctoral study; however, many students demonstrate fear, uncertainty, and little self-efficacy when engaging in these activities. Jessica was one of those students. When I looked at Jessica, I saw many untapped potentials and my goal was to help her discover those. I wanted Jessica to learn to trust herself for her personal and professional growth.

With the belief that she would grow from this experience, I decided to invite Jessica to partner with me in writing one of my peer-reviewed articles. Personally, I am selective of writing partners as I consider writing to be a relational and collaborative process where each author brings her unique styles and talents into the final product. With Jessica, I had complete confidence that she would learn how to exercise her talents and potential to pursue one of the most challenging scholarly activities—writing for peer-reviewed publications.

Jessica's Experience

At the time that Dr. Faii sent her invite, which happened to be a straightforward email with the subject line: "Possibility," I had little experience in academic writing for publication. My lack of experience stemmed in part from not reaching out to seasoned scholars for support and guidance. This inaction was just the tip of the iceberg. Under the surface I was dealing with a larger issue: I did not envision myself as being a scholar who could produce quality work.

I was suffering from what many novice students have termed, "imposter syndrome": wondering how I got into the doctoral program and dreading the day when others found out that I was a fake. Self-doubt, by far, was one of the most prominent "symptoms" of imposter syndrome that I experienced. In regards to writing for publication, I felt uneasy about each step of the process. I worried that I would fail to identify and include highly cited publications that readers would expect to see in our work. I also did not believe that I would be able to provide valuable suggestions and recommendations related to framing the paper because the line of inquiry was new to me. And, more so, I feared that once Dr. Faii received my written drafts that she would be disappointed in my writing ability.

Writing for publication, as part of the larger doctoral experience, seemed impossible and as a result I thought of numerous excuses that would keep me from accepting Dr. Faii's invitation. Yet, for as many voices that I had telling me I could not do it, there was one encouraging me to give this opportunity a shot because Dr. Faii believed in me as evidenced by her *reaching out to me*. Her gesture helped change my perception. She helped me realize that within the word "impossible" is the word "possible." By choosing not to focus on those first two letters (with some much needed support!), a space for growth emerged.

THE WRITING PROCESS

Growth is a process that best occurs in a nurturing environment. Take for example, caring for a plant. Without the necessary amount of light, the right temperature, quality soil, and tender care, the plant will inevitably wither and die. In the gardening world, we often refer to naturally talented individuals as having "green thumbs" – no matter what plant they tend to, it somehow happens to grow and thrive. It is that "somehow" that those of us with our first plants, and those of us with dying plants, are eager to learn more about. However, when asking seasoned gardeners to share their secrets to success, we are often times surprised about what they share.

Faii's Experience

Too often, students look up to their faculty members. Their admiration leads them to wanting particular faculty to serve as their mentors. Mentors then turn to be idealistic rather than realistic. In my view, idealistic mentors refer to perfect role models who are on an academic pedestal and are viewed unreachable or unobtainable, whereas realistic mentors are individuals to whom protégés can relate and perceive to have appropriate qualities as role models. In terms of writing and research, many students refer to me as their mentor and the fact is, I always feel hesitant to call myself their mentor. First, I personally feel ambivalent with the notion of being an idealistic person. Second, I do not believe I have strong mentoring skills. Mentoring holds such a profound meaning to those engaged in this relationship—protégés and mentors. Although I have helped many students successfully pursue their scholarship, I hardly consider myself a mentor.

I am very particular when it comes to writing and publication. What I had learned early on in my career is that writing and publication rely heavily on self-discipline including setting goals, developing plans, and executing tasks. I have particular ways to approach my writing and organization; however, I have no idea how to teach people to develop self-discipline. My approach to mentoring students in writing and publication is to help students believe in themselves. I believe that once one believes in themselves, she/he can then generate strategies on how to develop skills and approach tasks. That was also my goal for Jessica. I wanted Jessica to know that there is no green thumb and even if there were people with green thumbs, it did not matter what they say. It only matters if you think you have a green thumb! With this belief in mind, my goal was to help Jessica promote self-confidence which ultimately leads to self-sustainability.

Jessica's Experience

In the world of counseling scholarship, I viewed Dr. Faii as having green thumbs, fingers, toes, arms, legs – you name it! With her by my side, I had hoped to practice the attitudes and behaviors of successful academic writing. And, this is exactly what happened. At the onset of our writing experience, Dr. Faii presented me with a contract that delineated my role as co-author and provided me with clear-cut suggestions (for example, lists of keywords and journal names) that would help me move forward with my responsibilities. She also met with me on a regular basis, and if I needed advice or encouragement in between our scheduled meetings, she was always available by phone. At times when I needed additional time to finish my work, new mutually-agreed upon deadlines were established. As a result of her continuous support and guidance, I developed new skills related to conceptualizing and framing a manuscript, writing with intentionality, and overcoming personal and environmental barriers that hindered my writing progress.

Additionally, I experienced first-hand how a mentoring relationship can evolve in the midst of collaboration, mutuality, and respect. These conditions created the necessary environment for our relationship to grow and thrive. As more and more time passed, I felt increasingly comfortable sharing my thoughts and ideas, my vulnerabilities, and my successes. I also felt that Dr. Faii opened up to me as well, sharing about personal and professional experiences aimed at helping me grow as a scholar in the field. After experiencing numerous heartfelt conversations, with a click of a switch, the light went on: I was not only learning how to be a gardener in the sense of tending to our paper, but our mentoring relationship as well!

Becoming a *successful* gardener, as I learned from Dr. Faii's shared wisdom, as well as our experience together, is not the sole result of natural talent. Instead, successful gardening can best be viewed as a developmental process that entails the cultivation of natural talents *as well as* a commitment to learn and practice new skills.

WRITING OUTCOMES

The writing process is like gardening, and submitting scholarship for publication is like climbing a steep mountain. At times, we experienced personal hurdles (e.g., feeling lost and confused) and contextual hurdles (e.g., receiving a recommendation to revise our initial submission) that blocked, or redirected, our journey straight to the top. Despite these set-backs, we successfully managed to reach our destination as a result of our shared knowledge, skills, and passion for the project. The shared perspective at the end was worth the journey.

Faii's Experience

Too often, research mentoring focuses on the end result—publications. Because of this, protégés and mentors may lose perspectives of what is important. In my experience, collaborative, mutual, and respectful relationships are the primary product of mentoring, while publications are a by-product. The effective and meaningful mentoring experience should inform both parties of how this relationship dynamic affect them on a personal level. The experience should also foster their mutual admiration and respect for each other within the working alliance. That was (and is still) my hope when working with Jessica. I wanted her to know that developing a long-term collaborative relationship is the most important aspect of research mentoring.

It is not about finishing the project. It is about developing and maintaining our relationship. It is about showing my admiration and respect for her in achieving her professional goal—publishing in a peer-reviewed journal. It is about showing my appreciation of her hard work. It is also about expressing my sincere gratitude to my writing partner, not my research protégé.

Jessica's Experience

I vividly remember the day that Dr. Faii shared the final disposition letter with me. I was standing in the department and I heard her call out to me from her office, "Jessica, Jessica, Jessica!" As I walked toward her I could see the excitement in her eyes. After reaching her doorway, she motioned me to sit in her desk chair and read the letter on her computer screen. As soon my eyes hit the big news, Dr. Faii exclaimed "Jessica! This is your first publication!" Most touching to me was not only her words, but her facial expressions that relayed an important message to me: "*We* did it and I am proud of you."

Beyond her initial response, Dr. Faii shared with me an important lesson about the publishing process that I have kept with me to this day. She had reminded me how long and hard we had worked on our article and discussed the importance of celebrating successes. Her idea of success, however, was not a tangible acceptance letter (or in the context of mountain climbing: reaching the top), but being able to accomplish something meaningful, no matter the editorial decision (that is, appreciating the process that beautiful view no matter where you are standing on the mountain). To celebrate our success, she invited me to lunch for the very first time in our relationship. This was another first invitation from her that became another transformative experience—and another story to share altogether!

TAKEAWAYS FROM THE MENTORING EXPERIENCE

Reflecting upon, and sharing about, our first co-authored publication has helped us gain a deeper appreciation for the transformative nature of research mentoring relationships and each other. Beyond our shared interests, our appreciation for one another and our commitment to our project and relationship throughout various stages of the writing process contributed to our success. Although successful outcomes (e.g., publications) are important, appreciation for one another in the mentoring relationship is critical. We believe that the key for a successful mentoring relationship is mutuality and respect for each other which, in turn, fosters both personal and professional growth not only for the protégés, but also for the mentor. For example, in academia, both students and faculty who are in mentoring relationships typically experience a power differential. Although we are unable to remove this power dynamic completely, we have made our mentoring relationship work by listening and valuing each other's opinions, believing that we can voice our concerns, and acknowledging struggles and challenges emerged in our relationship. The benefits of these actions promote transparency in our mentoring relationship in a meaningful way for both of us.

AUTHOR NOTE

Correspondence concerning this article should be addressed to Jessica A. Headley, School of Counseling, 118 Chima, Akron, OH 44325. Email: jah66@zips.uakron.edu.

SUGGESTED REFERENCES

Borders, L. D., Wester, K. L., Granello, D. H., Chang, C. Y., Hays, D. G., Pepperell, J., Spurgeon, S. L. (2012). Association for Counselor Education and Supervision Guidelines for Research Mentorship: Development and implementation. *Counselor Education & Supervision, 51*, 162-175. doi: 10.1002/j.1556-6978.2012.00012.x.

Casto, C., Caldwell, C., & Salazar, C. F. (2005). Creating mentoring relationships between female faculty and students in counselor education: Guidelines for potential mentees and mentors. *Journal of Counseling & Development, 83*, 331-336. doi: 10.1002/j.1556-6678.2005.tb00351.x.

Hammer, T., Trepal, H., & Speedlin, S. (2012). Five relational strategies for mentoring female faculty. *Adultspan, 13*(1), 4-14. doi: 10.1002/j.2161-0029.2014.00022.x.

Lambie, G. W., Sias, S. M., Davis, K. M., Lawson, G., & Akos, P. (2008). A scholarly writing resource for counselor educators and their students. *Journal of Counseling & Development, 86*, 18-25. doi: 10.1002/j.1556-6678.2008.tb00621.x.

Rheineck, J. E., & Roland, C. B. (2008). The developmental mentoring relationship between academic women. *Adultspan, 7*(2), 80-93. doi: 10.1002/j.2161-0029.2008.tb00048.x.

Chapter Twenty

Better Together

A Personal Exploration of a Co-Counselor Relationship

Christy W. Land and Lauren J. Moss

We had recently attended the Southern Association for Counselor Educators and Supervisors (SACES) conference. Not only was the conference an amazing professional development and networking opportunity, it allowed us to spend quality time with one another after not seeing each other for months. During this time spent together we reflected on our professional and personal relationships and often were speaking about what a unique and powerful connection that we have. A connection so strong that drives us and influences us to strive for growth in many areas of our lives. We even began to brainstorm about writing and/or presenting on our positive working alliance. As the conference concluded we went our separate ways, back to different states, with a renewed sense of energy and wellness. It was about a week after the conference that the call for proposals on transformative experiences came to our attention via email. Needless to say, this was a timely opportunity for us to do what we had a burning desire to do, share the story of our relational connection.

Relational movement is the fluid process of fluctuating through relational connectedness and disconnectedness, back into advanced, transformative, and enhanced connections with others (Comstock et al., 2008). The following chapter will closely examine the evolution of a co-counselor relationship between a novice and veteran professional school counselor through a Relational-Cultural theoretical lens. Specifically, the chapter will explore the positive impact of this growth-fostering relationship and how, as a transformative experience, this connection heavily impacted both school counselors professional and personally (Comstock et al., 2008). Further, the following chapter will highlight a case conceptualization and critical incident, giving the reader a personal glimpse in to the school counselors' daily interactions and showcase the unfolding of their process as a series of transformative shifts precipitated by a critical incident.

CHRISTY'S VOICE "PRE-INCIDENT"

I was thrilled to learn that the counseling department at my middle school would be hiring a new school counselor due to the upcoming retirement of the previous school counselor, as this person was not invested nor believed in the value of implementing a comprehensive school counseling program to meet the academic, personal/social, and career needs of all students. At this time, I was in my fourth year of school counseling at my current school and in my ninth year as a professional school counselor and considered myself an advocate for the profession and the implementation of a comprehensive school counseling program (ASCA, 2013). Therefore, this news evoked many personal emotions—hope for a positive working collaborative relationship with the new counselor toward a common goal, excitement about revamping and reenergizing the school counseling department's initiatives, and the desire to work with a professional who was passionate about student success. Numerous discussions occurred between the administration and myself in regards to personal and professional characteristics that the ideal candidate would possess and how such qualities would impact the school counseling department. I anxiously awaited the announcement of the administration's decision on the person with whom I would be working closely; I felt that my professional fate was in their hands.

I was informed that Lauren, who had previously worked as a special education teacher at my current school, had been offered and accepted the position as a school counselor. While I knew, liked, and respected Lauren on a peripheral level, I had some concerns. Lauren did not have experience as a school counselor. Were her goals as a school counselor going to mesh well with mine? Was I going to be spending this first year training and guiding her, adding more to my already full plate? Did she fully understand the role of a school counselor and implementing a comprehensive school counseling program?

Lauren and I began to communicate over the summer about plans for the upcoming school year, dividing roles and duties, planning our yearly calendar, and brainstorming creative ways to revamp many of our school-wide initiatives. As we began to collaborate I realized that Lauren just may exceed the expectations for my ideal co-counselor and as we started to work closely together with students and families, I began to understand that she possessed qualities that I craved both professional and personally. Lauren is a strong social justice advocate, is able to find humor in the hardest of situations, and is amazingly caring and kind, not because she has to be, but because that is who she truly is. I felt amazed and appreciative by her creativity, knowledge, and work ethic. I also felt blessed to go to work every day and be in the trenches with someone I was learning from and who I knew I was growing to love as a colleague and more importantly, as a friend.

LAUREN'S VOICE "PRE-INCIDENT"

"What will I do?" I thought to myself as I learned of the news that the class I taught, a special education classroom for students with emotional and behavioral disabilities, was being relocated to another school building. Although I loved the students I worked with, I knew that if I were to follow my professional position to a new school my life would be very different. Over the previous three years I had grown very comfortable in my setting and was anxious to leave. Furthermore, I had a desire to transition from my role as a classroom teacher to that of school counselor, so making the shift to a new setting without transitioning into the role of school counselor felt like a step backward in my career. Although I love teaching students who were often marginalized due to their disability, I knew I would be able to make a greater difference with this and other marginalized populations working in the capacity of school counselor. After all, my professors in graduate school had consistently lectured that the role of the school counselor was to advocate for ALL students.

As the days passed and I prepared for the potential of leaving the middle school that had begun to feel like a second home, my principal invited me into her office for a meeting to determine how I might be afforded the opportunity to stay at the school. "What are you certified to do?" She asked quite directly. I rattled off a number of teaching certificates, but quickly disclosed that while I appreciated her support, she should know that I was mostly interested in a school counseling position (although I knew the current school counselors at the school were likely to keep their positions for years to come). The meeting essentially ended with a look of pity from my principal and me with shoulders in a perpetual shrug. I did not feel hopeless, but had a renewed sense of confidence in my desire to serve my school district as a school counselor, due to efficacy found from speaking candidly about my professional goals. On a professional level, this moment resembled the shift in my professional identity from educator to counselor. Yet, on a personal level, I experienced the desire to connect with other counselors, like Christy.

The next week I heard rumors that one of the two current school counselors had, unexpectedly, decided to retire. A thousand emotions raced through my mind: my dream job! I have a chance to serve more students! Will I even be considered for the position? Again, I met with my principal. She offered me the opportunity to interview for the position, but made no promises.

The following weekend, the unexpected occurred. I checked my email to discover a message from the school district's human resources department indicating that my professional role had been 'reassigned' to that of school counselor at my current school. I was confused, shocked, and excited. I wondered if someone was playing a practical joke! However, on Monday morning my principal confirmed that, in fact, the administration had made the decision to keep me at the school in the new role of school counselor. Of course I was elated, but feelings of doubt were also present. I had no professional counseling experience and would actually require a provisional certification from the state in order to operate as a professional school counselor until I graduated from the doctoral program in which I was currently enrolled. Would I be able to perform the job expected of me?

I knew immediately who I needed to talk to in order to get started on the right foot – Christy. Christy would be my co-counselor and serve as the chair of our little department. I felt that if we were aligned with our goals and philosophies, then everything else would likely fall into place. I was nervous, but excited. I knew Christy was young and energetic and that, like me, she had training in social justice. I hoped for the best. My hopes quickly became a reality as my new co-counselor and I met and planned in late spring and through the summer in order to prepare for the following school year. During that time I began to experience what I would later understand as the "Five Good Things", or essential attributes, outlined by Jean Baker Miller and Relational Cultural Theory as crucial to growth-fostering relationships. I experienced a sense of zest and energy (the first of RCTs 'good things') each time we had a planning session, but also when conversation turned personal or theoretical (Jordan, 2010). As our relationship and plans continued to blossom, I also noted an increased sense of self-worth (the second of RCTs 'good things') due to the contribution I felt I was able to make to my new profession, incoming students, and emerging friend, Christy. The relationship and action gave way to clarity and productivity (the third and fourth of RCTs 'good things') in a way which allowed me an increased understanding of myself and Christy and motivated us both to take action in our relationship and in our professional pursuits (Jordan, 2010). Ultimately, my time in Christy's company facilitated increased connection, which is the fifth and final element of RCTs growth-fostering relationships. I felt satisfied in the relationship we were fostering and the professional results we were yielding. Truly, I was engaging in a growth-fostering relationship with Christy, my co-counselor, and as the new school year began I looked forward to the work we would do together as school counselors.

THE TRANSFORMATIVE INCIDENT

We were in the first year working together in a middle school counseling department. One of us was brand new to the profession and the other was a seasoned school counselor. We both had extensive training in social justice and were interested in implementing interventions to support marginalized populations. To take case in point, we both really wanted to bring a Safe Space Program to our middle school. In fact, we both felt strongly that this initiative would provide needed support and guidance for many of the students at our middle school as several students and parents had reached out to us with issues around sexual identity.

As a way to provide appropriate resources to our stake-holders, we decided to collect information regarding how Safe Space kits could be provided to the school. After corresponding via email with a Safe Space representative, Lauren forwarded her correspondence to the principal, indicating that we would like to talk to the administration about implementing the program. However, the administration at the school was resistant to this program and expressed concerns in regards to the school communities' reaction to what the administrators deemed a questionable program. In fact, we were reprimanded for exploring this program as an option for their student population. We were both shocked and did not anticipate receiving this reaction from our administration. It was this very critical moment that we profoundly experienced a mutually empathetic connection driving us to voice our concerns to the administration on denial of the program, as well as serve as a united voice for a marginalized group of students.

CHRISTY'S VOICE "POST-INCIDENT"

After Lauren and I left our administrator's office and were reprimanded for exploring the Safe Space Program for our school, we went back to the counseling office and shut the door to process the interaction. It was at this very moment that I could feel the connection that we had as school counselors uniting to advocate for our students and as human beings connectively concerned and compassionate for a marginalized group of our students. While we may have not had the support from our administration to implement this program school-wide, there were Safe Space stickers placed in clear view in each of our offices that very day. Our emotions and statements literally seemed to mirror one another's; our connection had transformed in to one that was unbreakable and a force to be reckoned with.

As our professional connection strengthened so did our school counseling program. We truly felt that the two of us together could initiate beneficial change in our schools, communities, and society at large. We begin collectively seeking out opportunities to contribute to the field of counseling by presenting at professional conferences together, co-authoring literature to contribute to the field of school counseling, and serving as a united voice to advocate for our students and the profession. In fact, several colleagues began to refer to us as the dynamic duo and commented on how seamlessly we worked together for the benefit of our school and community.

Through professional time spent together our personal relationship continued to grow and blossom. We began to eat lunch together when possible, an albeit small break with this astonishingly wonderful friend and colleague rejuvenated me mid-day due to the synergy we created together, resulting in my development into a better, more effective school counselor. Lauren and I began to share our common interests outside of school by going on walks, sharing a meal, or just socializing and laughing. While we no longer work together, I am forever grateful for everything that Lauren taught me and the person she helped me become by emulating her outstanding professional and positive qualities. I still consider her a professional colleague as we continuously work on projects collaboratively from two different states. However, most importantly I am honored to call her my best friend.

LAUREN'S VOICE "POST-INCIDENT"

I vividly remember my administrator requesting my presence, along with Christy, in her office to discuss the Safe Space program. Naively, I believed that she wanted to discuss this intervention in the same way we had countless other interventions around topics like bullying prevention, study skills, or peer mediation. To the contrary, as soon as the door to the principal's office slammed shut, her tone changed from collegial to enraged. She spoke in a harsh tone about her feeling that I was trying to undermine her authority by suggesting the Safe Space program for our school population and questioned me about how parents might react if they saw a box of rainbow propaganda delivered to the front office. I was in shock. I conceptualized my intentions and efforts as such that they were in the best interest of students, not a way to control the school or push a personal agenda. At first I thought I must be confused by the principal's questions, but the more I attempted to clarify my thought process and actions the angrier she became. I began to feel trapped. What could I do? I was forced to either take a stand for what I believed in, the right for all students to feel safe and supported at school, or apologize for my actions that were perceived as the principal to be inappropriate. I looked at Christy, my colleague, mentor, and at this point in our relationship, my friend. I wondered if this moment would be the one to send everything spiraling in a negative cyclone. Would I lose my new friend? Would she distance herself from me as a way to avoid standing with me in a negative light in the eyes of our supervisor? Were the plans we made all summer pipe dreams? Most importantly, were we really able to make a difference for our students?

I looked to Christy, my glance begging for help. I did not know how to proceed. As if putting all my fears to rest, Christy calmly interjected with the principal, offering both a rationale for why we had taken the action we did and suggesting steps subsequent that were more digestible to the principal. I was relieved, yet wondered if we did the right thing.

Once dismissed from the principal's office, we returned to my office, behind closed doors, to discuss what had transpired. As the door closed we returned to the honest, private relational connection we typically enjoyed. As we processed our conversation with the administrator and how to proceed with supporting students, it was as if a mutual space was created. One that was outside of each of us, yet equally accessible to us both. The idea of mutuality, as RCT suggests, lies in the ability to be affected by someone while simultaneously affecting them (Jordan, 2010). While Christy and I had been developing mutual empathy during the months prior to the critical incident, it was actually in the resolution of the incident which brought us to understand our connection as having the ability to create a mutual space between us. This space does not exist when either of us are absent, and is far more deep, genuine, and powerful than when either of us are in our own personal space.

After creating and acknowledging the mutual space we had generated, Christy and I began exploring how to best leverage this space. Ultimately, the ability to exist in this space collectively allowed us to transform our department and school to become much more inclusive and meaningful. Furthermore, we were able to engage in scholarly activity, such as professional presentations and publications, as a way to push the social justice agenda forward in the field of school counseling, a journey we continue through to the present date. Finally, we have been able to use our mutual space as a tool for self-exploration and growth to ensure that we continue to cultivate RCTs Five Good Things in and among ourselves.

EXPLORATION OF IMPORTANCE

The connection between us, two school counselors, served as a powerful impetus, causing us to form solidarity and collectively serve as advocates. Experiencing the critical incident together empowered us to challenge the status quo and give voice to those in their school community who had none, which produced an undeniable shift in the two counselors professionally and personally. Our mutual empathetic connection propelled growth, increased each other's energy and sense of worth, helped us both develop clarity and productivity, and ultimately resulted in a desire for more wellness and strength-producing connection (Comstock et al., 2008). Subsequently, our school counseling department continued to grow and support students through an increasingly successful comprehensive school counseling program which was ultimately recognized by the American School Counselor Association as a RAMP school (ASCA, 2012). Further, we both began to serve as a voice for the profession through involvement in professional organizations at the local, state, and national levels. Their connection bled into their personal lives as their explored personal interests with one another outside of the work place, giving way to richer, more meaningful life experiences and positively impacting their overall well-being.

REFLECTION OF CHANGE

As our relationship continued to grow and become more authentic, so did our professional and personal identities (Comstock et al., 2008). The success of the school counseling program and us as individual counselors as a result of this transformative shift is undeniable. We and our school have been recognized for our work at the local, state, and national levels. Further, we are both active leaders and advocates for the school counseling profession. The significance of their connection is virtually 'tangible'; professional colleagues, coworkers, friends, and family have commented on the positivity and success that has resulted from their growth-fostering relationship.

REFERENCES

American School Counselor Association (2012). *ASCA national model: A framework for school counseling programs, third edition.* Alexandria, VA: American School Counselor Association.

Comstock, D.L., Hammer, T.R., Strentzsch, J., Cannon, K., Parson, J., & Salazar, G. (2008). Relational-cultural theory: A framework for bridging relational, multicultural, and social justice competencies. *Journal of Counseling & Development, 86,* 279-287. 10.1002/j.1556-6678.2008.tb00510.x.

Jordan, J. V. (2010) *The power of connection: Recent developments in Relational-Cultural Theory.* New York, NY: Routledge.

Chapter Twenty-One

My Process and Development through Group Process

Greg A. Meyer

The process I experienced while encountering a Group Process course during a summer semester of my graduate course work significantly awakened my awareness both personally and professionally. Developmentally, I experienced growth from feedback provided by the course professor, as well as the experiential process group, led by a graduate assistant and composed of peers. The honest and direct feedback I encountered through these varied experiences formed a transformational framework for me to more thoughtfully and honestly become aware of my own processes and motivations. I attempted to provide a rich description of the experience, as well as a personal reflection of the experience, which may provide contextual information for the reader.

GROUP PROCESS AS A CRITICAL INCIDENT

In the summer semester of 2008, I enrolled in a course entitled, "Group Process." The class met once a week with a lecture component followed by an experiential process group component for approximately 90 minutes. Various weekly tasks provided the structure to the course, as students were expected to hand in their written weekly chapter commentaries on the prepared reading, listen to a few prepared lecture notes from the professor, participate in or observe an in-class activity, then recess before reconvening with their experiential process groups.

The course structure, which felt objective and rigid, was juxtaposed by the professor's intentionality and genuineness in offering his critique of our work. The professor provided written weekly feedback, often short and direct remarks, following the required page-and-a-half commentary. These remarks provided insight to his judgment of my grasp of the material. I recall phrases written directly to me from the professor indicating my lack of thoughtfulness, understanding, and awareness in applying the material in a practical sense. Often, it was my goal to produce a commentary that manufactured no written feedback from the professor. The moment that taught me the value of this exercise occurred after the commencement of the course when I received feedback on my final commentary. We were not required to write a commentary for the final class; however, I only became aware of this upon handing in my prepared commentary. The professor explained this to me, then offered to still read it and provide feedback. I accepted, and received his feedback in the mail the following week. He wrote that he was glad to have gotten the chance to read what was my most thoughtful, intentional, and well-developed commentary. He could see how I made sense of the reading material, incorporated it into the broad sense of group practice, and gave exceptional effort in producing a written work demonstrating my understanding. He then remarked on my potential, and requested that I offer this effort throughout my career as a counselor.

Through this exercise, the professor developed an awareness of his students and perhaps their effort, study habits, and ability to critically engage the materials. I was routinely confronted for having not provided what he assumed I was capable of producing. Simultaneously, the lecture portion of the class was used by the professor to share his anecdotes and tales of leading groups in the field. He would receive questions about the prepared readings and converse with the class like an invited author speaking about his latest project. I recall never being engaged enough to comment or offer a question for this activity. In fact, there were two times in which my level of disinterest became worthy of comment by the professor. I had the tendency to embark on comedy competitions when sitting next to one particular student. The professor called on me to share my question or comment with the class. At the time, this felt mortifying; however, this became a lesson to which I drew immense awareness of maturity and professionalism.

The second half of class was devoted to an experiential process group. The entire class was split into four groups of approximately eight members. Each group was led by a graduate student in their second year, as part of their planned practicum coursework. Each leader was supervised by the course professor. The process group was the first time in my life I can remember feeling completely exposed, not only to my peers in the group but more significantly, to myself. The feedback given and received in the group was quick to reach discussion of the here-and-now process which provided a previously never experienced trust and vulnerability of one another. From the first session, the group worked to realize the tremendous value in reducing our defenses. The more each individual tried to feel comfortable, the more we each displayed our insecurities and fears. I recall speaking with my wife about being a part of something so unbelievably thrilling by learning about my peers in ways much deeper than I had ever known others before, yet not by their stories or explanations, but through their being. Inevitably, I had to recognize my own communication in this experience and reconcile my peer's perception of me with my own perception of myself.

In the final session of the semester, I had to arrive late due to a previously scheduled appointment. When I arrived, the group welcomed me into the discussion which was about 20 minutes old, and we jumped into where we left off the previous week. I felt as though I had missed nearly nothing. Approximately ten minutes later, the group leader asked the group if they had noticed the dynamics shift upon my arrival. He explained how he perceived the group to have spent the entire time prior to my arrival in surface-level casual conversations with significant tension or nervous energy. Upon my arrival, the leader explained how it felt as though the group breathed a collective sigh, and immediately began processing here-and-now vulnerability. Various comments confirmed the leader's observation, which led me to question my role in more of a macro-sense. I had not seen myself in this way at any moment of my life. I grew up believing I had a purpose, or a role, in the systems I inhabited, but the role I saw for myself was in sharp contrast to the role my peers were explaining to me at this moment. I saw myself as the nuisance or irritant within systems. My approach was to bother others which was always received in a negative manner. Here, I was still a catalyst, but in a positive fashion. This experience caused more reflection inward than anything I had ever experienced in my life. Reflection inward could potentially cause a person fear or pain; however, I would describe my experience of this inward reflection as the most alive I had ever felt.

Critical to this semester-long experience was the vulnerability by both peers and the group leader to share their experiences of one another with each other. Here, I learned my strengths, my weaknesses, my insecurities, my motivations, and most importantly my new professional identity as a counselor. Through my experience of this Group Process course, I was able to grow in awareness and responsibility regarding an interpersonal understanding of myself, specific behavioral patterns I engaged in, and insights into motivation for connecting with others. In addition, the nature of the course, specifically the direct feedback, produced greater awareness and accountability for my own future goals and aspirations.

PERSONAL REFLECTION OF THE GROUP PROCESS EXPERIENCE

This reflection provides the opportunity to consider the ways in which significant moments impact our journeys. This single experience is one of many different moments that facilitate development, decisions, and motivation along the path to what is taking place in the current moment. As I call to mind the moments during my Group Process course, I am amazed by what appears to be relatively mild instances, over time, becoming driving forces behind career aspirations and goals. Becoming aware of my capabilities through feedback from an intentional professor and witnessing peers' vulnerable explanation of their perception of me during a process group may have provided some of the most powerful moments of my life. These moments may have allowed me to not be afraid to seek bigger career goals.

The feedback received from the professor launched many existential dialogues in my own mind. His expectations seemed drastically higher than my own and additionally, the words appeared to lack social politeness. His feedback expressed his experience of me through my work. This was the moment I grasped authenticity and the transformative experience of hearing someone's authentic perception of me. Likewise, in the process group, I experienced feedback from my peers and the group leader regarding the way my presence in the group impacted the individuals in our group. Occasionally this feedback was embarrassing or caused me to feel exposed. The group experience alone allowed me to question my motives for interacting with others in general, prior to ever using verbal communication. Until this experience, I had not asked myself this. To ruthlessly shed light on my motivations for something as simple as opening my mouth to verbally communicate was startlingly freeing.

The experience of the process group allowed me to realize my ability to understand the here-and-now process of human interaction, and subsequently affirmed my theoretical paradigm as a counselor. As I reflected during the process group, on myself and others, I recognized the direct link here-and-now moments have toward existential themes and ultimate concerns for one's existence. Specifically, I recognized my own concern for control, direction, and fulfillment. Coupled with the professor's sharp and accurate feedback, I began taking responsibility for my education during the program. It was during this semester that I recognized a shift in my professional identity. I saw myself as less of a student and more of a professional counselor-in-training. My behaviors shifted in both personal and professional situations.

Currently, as a counselor educator, I consciously make a point in each course I teach to introduce and discuss shifting ones professional identity from a student to a professional counselor-in-training. It is because of this critical moment, and the subsequent shift in professional identity I experienced, that I recognized the potential impact an awareness of these moments can have on a counselor's growth and development.

DISCUSSION

Various experiences have impacted my professional and personal growth as a counselor and counselor educator, but perhaps none more than my experience of my Group Process course. Through the feedback provided by the course professor, which was honest and pointed, I developed more awareness of my capabilities and the way my professor had viewed my effort. Additionally, I was confronted on my immaturity and lack of professionalism in class. I recognized the expectations others had of me and noticed the obvious inconsistency with my own expectations.

In addition, the experiential component of the course provided my first opportunity to examine my intentions, motivations, and interpersonal patterns which was both exciting and freeing. Also, experiencing the feedback offered by my peers, as well as their perceptions of me, produced a new framework of viewing my interpersonal style in a positive manner, dispelling the notion I had come to accept throughout my life. The group experience allowed me to come to an awareness of my defenses as well as recognize the deep ultimate concerns of those around me. I began developing an understanding of others and their unique ways of communicating through process.

Through the entirety of the transformative experience I recognized the impact this course had on my theoretical orientation and eventual career. This course was the first time I can recall truly considering my professional identity. I became interested in the profession of counseling and considered my career as a professional, rather than a student. More importantly, the feedback I received from those around me instilled a sense of confidence in myself, and raised my belief in my capabilities. Because of this, I stepped out of the fear that hindered me from creating loftier career goals and began embracing my unique personal abilities.

Chapter Twenty-Two

Counselor, Know Thyself

Sudha Nagarajan

I begin my chapter on transformational personal growth experiences with some relevant words by the Dalai Lama, who said,

> I believe that it is essential to appreciate our potential as human beings and recognize the importance of inner transformation. This should be achieved through what could be called a process of mental development. Sometimes, I call this having a spiritual dimension in our life (in Cutler, 2009).

One experience that allowed me to develop my personal and professional identity was my exposure to a natural disaster in India. I was in Chennai, a city in south India, on the 26th of December, 2004, and felt the earthquake in the early morning hours that preceded the devastating tsunami. We heard accounts of fishermen and their families being swallowed by the ocean, of people out on their early morning walk at the beach being swept away, of the ocean encroaching insidiously onto the beachfront and low lying areas of the city, of miraculous escapes, of the daring of rescuers, of the selflessness of lay people, and the incongruity of life experiences. Thousands of people perished in India alone, and many more were displaced in terms of homes and livelihood (NDMA, 2015). The psychological impact of such devastation can be realized by understanding the fear and uncertainty of the survivors. The aftermath of the tsunami was bewildering, though we were safe in the middle of such a devastating experience. Apart from feeling the earthquake very distinctly, we were in a part of the city that was largely unaffected by it and the tsunami. I had had previous experiences with powerful earthquakes since I lived in an earthquake prone zone in India, but this was my first exposure to a tsunami, albeit vicarious. Being spared any harm and yet hearing such heartbreaking stories of suffering, I wondered if that was my karma?

Perhaps that experience was embedded in the recesses of my mind as I sought a career in the helping profession a few years later.

India is very diverse in terms of ethnic composition, language, religion, and socioeconomic class (Catalyst, 2013). For me, living in India until adulthood was instrumental in the development of awareness of diversity and disparity. I am very cognizant of the privileged classes that have access to resources and the unfortunate plight of the disadvantaged. For a conscientious person, it is very hard to enjoy privileges while acknowledging the dire circumstances of the surrounding humanity. Yet, one becomes hardened to some realities in order to desensitize oneself because change is systemic and often very difficult to achieve. On the contrary, lasting change can be initiated through awareness and empowerment beginning with the self.

Although there have been many experiences that have allowed me to grow, I would like to share a rather serendipitous experience of my participation in an international exchange that sharpened my self-identity. It allowed me to practice ambassadorship of my country of origin with objectivity, as well as that of my adopted country. While enrolled in a graduate program in mental health counseling, I participated in an immersion experience with the international delegation People to People Ambassador Program (2012) to understand India's psychosocial approach to disaster mental health management. Since I was drawn to issues of global diversity and disparity, this cultural exchange opportunity aroused my curiosity regarding India in terms of disaster-preparedness, something I had never given my focused attention to. Revisiting the event (tsunami of 2004) in 2010 with the international delegation (People to People Ambassador Program, 2012) focused on disaster mental health allowed me to understand the preparation and response required for such an overwhelming experience. I did not quite understand the emergency preparation needed to address the requirements of a populous of such magnitude until I interacted with the officials who created and refined the governmental disaster response guidelines. This exposure was quite revealing for me because I didn't realize the enormity of the country's vulnerability to disaster, and I did not appreciate the natural resources of communal strength, faith, and innovation that marks the resilience of Indian citizens.

My fellow delegates on the People to People Ambassador Program (2012) were seasoned mental health professionals, practitioners, educators, pastoral counselors, and fellow students. I perceived myself as one of the junior-most delegates since I was still a counselor-in-training. That experience though, was a mile marker for me because I saw my country-of-origin through the eyes of an external observer for the first time. As an international delegate, I was able to perceive India from a distance and yet with a nuanced sense of belonging. It was a sort of surreal experience because I realized that as a natural born citizen of India, I had taken so much for granted. As a member of a privileged class, I had been shielded from some of the stark realities of life in India and had never focused my attention on state-sponsored efforts towards disaster management even though India is constantly under the threat of some form of natural or man-made disaster. But, returning as a naturalized citizen of the United States of America, I became more acutely aware of my "dual" citizenship. And as a result of this, I could now perceive some aspects of my country-of-origin from "the outside-in."

This immersion into India's disaster mental health response gave me a new perspective of the complexity of the country's structure and demographic distribution. For example, I became more acutely aware of the similarities and differences between people in general and communities in particular, when responding to trauma. Prior to the trip I think I was a naïve and a passive observer, never having been involved in public service. But as with any personalized trauma, even if it is vicarious, it hits home and suddenly, the meaning-making seems very appropriate. Vicarious traumatization is a powerful factor to consider in reactions to events that are impactful, and often personality characteristics including resiliency, spirituality and environmental factors determine the ability to heal and recover from such experiences (Adams & Riggs, 2008; Newell & MacNeil, 2010; Palm, Polusny & Follette, 2004; Trippany, Kress & Wilcoxon, 2004). As a result of my increased sensitivity to disaster exposure and response in India, I began to understand the implications of the phenomenon and appreciate the human capacity to recover and heal through internal and external resources.

Although ancient in history, India, is a young republic, and a developing country with limited financial and institutional resources to provide for its population of over a billion people. There are many features that increase the vulnerability of the country to disasters including geographic exposure to earthquakes, landslides, floods, drought, hurricanes and devastating heat waves, compounded by poverty and illiteracy (NDMA National Policy on Disaster Management, 2009). Responding to such a challenging and constant demand requires creative planning and optimal utilization of limited resources.

Furthermore, India is a microcosm of issues of diversity, and a land of starkly contrasting land structure, languages, religions, economic development, cultural expression, and food habits (Mahajan, 2010). Managing a developing nation requires dedicated planning and implementation to build and sustain the infrastructure with restricted resources while responding to the many risks (Agarwal, 2013; Federation of Indian Chambers of Commerce & Industry, 2015; Xu & Albert, 2014). It requires strategies such as frugality, inclusion, collaboration and flexibility in thinking to generate movement in situations that can prove challenging in scope (Barodawala, Banerjee, Roy & Kapur, 2015; Radjou, Prabhu, & Ahuja, 2012). A case in point of this resourcefulness is the improvisation of community level workers (CLW) in disaster response due to an acute shortage of trained professionals.

Other instances have been the inclusion of medical and psychiatric resources in the field for the rural population that would otherwise not have access to it. Furthermore, there are many non-governmental organizations that provide care at the grassroots level and train local people identified in the community for sustainability of programs. An example of community work initiated by a non-profit would be the Ananya project conducted by the Bill and Melinda Gates Foundation (Gates Foundation, 2015) and sustainable healthcare initiatives through innovative approaches in ideology and processes to find indigenous solutions to reduce costs (DeLoitte, 2012). Organizations such as these provide ongoing support and access to services that otherwise would not be available.

My visit to India in 2010, organized by the People to People Ambassador Program, was led by a prominent member of the counseling profession in the United States with extensive experience in the field of disaster mental health. People to People Ambassador programs are led by members of the academic and professional communities in order to provide opportunities for students, researchers, and professionals to avail in educational travel (People to People Ambassador Programs, 2012). During our visit, the team met with Indian senior government officials and members of their advisory team for disaster management including heads of department of public and private mental health institutions in India. We visited a state-sponsored mental health research institute in the capital, New Delhi, non-profit organizations, a school for physically and intellectually challenged children, the psychology department of a university, and participated in cultural experiences in terms of food and folk culture. Through this immersion, my view of human suffering shifted from an externalized one to a more internalized experience because I was no longer insulated from the physical, mental and emotional challenges of human existence.

I also took the opportunity to visit one of the premier mental health teaching hospitals in the country following up my connection with one of the department heads of the school of psychiatric social work. While I was at the hospital in the southern city of Bangalore, called the National Institute of Mental Health and Neurosciences (NIMHANS, 2015), I met with the head of the department of Psychiatric Social Work, who took me on a tour of a residential facility for boys who were displaced from their homes due to running away. Some had been rescued from child labor and exploitation or abusive situations, and some were in pursuit of employment. These were young boys from all over India who had somehow found their way to the facility and were cared for by the staff. The director of the facility shared with me that many of these young men had been rescued by social workers who came across them homeless in the street or as a result of traumatic events. During their stay, every attempt was made by the hospital to reintegrate them with their families and with society. Seeing their journey made me realize how vulnerable these children were, and I became acutely aware of the dire circumstances that would force these children into leaving their homes and leaving them so vulnerable to experiencing trauma. I also worried about the emotional health of these children and the long-term scars that these life-changing experiences would expose them to. Although their displacement was not always directly related to a disaster, I could think of many instances in which children especially, could become destitute as a result of calamities such as the frequent earthquakes, the tsunami of 2004, and sadly, even communal riots.

Burdened with a huge rural population, inadequate infrastructure and divisive sociopolitical forces, the administrators of the country need to rely on trained professionals to provide effective response in emergency situations (Bhandari, 2006; Madan, 2005). But strong leadership needs able delegates at the community level. Since the resources for such delegations are limited by a lack of trained mental health professionals, the model used is one based on community support. It is an empowerment approach using Community Health Workers (CHW) who are local citizens trained in basic skills to administer education and support to residents through local connections while working closely with health services agencies (UNICEF, 2004). In India, accredited social health activists (ASHAs) are also chosen and trained to supplement the lack of competent health professionals especially in rural areas to provide liaison services between the community and healthcare agencies (World Health Organization [WHO], 2013). It utilizes a hierarchical structure that branches from federal directives to state level mandates and community level responsibility and finally down to the common able-bodied person who can be trained to provide stabilizing support (NDMA, 2009a).

Visiting governmental representatives with the delegation, I learned about the National Disaster Management Authority (NDMA), an initiative of the Government of India, that has published specific and detailed guidelines for Psycho-Social Support and Mental Health Services (PSSMHS) in disaster situations (NDMA, 2009b). It was illuminating for me to learn about ongoing standardized training of mental health professionals as well as paramedics, community level workers, and representatives of non-governmental organizations (NGOs). Additionally, in view of the acute shortage of psychiatrists, medical personnel are trained to recognize psychological symptoms and direct patients to appropriate healthcare centers for treatment and prevention. The use of CLWs is very appropriate because they are sometimes welcomed more than trained professionals. CLWs are better positioned to accurately read the pulse of the local people, establish rapport and build trust with them, instill hope, and help them to understand the vulnerability in the face of local hazards.

For me, personally, it was illuminating and a great opportunity to learn more about psychological first-aid, cultural barriers, and the specialized training required to deploy personnel who can speak the local language and can be trusted by the affected populations. For instance, I came to learn that during the aftermath of the Indian tsunami in 2004, members of differing religious communities hesitated to be housed together in temporary shelters, possibly because of socialization practices that discourage mingling with people of differing religions, cultures, or socio-economic status. According to Subbaraju, Siva Krishna Raju, Prudhvy Raju and Anudeep, (2015) the Dalit community, considered of 'low caste' socially, was particularly marginalized due to long-standing oppression based on caste segregation (p. 29).

Through such exposure, I began to make similar connections between my personal and professional identity and my own wellspring of resilience. I discovered that serving humankind is one way I could fulfill personal and altruistic goals. While my training has been to help people achieve psychosocial and emotional wellbeing, I wanted to use my exposure to India in a way that would allow me to serve a community often underserved by mental health professionals. The realization that people from my community do not access mental healthcare deepened my focus to work with the South Asian population in the U.S. As I researched more into the attitudes of South Asians towards mental and emotional wellbeing, I found strong evidence that indicated much lower utilization of professional resources because of denial, stigma, shame, lack of awareness about mental illness, and faith-based or spiritual and philosophical outreach (Bhattacharya, 2004; Frey & Roysircar, 2006; Khanna, McDowell, Perumbilly, & Titus, 2009; Lawrence et al., 2006; McAuliffe, 2008; Sandhu et al., 2013).

Asians in America are considered the 'model minority' because it is felt that their higher academic achievements suggest reciprocal achievement of successful acculturation (Wu, 2015). An explanation of the concept of model minority as it pertains to Asians in particular in America, refers to stereotypical perceptions of being smart, self-sufficient, submissive, pursuing academic excellence, good at mathematics and technical subjects, hard-working, spiritually enlightened and not having any problems. There are negative stereotypes of this very broad cultural group as well, of being selfish, cunning, unemotional, socially awkward and often experience prejudice and discrimination based on these ambivalent perceptions (Maddux, Galinsky, Cuddy & Polifroni, 2008; Wong & Halgin, 2006). Some common misconceptions in this regard refer to the perception that all Asian Americans are the same, they are not considered ethnic minorities in terms of education, they do not face major challenges like other races, they do not need supporter resources, and that academic achievement of Asian Americans denotes success (Lee, 1994; Museus & Kiang, 2009). Furthermore, the perception of belonging to the 'model minority' raises expectations for people from such communities to practice higher social and moral standards, resulting in denial of mental and emotional problems, substance abuse, and physical abuse and violence (Das & Kemp, 1997). This community experiences many forms of microaggressions, perpetuating the model minority myth. Microaggressions are described as subtle, derogatory verbal and behavioral expressions that could be intentional or unintentional, which cause the victim to feel insulted and invalidated and question their experiential reality (Sue, Bucceri, Lin, Nadal & Torino, 2007).These discoveries prompted me to volunteer with the South Asian affiliate of the National Alliance on Mental Illness (NAMI-NJ) called South Asian Mental Health Awareness in Jersey (SAMHAJ, 2014). As a volunteer I have worked with the group as a support group facilitator, crisis hotline responder, trained volunteers, organized community education events, provided cultural competency training for mental health agencies and educational institutions, and am now a member of their Professional Advisory Group focused on furthering the vision and mission of SAMHAJ to provide support to an underserved community here in the U.S.

As a professional counselor and educator, my internal compass orients itself towards ongoing self-awareness as well as attunement to those around me in order to respond effectively to the unique needs of people. It also requires the integration of self-awareness and cultural knowledge with appropriate intervention skills, (Ancis & Marshall, 2010; Estrada, Frame & Williams, 2004) in order to be an effective force in the development of wellness, resilience, and empowerment in my clients. Pursuing a career in counseling has helped me develop my self because I am continually assessing my self-awareness in the context of my experiences. This is crucial to personal growth as I learn to accept the dynamic realities of life.

Learning about Indians in particular through personal experiences and the lived experiences of others from my community in the U.S. has given me pause for thought as a counselor and counselor educator. Reducing stigma, acknowledging mental and emotional problems, seeking help before a crisis situation develops, and offering my services as a member of the community is my professional endeavor. Personally, I would like to continue working on myself by focusing on my own identity development and self-concept. Knowledge of oneself in the context of others is the basis for developing a multicultural orientation to living that is essential in a globalized world and I hope to continue on the journey of self-awareness.

REFERENCES

Adams, S. A., & Riggs, S. A. (2008). An exploratory study of vicarious trauma among therapist trainees. *Training and Education in Professional Psychology, 2*(1), 26. http://dx.doi.org/10.1037/1931-3918.2.1.26.

Agarwal, M. (2013). *A passage to modernity.* Gridlines. Pricewaterhouse Coopers. Retrieved from www.pwc.com/gx/en/capital-projects-infrastructure/assets/gridlines-india-article-2013.pdf.

Ancis, J. R., & Marshall, D. S. (2010). Using a multicultural framework to assess supervisees' perceptions of culturally competent supervision. *Journal of Counseling & Development,* *88*(3), 277-284. doi: 10.1002/j.1556-6678.2010.tb00023.x.

Barodawala, B., Banerjee, R., Roy, S. & Kapur, V. (2015). Jugaad. The perennial short-term solution. *World Journal of Social Sciences, 5*(2), 163-176. ISBN: 978-1-922069-22-1.

Bhandari, R. K. (2006). Disaster management in India, a new awakening. *Journal of Disaster Development, 1*(1), 1-26.

Bhattacharya, G. (2004). Health care seeking for HIV/AIDS among South Asians in the United States. *Health & Social Work,29* (2) 106-115. DOI: http://dx.doi.org/10.1093/hsw/29.2.106.

Catalyst. (2013). *First step:India overview.* Retrieved from http://www.catalyst.org/knowledge/first-step-india-overview.

Cutler, H. C. (1998). *The Art Of Happiness.* New York, NY: Riverhead Books.

Das, A., K & Kemp, S. F. (1997). Between two worlds: Counseling South Asian Americans. *Journal of Multicultural Counseling and Development, 25*(1) 23-33. doi: 10.1002/j.2161-1912.1997.tb00313.x.

DeLoitte. (2012). *Innovative and sustainable healthcare management: Strategies for growth.* Retrieved from http://www2.deloitte.com/content/dam/Deloitte/in/Documents/life-sciences-health-care/in-lshc-innovative-healthcare-noexp.pdf.

Estrada, D., Frame, M.W., & Williams, C.B. (2004). Cross-cultural supervision: Guiding the conversation toward race and ethnicity. *Journal of Multicultural Counseling & Development, 32,* 307-319.

Federation of Indian Chambers of Commerce and Industry (2015). India Risk Survey. Retrieved from http://ficci.in/surveys.asp.

Frey, L. L. & Roysircar, G. (2006). South Asian and East Asian international students' perceived prejudice, acculturation, and frequency of help resource utilization. *Journal of Multicultural Counseling and Development, 34*(4), 208-222. http://dx.doi.org/10.1002/j.2161-1912.2006.tb00040.x.

Gates Foundation. (2015). *Our work in Bihar.* Retrieved from http://www.gatesfoundation.org/Where-We-Work/Our-Work-in-India/Our-Work-in-Bihar.

Khanna, A., McDowell, T., Perumbilly, S. & Titus, G. (2009). Working with Asian Indian American families: A Delphi study. *Journal of Systemic Therapies, 28*(1), 52-71. doi: 10.1521/jsyt.2009.28.1.52.

Lawrence, V., Banerjee,S., Bhugra, D, Sangha, K, Turner, S. & Murray, J. (2006). Coping with depression in later life: A qualitative study of help-seeking in three ethnic groups. *Psychological Medicine, 36,* 1375–1383. doi: http://dx.doi.org/10.1017/S0033291706008117.

Lee, S. J. (1994). Behind the model-minority stereotype: Voices of high-and low-achieving Asian American students. *Anthropology & Education Quarterly, 25*(4), 413-429. doi:10.1525/aeq.1994.25.4.04x0530j.

Madan, D. (2005), Disaster Management in India. In *Catastrophic Risks and Insurance.* (The Office of Economic Co-operation and Development OECD Publishing. doi: http://dx.doi.org/10.1787/9789264009950-22-en.

Maddux, W. W., Galinsky, A. D., Cuddy, A. J., & Polifroni, M. (2008). When being a model minority is good and bad: Realistic threat explains negativity toward Asian Americans. *Personality and Social Psychology Bulletin, 34*(1), 74-89. doi: 10.1177/0146167207309195.

Mahajan, G. (2010). *Negotiating cultural diversity and minority rights in India.* Institute for Democracy & Electoral Assistance-IDEA. Retrieved from http://www.idea.int/publications/dchs/upload/dchs_vol2_sec3_4.pdf.

McAuliffe, G.J., (2008). *Culturally alert counseling: A comprehensive introduction.* Thousand Oaks, CA. Sage.

Museus, S. D., & Kiang, P. N. (2009). Deconstructing the model minority myth and how it contributes to the invisible minority reality in higher education research. *New Directions for Institutional Research, 142,* 5-15. doi:10.1002/ir.292.

National Disaster Management Authority (2009a). National Disaster Management Guidelines: Psycho-Social Support and Mental Health Services in Disasters, 2009. Government of India. New Delhi. Retrieved from http://ndma.gov.in/images/guidelines/pssmhsguidlines.pdf.

National Disaster Management Authority (2009b). National Disaster Management Guidelines: Psycho-Social Support and Mental Health Services in Disasters, 2009. Government of India. New Delhi. Retrieved from http://ndma.gov.in/en/irs-training/introduction.html.

National Disaster Management Authority. (2015). Retrieved from http://ndma.gov.in/en/media-public-awareness/disaster/natural-disaster/tsunamis.html.

National Institute of Mental Health and Neurosciences (2015). Retrieved from http://nimhans.ac.in/.

Newell, J. M., & MacNeil, G. A. (2010). Professional burnout, vicarious trauma, secondary traumatic stress, and compassion fatigue. *Best Practices in Mental Health, 6*(2), 57-68.

Palm, K. M., Polusny, M. A., & Follette, V. M. (2004). Vicarious traumatization: Potential hazards and interventions for disaster and trauma workers. *Prehospital and Disaster Medicine, 19*(01), 73-78.

People to People Ambassador Programs (2012). Retrieved from http://citizens.peopletopeople.com/AboutUs/Pages/default.aspx.

Radjou, N., Prabhu, J., & Ahuja, S. (2012). *Jugaad innovation: Think frugal, be flexible, generate breakthrough growth.* Jossey-Bass. San Francisco, CA.

Sandhu, S., Bjerre, N. V., Dauvrin, M., Dias, S., Gaddini , A., Greacen, T., Ioannidis, E., Kluge, U., Jensen, N.K., Lamkaddem, M., Puigpino's i Riera, R., Ko´sa, Z., Wihlman, U., Stankunas, M., Straßmayr, C., Wahlbeck, K., Welbel, M. & Priebe, S. (2013). Experiences with treating immigrants: A qualitative study in mental health services across 16 European countries. *Social Psychiatry & Psychiatric Epidemiology,48*(1), 105–116. doi: 10.1007/s00127-012-0528-3.

South Asian Mental Health Awareness in Jersey (SAMHAJ). (2014). Retrieved from http://www.naminj.org/programs/multicultural/samhaj/.

Subbaraju, Siva Krishna Raju, Prudhvy Raju & Anudeep. (2015). Disaster management in India. *International Research Journal of Management Sociology & Humanities,6* (7)15-31. ISSN 2277 – 9809.

Sue, D. W., Bucceri, J., Lin, A. I., Nadal, K. L., & Torino, G. C. (2007). Racial microaggressions and the Asian American experience. *Cultural Diversity & Ethnic Minority Psychology, 13*(1) 72-81. http://dx.doi.org/10.1037/1099-9809.13.1.72.

Trippany, R. L., Kress, V. E. W., & Wilcoxon, S. A. (2004). Preventing vicarious trauma: What counselors should know when working with trauma survivors. *Journal of Counseling & development, 82*(1), 31-37. doi: 10.1002/j.1556-6678.2004.tb00283.x.

United Nations International Children's Education Fund-UNICEF. (2004). *What works for children in South Asia: Community health workers.* Retrieved from http://www.unicef.org/rosa/community.pdf.

Wong, F., & Halgin, R. (2006). The "model minority": Bane or blessing for Asian Americans?. *Journal of Multicultural Counseling and Development, 34*(1), 38-49. doi: 10.1002/j.2161-1912.2006.tb00025.x.

World Health Organization-WHO. (2013). *Assisting community health workers in India.* Retrieved from http://apps.who.int/iris/bitstream/10665/92802/1/WHO_RHR_13.18_eng.pdf.

Wu, E.D. (2015). *The Color of Success: Asian Americans and the Origins of the Model Minority.* Princeton University Press. Princeton, NJ.

Xu, B. & Albert, E. (2014). *Governance in India: Infrastructure.* Retrieved from http://www.cfr.org/india/governance-india-infrastructure/p32638.

Chapter Twenty-Three

Learning Not to Work Harder Than Your Clients

Alyson Pompeo-Fargnoli

As a novice counselor, I wanted all of my clients to be success stories. After all, if my client had great, groundbreaking changes in therapy, then that meant I was a good counselor. Or at least this is what I believed at the time. Reflecting back, these were the thoughts that were running through my head as a fresh new counselor, right out of my Master's program. Skovholt and Ronnestad (2003) have also noted this concerning belief of novice counselors, "...the beginning counselor/therapist is highly vulnerable. Professional self-worth closely coexists with client improvement" (p. 53). In addition, beginning counselors often have unrealistic expectations that if their client improves, it means they are a good counselor (Skovholt & Ronnestad, 2003).

When working with one client in particular, who I will call Lisa, I was working much harder than she was in the session—but I did not realize this at the time. With each session, Lisa came to me seeking more specific direction and advice. As much as I tried to support her working on developing her coping skills, self-reflection, and personal growth, these seemed to require too much effort on her part (as she actually told me once). She was the client who wanted that "quick fix." I would leave each session feeling mentally and emotionally exhausted. I also felt frustrated, but I could not figure out why. I liked this client and I genuinely wanted her to feel better but there seemed to be little progress resulting from our sessions.

Good training and previous supervision had taught me to listen to my feelings following sessions. These mentioned feelings of mental and emotional exhaustion and frustration were my trigger to self-reflect upon the sessions and situation. Such an event or catalyst which triggers the counselor's self-reflective process has been referred to in the literature as a causal

179

condition or trigger event (Holloway, 1982; Strauss & Corbin, 1990). Such a catalyst or trigger is also the first step to the Path of Counselor Self-Awareness, which outlines a route through aspects and requirements of counselor self-reflection to ultimately achieving counselor self-awareness (Pompeo & Levitt, 2014).

Through my own personal self-reflection I realized that I was associating Lisa's success with my own value as a counselor. This awareness was extremely important, as personal self-reflection can also lead to professional reflection (Griffith & Frieden, 2000). Through further self-reflection, consultation, and supervision, I began to understand that I was taking on all of the responsibility of the sessions and in many ways enabling her history of getting other people to just "fix her problems." This professional reflection helped me to realize that I was actually impeding her progress by enabling her problematic behavior.

Within my own supervision, I gained awareness as to why I was associating Lisa's progress with my competence as a counselor. I realized that for most of my own life, my accomplishments were measured by positive outcomes. For example, years of successful academia were measured by resulting positive grades. I had learned that if positive outcomes occurred, then I was successful. And, as many do, I had tied these feelings of success to confidence, self-esteem, and competence. As a result of this, I had been connecting being a good counselor to my clients' own positive success. I was falsely believing that being a "perfect" counselor meant that all of my clients were successful in counseling. Such realizations encouraged me to seek my own counseling and continued self-care. Learning that confidence in my ability as a counselor and lack of self-care can impact the session was a great lesson for me as a novice counselor. To this day, I am sure to set aside time for my own self-reflection, self-care, and personal counseling as needed. I strongly encourage this for all counselors, at all stages of their professional journey.

Being so honest with myself had allowed me to gain powerful self-awareness and to take the steps needed to work on myself. Therefore, I decided to also be honest with Lisa in hopes of using honesty in the counselor-client relationship as a catalyst for her own self-awareness and growth. I had an open discussion with Lisa about my perception of her lack of engagement in the therapeutic process. I was also open with her about how this lack of engagement in the sessions made me feel, including that while I wanted to help her and see her grow, I felt frustrated and at a loss for how to best help her given her resistance. I also spoke about her responsibility in the counseling process and that I did believe that she had the power to make changes in her life if she was ready to work hard and commit to it. This was a breakthrough moment for her. She said that people were never so honest with her about her responsibility to fix her own life and that this actually made her feel powerful to make changes. She was able to make associations between her level of participation in counseling and in other areas of her own life. She realized that she was the only thing holding herself back.

My own reflection and awareness had become a catalyst for Lisa's self-awareness. In line with this, it has been suggested that as the counselor chooses to self-reflect to promote professional growth, clients may be engaged in a parallel process of their own self-reflection (Pompeo & Levitt, 2014), as clients can experience challenges to personal growth (Skovholt & McCarthy, 1988). Through Lisa's own self-awareness, she was able to be more honest with herself and realize that she looked to others to alleviate her problems. Now, understanding her deeper issue, she was motivated to change. The session dynamics then changed as Lisa took on the more active role. I then comfortably facilitated and supported her progress. She made great strides and was able to use the counseling session as a microcosm to apply change to her own life and interactions with others. Yalom (2005) has alluded to this same microcosm phenomenon in which the counseling session can have parallel applicability to other relationships in the client's life, such as family, other relationships, and even society as a whole.

I often think back to my early career experience with Lisa. Through allowing myself to not be that "perfect" (in my mind at the time) counselor, I became a better counselor. Through my own self-reflection, I realized that my value as a counselor is not, and should not, be dependent on client success. Clients will make their own decisions and choose when they are ready to make changes in their lives. I needed to relinquish this misperception that I had some control in this. I grew to realize that not only is this up to the client to make changes and improvements, but this is an important personal growth journey that the client must walk. We can be there to support them, but they must lead. In a study of beginning counselors (Woodside, Oberman, Cole, & Currath, 2007), it was found that many of them believe that an important lesson to learn early on in the counseling profession is to empower clients with support and confidence to solve their own problems, or "help the client to help themselves" (p. 22). While it appears that novice counselors understand the importance of empowering clients to help themselves, bridging this with action may be more difficult.

Furthermore, I believe that many counselors are drawn to the profession because they want to help others and see them succeed. Therefore, I think many counselors have an innate desire to want to see our clients do well and positively progress. This counselor drive can be helpful at times, but harmful too if we are unaware of it. In attempts to strive for awareness, counselors may want to ask themselves, "Who wants the client to succeed more, me or the client?" The answer should always be that the client wants it more and wants to work for it. Otherwise, we as counselors (albeit with good intentions), walk a blurry and dangerous line of enabling and actually impeding client self-progress. Again, as many counselors have an innate drive and personality to want to help others, this may cause an internal conflict of what is actually the best way to help clients—by helping by doing, or by helping by stepping back. In this respect, it is also helpful to ask ourselves, "Who is working harder, me or the client?" We must not only encourage our clients to "do the work," but we also must be comfortable with trusting them to make the right decisions for themselves and their own growth. I have also heard novice counselors leave sessions noting, "that session was like pulling teeth." By this they mean that they are doing most of the work in the session and straining to get the client to take an active role. This type of structure is not only of little help to the client, but can also cause emotional strain, frustration, and burnout on the part of the counselor. Learning to encourage and allow clients to help themselves is an important piece of the professional development of beginning counselors. As Skovholt and Ronnestad (2003) noted in regards to the novice counselor, "professional development can be conceptualized as a self-other differentiation process where the counselor or therapist gradually increases in ability to differentiate client and practitioner responsibilities and to relate in functional ways" (p. 48).

All of this being said, through my experiences with Lisa I gained awareness of the importance of not working harder than my clients—supporting and encouraging them to make their own changes even if they may struggle is an important part of their growth process. I realized that my value and skill as a counselor is not dependent on my client's progress and that letting go of this idea of being a "perfect counselor" actually enables me to become a better counselor. No counselor is "perfect," and perfection does not equal competence. Furthermore, while there is much to be learned in the profession and a great value in research, often times I consider counseling more of an art than a science. Each counselor will bring a unique style and personality into the session, and true counselor growth is achieved through things such as experience, professional development, supervision, self-reflection, and self-awareness.

I also developed a greater appreciation for personal and professional self-reflection. I learned to trust my feelings, both positive and negative, in the session to be a trigger for self-reflection. I realized the importance of consultation and supervision in a counselor's professional growth. As do many other professionals in our field I believe that continual self-reflection is an ethical and professional obligation (Schmidt & Adkins, 2012). Looking back on challenges experienced during my counseling career, and what I learned from them, helps me to continually grow as a counselor and help my clients, counseling students, and supervisees.

REFERENCES

Griffith, B. & Frieden, G. (2000). Facilitating reflective thinking in counselor education. *Counselor Education and Supervision, 40,* 82–93. doi: 10.1002/j.1556–6978.2000.tb01240.x.

Holloway, E. L. *(1982). Interactional structure* of the supervision interview. *Journal of Counseling Psychology,* 29, 309–317. doi: doi.org/10.1037/0022–0167.29.3.309.

Pompeo, A., Levitt, D. (2014). A path of counselor self-awareness. *Counseling and Values, 59* (1), 80–94. doi: 10.1002/j.2161–007X.2014.00043.x.

Schmidt, C. & Adkins, C. (2012). Understanding, valuing, and teaching reflection in counselor education: A phenomenological inquiry. *Reflective Practice: International & Multidisciplinary Perspectives, 13,* 77–96. doi: 10.1080/14623943.2011.626024.

Skovholt, T. & McCarthy, P. R. (1988). Critical incidents: Catalysts for counselor development. *Journal of Counseling and Development, 67,* 69–72. doi: 10.1002/j.1556–6676.1988.tb02016.x.

Skovholt, T. M., & Ronnestad, M. H. (2003). Struggles of the novice counselor and therapist. *Journal of Career Development, 30* (1), 45–58. doi: doi: 10.1177/089484530303000103.

Strauss, A., & Corbin, J. (1990). *Basics of qualitative research.* Newbury Park, CA: Sage.

Woodside, M., Oberman, A. H., Cole, K. G., & Carruth, E. K. (2007). Learning to be a counselor: A prepracticum point of view. *Counselor Education and Supervision, 47*(1), 14–28. doi: 10.1002/j.1556–6978.2007.tb00035.x.

Yalom, I.D. (2005). *The Theory and Practice of Group Psychotherapy* (5th ed.). New York, NY: Basic Books.

Chapter Twenty-Four

To Walk in Humility

Lesson Learned in Indian Country

John Yasenchak

The Wabanaki tribes of the Northeast are comprised of several groups; Penobscot, Passamaquoddy, Maliseet, Micmac, and Abnaki. As a doctoral student in counselor education at the University of Maine during the 1990's, I noted that the Northeastern Tribes were not mentioned in many introductory textbook chapters on "multicultural counseling". Since the northeastern tribes were the first to encounter Europeans on this continent, my guess was that assimilation had caused this invisibility. I made a practice of writing to editors whose chapters on "Counseling Native Americans" failed to include the northeastern woodland tribes. But in addition to this large population not showing up in our textbooks, I also discovered that the Wabanaki people were also invisible to our counselor education students in a state where they often lived as neighbors.

My interest in "Indian Country" probably began when I was a young boy. I grew up in a Pennsylvania town named after a Lenape community that once lived in the region. Slate arrow heads could be found in the woods and among the piles of anthracite coal. During the annual "Indian Days" celebration, the townsfolk (all white) got to paint their faces red, dress in regalia, and dance in parades. Parents made "teepees" in their backyards while kids played toy drums. But there was not a "real" Indian anywhere in sight.

I always thought there was something more to be learned so as a college student, I applied for a summer work study position on the Pine Ridge Reservation in South Dakota. I had no knowledge of the Lakota people or their history. I knew nothing about great warriors like Red Cloud, Crazy Horse, and Sitting Bull. Although I had heard of both the first and second Wounded Knee, I really did not know (I mean really *know*) about the history, events, culture, the American Indian Movement, or the political issues (I may have seen 'Free Leonard Peltier' bumper stickers). At that time, I had only a vague sense of wanting to "work with Indians" that was, unbeknownst to me, coming from a place of White privilege that had not yet recognized in myself. I was sure "they" would be excited to receive me. But I received a letter back that told me I was not wanted if I could not commit to more than three months since short-term people seemed only interested in taking what they could learn rather than making a real contribution. Although I felt disappointed, I was vaguely aware of an invitation to really examine my motives and my intention. Who did I really want to serve? What did I really know? Subsequently, these questions grew deeper over the next several years.

Anyone who has hiked the Appalachian Trail from the beginning (or at the end depending on your perspective) knows the rugged beauty of Mount Kathadin. My first experience of the mountain was in 1988, the year before I moved to Maine for my doctoral program. While hiking in Baxter State Park, I was drawn into the mountain's energy and beauty and felt deeply "at home." I later discovered that Kathadin was the highest point on the east coast and received the first light of each morning. I learned that the Wabanaki, the "People of Dawnland" considered Kathadin to be the sacred home of the 'first person.' The beautiful Penobscot River flows from the Kathadin region and embraces a small tribal island that is the home of the Penobscot Indian Nation. In 1992 while still a doctoral student, I was hired as a counselor to be part of a multidisciplinary team at the tribal primary health care center (Indian Health Service facilities were practicing "integrated care" long before its popularity). For the next twenty years, I had the privilege of listening to stories and participating in the life of a community that both challenged and welcomed me.

In order to get to work, I had to cross over a bridge that connected the tribal island to the surrounding non-Native community. I saw the river change through its many seasons and was always moved by its beauty. Some days, an eagle would be sitting atop the tallest tree on the bank. I told a Native friend one day about how the river moved me, and the response was, "Of course! It's alive!" I soon found out that the community was like the river. Life flowed through the community in ways that were both familiar and new. As a counselor (and as a person) I found that, despite years of prior clinical experience, I had much to learn. I also thought I knew myself fairly well. But as a non-native professional working in a Native community, I had to let go of my dominant culture assumptions about what works in counseling. Tittles and degrees did not automatically provide credibility. Respect had to be earned. The counseling process itself did not operate according to linear goal-based treatment plans. Relational loyalty, both in families and the community, were most important even when there were challenges.

After several "interesting" encounters during my first few months on the job, I learned to "walk lightly" in my role. For example, one of my very first clients raged at me during the initial appointment because of my presence there as a "White man." Rather than react, I quietly listened and tried to show my willingness to understand. Over time, a strong therapeutic relationship developed as I learned to "hold the space" for these feelings. On other occasion while attending a community concerns gathering with about 50 people present, a tribal council member asked about my experience. I indicated that I would be happy to learn whatever I need to learn in order to work with Native Americans. Someone in the crowd yelled out, "Yeah, but would he be happy to work with Indians?" The entire room broke into loud laughter. As a result of these early experiences, I began to pay attention to what I called "critical incidents" (or "critical encounters") that occurred in the form of interpersonal encounters that not only changed how I did things as a counselor but also changed me as a person. These encounters created a deep emotional impact and began to shape my identity as both a cultural person and a professional counselor working across cultures. They resulted in my belief that counseling is a practice that cannot be abstracted, either by technique or in theory, from the culture in which it is embedded. Critical incidents shared with me by my clients, as well as those I myself experienced, taught me that mental health and social justice are one and the same.

CRITICAL INCIDENTS IN COUNSELOR DEVELOPMENT

The term "critical incident" often conjures up the image of an emergent crisis situation. This is an apt term for the incidents to which I am referring since they often *feel* like an emergency and often create a crisis of identity. Critical incidents in counselor development are interpersonal encounters (in this case, cross-cultural) where the ideas we use to construct meaning are challenged and often fall apart. This crisis situation throws us into a somewhat perilous transitional space where the task is to create a new understanding and perhaps a different way of doing things. Research on counselor development has provided tools for negotiating this transitional space through cognitive learning, skill development, and increased self-awareness (Furr & Carrol, 2003). But the critical incidents to which I refer are experiences primarily characterized by the word "felt"; they are deeply emotional experiences that changed my life as a counselor. Furr and Carroll (2003) defined a critical incident as a positive or negative experience recognized as significant because of its impact on counselor development. In regard to counselor supervision, Fukuyama (1994) defined a critical incident as a meaningful behavioral or emotional event that impacts the supervisee. In these and other definitions of critical incidents, the identified event or encounter has a deep emotional impact on the counselor. Learning can result from reflection on the encounter in the context of supervision (or the counselor's personal counseling). But the key is that the focus of a critical incident approach is on events that are a catalyst for change, rather than on the developmental nature of change. Critical incidents may indicate a turning point – or what I like to call a "conversion" – in the counselor's deeper understanding of themselves, others, and the counseling relationship. Over the course of my twenty years of work in Indian Country, the flow of life brought many surprises and I experienced countless "critical incidents." Some were small and others were large. Some made me laugh, and others made me cry. All of them made me change. The following are just a few examples of critical incidents that changed me as a counselor and a person during my work in Indian Country.

The Lodge Is My Home

I was raised in a small Northeastern Pennsylvania coal mining town during the 1960's. All four of my grandparents emigrated from the Carpathian Mountain Region of Slovakia. Arriving with their peers in the early 1900's, they brought their Eastern European culture, traditions, and identity. The Carpathian Ruthenians (as they are called) established a close community centered on family, religion and work. The "elders" were mostly non-English speaking. Most worked very hard in the coal mining industry and lived in what were once coal-company owned homes. The Byzantine church, built as an exact replica of the building left behind in Europe, was the center of just about everything. Melodious Old Slavonic chants and the sweet smell of incense filled the church and uplifted the spirit every Sunday. My parents encouraged my participation and taught me about "faith." Our beloved cantor taught me chants that were passed on from one generation to the next. Life could be hard in the coal region but I remember feeling proud as I stood with my hard working people every Sunday morning, allowing myself to be filled with both music and dignity.

Things began to change, however, during my adolescence. I began to distance myself from my community. The pop culture of the 1960's presented a different kind of music and my peers were not like the Slavic ethic family of my childhood. I became confused. I saw my friend's families as "modern" whereas "my people" were "old fashioned." My family's expectations for me began to conflict with an internal craving for an independent identity. I saw a counselor who helped me to explore an emerging sense of self. That encounter, as well as the pain of separation occurs when hammering out an identity, most likely propelled me into the counseling field. But as my childhood identity seemed to be falling apart, I was creating a new identity that involved a denial of my cultural roots. I distanced myself from my family and my cultural roots. A self-inflicted cultural wound occurred as a result of my physical and emotional "cut-off" from "home." The price of my new identity was a gnawing little spot of emptiness deep in my soul.

I was in my late thirties when I began working for the "People of the Dawnland." Many years had gone by and many changes had occurred since I had "left home." During those years, I rarely visited my home town and when I did, I felt uncomfortable walking those old familiar streets. But the critical encounters I experienced in my work as a tribal counselor challenged me to really look at myself. Initially bewildered by the anger that was sometimes directed toward me as a "White" counselor, I began to think about what "White" means in terms of both privilege and identity. I listened to my clients' tales about grandmothers and grandfathers. I heard about the importance of place, the land and the river, as home. Spirituality and feelings about the Creator were freely shared. I bore witness to racism's past and present day effects. I learned that in addition to post traumatic stress, people suffer from historical trauma that occurs when there is a cultural history of genocide and displacement from the homeland. Subsequently, my desire to know more about my clients and Native culture grew. And so did my desire to learn more about myself as a cultural person. My healing journey had begun.

Sometime during my first year of work I read a book by Carl A. Hammerschlag, M.D., entitled: The *Dancing Healers: A Doctors Journey of Healing With Native Americans* (1988). Hammerschlag, a western trained psychiatrist, relates his own story of transformation that occurred while working among the Southwest tribes. He describes encounters that not only surprised and perplexed him, but that also touched him on a deep emotional level. For example, one encounter occurred when he visited an elder traditional healer named Herman who was a patient in a hospital. He was introduced to Herman as "a doctor who knows about the mind." When Herman asked him, "What do you know about the mind?" Hammerschlag was stunned. He had never been asked that question. The healer went on to say that what he knew of the mind could be said in one word: "Mysterious."

Hammerschlag's "critical encounter" with Herman helped me to let go of "certainty" and open more to mystery. My client's revelations taught me that I did not did not know everything, nor was I the expert regarding their lives. My way of looking at things was not the only way. Additionally, I was deeply touched by Hammerschlag's own struggle with his identity. His work and relationships with his native clients continued to remind him of his old Jewish home. As a young man during the 1960's he rejected his roots and cultural traditions in search of better answers – "throwing out the baby with the bathwater." But while trying to raise his children as universal members of one tribe, humankind, he describes the following incident:

> Then one day the children decided they wanted to go to church with their friends in this very Catholic town (Santa Fe). I suddenly rediscovered the force

of my attachment to the old connection. This happened at the same time that I was learning another dance from the Pueblos and the power of their connections. The reality hit me: my children didn't know what they were. They didn't really know what it meant to be a Jew. I discovered that it mattered to me what they were, what I was. It was a connection of truth and one of credibility. This is my tribe. So we began going to the synagogue again. In the absence of our circuit-riding rabbi, I even filled in for him. (p., 145)

Hammerschlag continues to describe how he accepted and re-created his identity. He pulled together parts of himself that were rejected long ago and integrated them into a meaningful cultural identity. He found that by reclaiming his own identity, he was in a better position to appreciate "others" within the human family:

. . . I came to realize that you have to know who you are before you can become a universalist; it's what makes us each unique that lets us appreciate the universalities among us. It you can realize that your heritage is part of what makes you special, then you can realize that others are special too. (p. 146)

Shortly after my "critical encounter" with Hammerschlag through his book, I was invited to my first sweat lodge ceremony. The lodge is a low, dome shaped structure made of natural materials and covered so that it is completely dark inside. A pit in the middle of the lodge holds glowing hot rocks. The medicine leader pours water over the rocks creating a cleansing steam while prayers and songs are chanted by participants. Tentative at first, I gave myself over to the heat, the steam, and the prayers. While the leader prayed to the four directions, I thought of the Carpathian Ruthenian Byzantine church I had distanced myself from years earlier in my life. The structure of the sweat lodge and the church seemed similar. The Eastern direction is the direction of light. The ancestors and the saints are present, living just above the entrance. The smoke of incense and sweet grass filled the spirit. The songs and prayers in the lodge reminded me of the chants taught to me by our cantor. But most importantly, I experienced the presence of my grandparents in that sweat lodge. The sacrifices they made, the struggles they endured, and the love they passed on to my parents and me appeared to me in a way I had never before experienced. From that day forward, I decided to heal the cultural wound I had created in myself and to more thoroughly explore my cultural identity. I began to appreciate the gifts of my ancestry which in turn helped me to appreciate the culture in which I was now working.

As relationships with tribal colleagues deepened, so did my relations with my own family. I began to "go home" more frequently. Like my clients, my father enjoyed telling stories about "the old days." I began to listen more attentively. Both my maternal and paternal grandparents had died long ago, but Dad regularly visited the "ancestral" cemetery and offered prayers. I accompanied him there on one visit home and watched him slowly walk toward my grandparents graves. I wanted to stand by his side and pray with him, but years of painful distance made this desire a struggle. But I remembered the sweat lodge and found the courage to walk over to him. Placing my arm around his shoulder I recited the "Our Father" with him in Slavonic, the language of my grandparents. When finished, he turned to me and said, "This is the best visit we've ever had." A cultural wound was healed in me that day. My father's blessing, which I was able to accept, initiated a period of conducting what I called my personal "cultural archeology." I subsequently learned more about my ancestors and my own cultural heritage and began to visit "home" more often. My sweat lodge was my home. I began to appreciate more deeply my own culture and subsequently the culture in which I was working as a professional counselor.

This Is Not the Way Our People Do Things

While working for the tribes, I regularly travelled to Native American Mental Health conferences attended by people from all over Indian Country. Early in my career, I submitted a proposal to present at a Native Spirituality and Wellness Conference in Tucson. The proposed presentation was entitled "Multicultural Awareness in Counselor Development" and my intention was to share my cross-cultural experience and received feedback from Native participants. In particular, I wanted to share what I had learned about my own cultural history through my work and how my cultural healing impacted my relationship with my Native clients.

I was surprised to hear that my proposal was accepted and I assumed (again) that I would be warmly received. Upon arrival at the conference, I was expected to present twice on that same day and also, I was one of the few White people attending among several hundred Native attendees. My morning session included about 25 participants who were mostly silent. I learned that the participants were from a variety of small Southwest pueblo communities and, to my surprise, spoke different languages. I had not anticipated this between-group difference. I began my session and distributed a paper handout that I hoped would engage the participants in conversation. I often used a handout in order to engage students in the counselor education classes I was teaching at the time. As I began to tell what I thought was my compelling life story, a tall Lakota young man from Pine Ridge with long hair and a very angry expression stood up, crumbled my handout into a ball, threw it on the floor and glaringly said, "This is not the way our people do things." He, along with two companions, stormed out of the room. The remaining group silently watched expressionless as, with voice trembling, I continued on with my story.

Needless to say, I was not looking forward to repeating my presentation in the afternoon session. Clearly my usual method of teaching did not work during the morning. Clearly no one was interested in my cultural story. Clearly I was another "White man telling us how to do things." But during lunch, I fortunately ran into a Wabanaki friend from home who was a traditional healer. I said, "Hey Frank, can you help me out here?" Frank suggested presenting the afternoon session as a "talking circle." I asked him if he would be willing to open the session with a ceremony and he agreed. Frank began the afternoon "talking circle" with a prayer and smudge ceremony and, to my surprise language was suddenly no longer a problem. I told my story of what it was like for me being a "white guy" working in Indian Country. The participants told me what it was like being "Indian" working and living in a society where "White" is dominant. There was mutual respect and listening in all directions and I was deeply touched. The circle was closed and the connections felt strong. Frank's ceremony made all the difference in the world.

This critical incident taught me a lot about between-group and within-group differences as we talk about them in multiculturalism. I assumed that my audience would be a homogeneous group because everyone was Native American. Wrong. But more importantly, the young angry Lakota did me a big favor, as painful as it was, and awakened me. At that time, I knew only a little more about the great Sioux nations than I did when I celebrated "Indian Days" as a kid. The man's family and perhaps he himself may have been around Pine Ridge during the difficult Wounded Knee days in the 1970's when conflict with the federal government broke out over a long history of violated treaties. I liked to think of myself as a humble person, but he must have thought of me as yet another pretentious White man. But the discomfort I felt over the interaction – actually, the pain I felt – was the beginning of a more respectful humility. I was on sacred ground.

What Do You Think I've Been Talking About for the Last Two Hours

When attending yet another large Indian Mental Health Conference in the Southwest, I encountered another young man who was an Indian Health Service clinical counselor by day and a Navajo Blessing Way chanter by night. Again, there were several hundred Native participants and only a handful of non-Natives attending. The conference opened on a contentious note since many tribes had been claiming their right to manage their own health care funding in their own way, much to the dismay of the Indian Health Service Officials (who ironically always appeared in their military-like public service uniforms). The Blessing Way Chanter opened the conference with a prayerful song that reminded me of the traditional Carpathian Ruthenia chants I learned as a young man. When I heard that he would be doing a two hour presentation on the Navajo Blessing Way, I decided to attend.

By the time of this conference, I traveled to such events in Indian Country with a clear intention to learn something about which I knew nothing. This time I wanted to ask as many Native people as possible what it means to "Walk in Beauty." "Beauty before me, beauty behind me, beauty above and beauty beneath me" . . . what did that mean. I carried my intention and question to the Blessing Way Chanter's presentation. There were about 50 people in the room. I was the only "White" person. The Blessing Way Chanter told stories about the "*Dine*," the First People. He talked about how his ancestors emerged from the earth and he drew complex diagrams representing Navajo cosmology and history. He defined mental health as connection to the earth, the ancestors, and the community. Depression is a disruption in those sacred connections. He described how he would work the DSM during the week at the Indian Health Service Clinic, and how on weekends he would visit the hogans (homes) of elders who were depressed, continuously chanting from the Blessing Way until all connections had been restored.

At the end of his talk, the Blessing Way Chanter asked, "Are there any questions?" The room was quiet. Slowly and tentatively, I raised my hand. He recognized me and I asked, "Can you tell me what it means to "Walk in Beauty?" The silence was probably only a few seconds but it seemed to go on forever. I felt my face turning red. Finally, the Blessing Way Chanter said to me, "What do you think I have been talking about for the last two hours." The room burst into hearty Indian laughter as I sank under my seat. But when the session ended, many of the participants greeted me with a hug and the familiar Indian handshake. People were not laughing at me as much as at the situation which was funny in a twisted sort of way. After all, now it was the "white guy" who was in the "minority" position asking a question "in class" that had such a clear answer. I thought of my Native clients back home who told me humiliating stories about how their university professors often singled them out in history classes. But now the tables were turned. It was funny. And it was beautiful. I learned, from this incident, a little more of what it means to lightly "Walk in Beauty." But I also learned a little more about what it means to walk in humility as a cross-cultural counselor.

"I Don't Want Her Talking about That – We've Had Thirty Years of Peace!"

The community where I worked has an elementary and middle school, but does not have a high school. Instead, the tribal youth attended a non-Indian public school in the larger mostly White community on the other side of side of river. At that time, the high school mascot was an image of an Indian wearing a southwest headdress—a headdress not even indigenous to the local

Native community. As a counselor, I worked with native youth who experienced the stigmatizing effect of the mascot, both in the classroom and on sports fields. Drop-out rates were high and my colleagues and I believed this was due, in part, to the stigmatization.

One day, the school referred a 16 year old tribal girl to me for counseling. This young sophomore was having some academic difficulties in school. Her difficulties were compounded when she, along with several of her native classmates, refused to participate in the "pledge of alliance" to the American flag. This refusal was a protest of the mascot. As the students struggled with how to be Native in the middle of a large and mostly White community, they were also becoming more aware of the political movements within Indian Country. One thing led to another and the young women referred for counseling showed up at my office with a school psychologists' diagnosis of Oppositional Defiant Behavior Disorder (rule out political conflict and racism).

The girl came in for the appointment with her grandmother. Both sat across from me as I tried to engage the student in a conversation. I asked about her classwork, activities, and her relationships with peers. We talked about study habits and suggestions for improving her grades. Her grandmother listened with quiet approval. Finally, I asked her about the incident that precipitated the referral. "Tell me about turning your back on the flag." At that point, her grandmother suddenly leaned forward, reached across, and covered her granddaughter's mouth with her hand. "I don't want her talking about that . . . we've had 30 years of peace around here…I don't want her doing that."

This incident was a striking example of both the impact and transmission of historical trauma. As a tribal counselor, I heard many elders talk about the impact of racism on their lives. Some would identify themselves as from Mediterranean descent rather than Native when seeking employment. Others talked of name calling and beatings that sometimes occurred when they went "to town" as kids. As a counselor, I watched the current generation struggle with their identity, growing in pride and knowledge of their Native history while at the same time trying to adapt to the dominant culture. Students seemed to go through various phases of anger, acceptance, and integration. As they learned to re-write their histories from a Native perspective, the "mascot issue" became more pronounced as a form of racism that imposed yet another media identity for the sake of dominant culture entertainment. But that grandmother only remembered how it was for her when she was her granddaughter's age, and she most definitely did not want the girl to have the same experience. Her gesture, to me, was a powerful symbol of how the experience of the past can impact the present, and how traumatic memories can be passed from one generation to the next in a very tangible way, with the touch of a hand.

MENTAL HEALTH IS SOCIAL JUSTICE

The above critical incidents as well as many others over the course of 20 years had a deep and lasting impact on my "self" and my philosophy of counseling. Initial encounters with my clients and the community in which I worked propelled me towards my own cultural healing. I came to know the cultural parts of myself that I buried long ago and became more comfortable. That in turn helped me in my work with others who were struggling with their own cultural identities. I learned through experience that some of what I had been taught in my counselor training did not really work all that well in Indian Country. I discovered hidden assumptions in my early work like "our way is THE way" and "THIS technique works everywhere" and "WE have a lot to give you." Mostly I learned to "walk in humility" through encounters with people who taught me how to listen quietly, how to respect the experience and gifts of another culture, how to acknowledge the impact of racism and historical trauma, how to hold spirituality and moments of life together, and finally, how to laugh at myself and silly situations where the "White guy" (as I was called) is the not-so-privileged minority.

I am still learning. I recently read two books. In *The Heart of Everything That Is*, Bob Drury and Tom Clavin (2013) tell the story of Red Cloud, the great Oglala Lakota Chief. Red Cloud's leadership of the Sioux through battles that were the result of "the trail of broken treaties" ultimately led to victory against the United States Army. This victory, however, was short-lived with the gradual encroachment of United States technology (the steam locomotive), the continued takeover of land, and the gradual removal of people to reservations. Moved by the story, I Googled Red Cloud's name and saw online a photo of his humble gravesite atop a hill on the Pine Ridge Reservation. Why is there not a large monument in honor of this great warrior and other Native heroes in Washington DC? The other book was Peter Matthiessen's *In The Spirit of Crazy Horse* (1992*)*. This book and others like it (Dee Brown's 1970's *Bury My Heart At Wounded Knee*) have been around for many years. But reading the story now of what happened at Pine Ridge during the 1970's reminds me of that young man at the conference. I will never forget his face. I learned so much from that encounter. I will also never forget my grandparents and my family, the cantor, and what *my* elders taught me. I have come to believe that the people who come before me when I am in my role as a counselor are not problems to be solved but are ever-unfolding mysteries to be appreciated and respected. Life does not always flow like a linear treatment plan. I am still learning.

As I continued to work as a counselor and prepare for my counselor education degree, I noticed that my experience resembled some of what was being talked about in the field of multicultural counseling. I was learning about a culture different from my own by listening to stories told by my clients and colleagues. I was also learning about what worked and what did not work in cross-cultural counseling through critical encounters like those I have described here. And finally, I discovered through critical encounters with authors like Carl Hammerschlag (1988) and encounters in my relationships that the most important factor was to know and accept myself. I learned that the degree to which I was comfortable in my own cultural skin was related to the degree to which my clients were comfortable with me. These three themes – cultural knowledge, culturally appropriate techniques, and most importantly self-knowledge –were beginning to be studied by the profession in a variety of ways (Wing Sue, Arrendondo, & McDavis, 1992). As a person, the critical incidents and encounters I experienced helped me to connect with my home. As a professional counselor, they taught me that mental health and social justice are one in the same and can never be separated. This is a conviction that I bring to my teaching as a counselor educator today. I will always be grateful for each and every "critical incident" I experienced in Indian Country and for the friendships I experienced there, as well as for the gifts I received from my own people.

REFERENCES

Drury, B & Clavin, T. (2013). *The heart of everything that is: The untold story of Red Cloud, an American legend.* New York, NY: Simon & Schuster.

Ellis, M. V. (1991). Critical incidents in clinical supervision and in supervisor supervision: Assessing supervisory issues. *Journal of Counseling Psychology, 38*, 342-349. doi: doi.org/10.1037/1931-3918.S.2.122.

Fukuyama, M. (1994). Critical incidents in multicultural supervision: A phenomenological approach to supervision research. *Counselor Education and Supervision, 34*, 142-151. doi: 10.1002/j.1556-6978.1994.tb00321.x.

Furr, S. R., & Caroll, J. J. (2003). Critical incidents in student counselor development. *Journal of Counseling and Development, 81*, 483-486. doi: 10.1002/j.1556-6678.2003.tb00275.x.

Hammerschlag, C.A. (1988). The dancing healers. San Francisco, CA: Harper & Row.

Matthiessen, P. (1992). In the spirit of Crazy Horse. New York, NY: Penguin Books.

Wing Sue, D., Arrendondo, P., & McDavis, R. J. (1992). Multicultural competencies and standards: A call to the profession. *Journal of Counseling and Development, 70*, 477-486. doi: 10.1002/j.1556-6676.1992.tb01642.x.

About the Authors

ARCURI, NICOLE M.

Nicole M. Arcuri, Ph.D., is a Counselor Educator and Supervisor doctoral adjunct faculty member at Capella University and Lock Haven University of Pennsylvania. Nicole is an Approved Clinical Supervisor, Licensed Professional Counselor, Nationally Certified Counselor, Distance Credentialed Counselor, Substance Awareness Coordinator, as well as a Certified School Counselor. Currently, Nicole serves her community as a Military Liaison District Counselor. In her free time she loves to practice in such self-care as jogging, yoga, relaxing on the beach, and spending time with friends and family.

BAKER, RIA E.

Ria E. Baker, Ph.D., LPC-S, a graduate of the University of Texas at San Antonio, has over 15 years of experience working in clinical, community, ministry, and university settings addressing various mental health and social service needs of diverse populations. She has served as adjunct faculty at the University of Texas at San Antonio, Texas A & M San Antonio, and Walden University. Ria takes an active role in addressing the needs of refugees resettled in Texas and has established a non-profit organization, namely the Center for Refugee Services, in San Antonio, Texas. She is currently an Assistant Professor of Counselor Education at the Houston Graduate School of Theology.

COLISTRA, ANGELA

Dr. Angela Colistra is an Assistant Clinical Professor in the Behavioral Health Counseling Department at Drexel University. She holds a Ph.D. in Counselor Education and Supervision from the University of North Carolina at Charlotte. Dr. Colistra is a Licensed Professional Counselor, a Certified Advanced Alcohol and Drug Abuse Counselor, and a Certified Clinical Supervisor in North Carolina and Pennsylvania. Her work in Kathmandu, Nepal and Beijing, China, under the direction of the late Dr. David Powell, focused on the training and certification of the substance use disorder workforce and gained her recognition from the United States Embassy. Dr. Colistra provides clinical services to adults and adolescents treating those managing co-occurring disorders. Dr. Colistra worked in a variety of treatment settings, which included in-patient, out-patient, intensive outpatient, intake, and psychiatric units as well as extensive experience providing clinical supervision to professionals and students within the counseling and substance use disorder professions. She is published in the areas of cultural competence for clinical supervisors, addiction related cognitive impairment, and best practices for adolescent addiction treatment.

DAVIS, ERIC S.

Dr. Eric S. Davis is a counselor educator in the Counseling and School Psychology department at the University of Nebraska, Kearney. Eric entered the profession as a school counselor for 4 years at the high school level before earning his Ph.D. in Counselor Education at the University of Florida. He has been a counselor educator for 5 years with an interest in school counseling pedagogy, play therapy, illness-related trauma, creative counseling, and education techniques. Eric lives in Kearney, Nebraska with his wife, Amanda, and daughter, Annalie.

DAWSON-FEND, LAURA

Dr. Laura Dawson-Fend Ph.D., LPCC, is an Assistant Professor of Counseling at Eastern New Mexico University, Portales, NM. with research interests in human trafficking, gender violence, rape culture, and military issues. Dr. Dawson-Fend graduated from Texas Tech University with her doctorate in Counselor Education and Supervision. Dr. Dawson-Fend is the mother of a beautiful and smart 21-month old little girl Emmalyn.

DUNBAR DAVISON, KELLY

Dr. Kelly Dunbar Davison earned her Ph.D. in Counselor Education & Supervision from The University of Arkansas and her M.S. in Counseling Psychology from Northeastern State University. Dr. Dunbar Davison studied Art Therapy at the University of Oklahoma. She is a Licensed Professional Counselor and board approved supervisor in Oklahoma. Additionally, she is a Nationally Certified Counselor, and a Certified PreK-12 School Counselor in Oklahoma. Dr. Dunbar Davison has experience providing counseling for individuals of all ages, groups, and families. She has provided consultation to universities, community mental health agencies, and individual professionals. She is currently a Core Faculty member at Walden University in the MS in Clinical Mental Health Program.

EDWARDS, CHARLES C.

Charles C. Edwards holds a Ph.D. in Counselor Education and Supervision from Oregon State University. He holds graduate degrees in political philosophy and school counseling from Brooklyn College and The University of the West Indies, Jamaica, respectively. Dr. Edwards has over 15 years of experience working as a teacher, a school counselor and counselor educator. He is employed as an Assistant Professor of School Counseling at Brooklyn College, City University of New York. His research focuses on school counselor effectiveness in supporting students' academic, personal-social and career development within urban school systems and communities.

FALL, KEVIN A.

Kevin A. Fall, Ph.D., is Professor and Program Coordinator in the Professional Counseling Program at Texas State University. He has co-authored books on group counseling: *Group Counseling: Concepts and Procedures, Alternatives to Domestic Violence, Choosing Nonviolence, and Modern Applications to Group Work;* counseling theory: *Theoretical Models of Counseling and Psychotherapy,* and advanced clinical training: *Translating Theory into Practice.* He has published numerous journal articles and book chapters and presented nationally on the topics of domestic violence, group counseling, Adlerian theory, and clinical supervision. Dr. Fall is a Licensed Professional Counselor and maintains a small private practice in Austin, TX.

FLORES LOCKE, ANNA

Not only am I a Latina doctoral student in counselor education, I am also a mother of three-year-old twins, a wife, a daughter, and a licensed professional counselor with 10 years of experience as a mental health community counselor. I identify as a multicultural, social justice counselor who advocates for the rights of all counselors. I am the student representative on the board of Counselors for Social Justice (CSJ) division of the American Counseling Association (ACA), a 2014 recipient of the emerging leader award of the North Atlantic Region Association for Counselor Educators and Supervisors (NARACES), and a member of the Association for Multicultural Counseling and Development (AMCD) and the New Jersey Counseling Association (NJCA).

GREEN, LEIGH ANNE

Dr. Leigh Anne Green, LPC, NCC is an Assistant Professor of Counseling at West Texas A&M University, Canyon, TX. Dr. Green is in her third year as a professor at West Texas A&M University, with research interests in veterans including PTSD, MTBI, transition to civilian and university life, and women particularly rape culture and infertility issues. Dr. Green graduated from Texas Tech University with her doctorate in Counselor Education and Supervision.

HARRIS, SHAYWANNA

Shaywanna Harris is currently a doctoral student in the Counselor Education program at the University of Central Florida. She received her master's degree in Marriage and Family Therapy from the University of Akron and her research interests include adverse experiences in childhood, neurocounseling, and neurofeedback in counseling.

HINOJOSA, TAMARA

Tamara Hinojosa earned her bachelor's degree in education from the University of Texas at Austin and earned her master's and doctorate degrees in counseling at Penn State University. She has worked in higher education since 2004 and has worked in community mental health with a focus on academic advising, career counseling, women's issues, and crisis intervention counseling. Her research interests incorporate gender issues, identity development, and exploring innovative counselor training techniques.

HEADLEY, JESSICA ANN

Jessica Ann Headley is a doctoral candidate in the Counselor Education and Supervision Program at The University of Akron. She is also a Licensed Professional Counselor in the state of Ohio. Her dissertation, inspired from her own experience as a protégé, is focused on the role of mentoring in facilitating leadership development among women counselor educators. Headley has also presented and published on mentoring among graduate students and new professionals to promote their career satisfaction and success.

HODES, JACQUELINE S.

Jacqueline S. Hodes is an Assistant Professor in the Department of Counselor Education at West Chester University. She is the coordinator for the higher education counseling/student affairs graduate program in the department. Previous to her work as a faculty member, she worked in student affairs for 26 years in a variety of roles including LGBTQA Services, Wellness Education, Orientation, Fundraising and Development, Paraprofessional Supervision and Student Learning Outcomes Assessment. Her scholarship includes understanding best practices in graduate student education, strengths-based education and creating change in higher education.

JOHNSON, VERONICA I.

Dr. Veronica I. Johnson is an Assistant Professor in the Department of Counselor Education at the University of Montana. Her degrees were earned at the University of Montana. After graduation, Veronica taught for 5 years at Winona State University before returning home to Montana. Her teaching interests include intimate relationship development and maintenance, research methods for counselors, and professional ethics. Her research revolves around intimate relationship issues and clinical supervision. Veronica is passionate about promoting healthy intimate relationships, and has completed training in Gottman Method couples therapy, levels I and II. In her free time, Veronica enjoys spending time with her family, camping, and playing Scrabble.

KRAFCIK, DREW

Drew Krafcik, Ph.D., is an Assistant Professor in the Counseling Department at Saint Mary's College of California. He is the Interim Coordinator of the Marriage and Family Therapy/Professional Clinical Counselor (MFT/PCC) specialization. He teaches counseling older adults and their families, advanced clinical practice, human development and family relationships, and field placement seminar. Previously, he taught courses at Stanford University. Drew has worked professionally in hospice, as a counselor and mentor for adolescents and young adults, as the associate director of youth and family programs, and as a psychotherapist in community nonprofits and private practice. Drew holds a doctoral degree in Clinical Psychology and master's degrees in Pastoral Care and Counseling and Psychology. His research interests include the integration of psychotherapy and spirituality, aging well, contemplative pedagogy, counselor education and mentoring, and the development of wisdom across the lifespan. He can be reached at aek3@stmarys-ca.edu.

LAND, CHRISTY W.

Dr. Land is in her twelfth year as a professional school counselor. She currently works in a middle school setting but also has extensive experience at the elementary school level. Dr. Land also maintains a small private practice, where her work focuses on clients through counseling, consultation, and supervision. Her areas of expertise include bullying prevention, stress and anxiety management with children/adolescents, group counseling, and supervision. As a counselor Dr. Land recognizes the unique position she holds and works to advocate for equity, access, and success for all of her students and clients.

MEYER, GREG A.

Dr. Greg A. Meyer is an Assistant Professor of Psychology and Counseling at Northeastern State University in Broken Arrow, Oklahoma. He earned a Ph.D. in Counselor Education and Supervision from Auburn University. He has worked in Kansas, Nebraska, Georgia, New Mexico, and Alabama, in various community mental health clinics, hospitals, group homes as well as private practice. He is a full-time educator and supervisor of graduate-level counselors-in-training.

MOSS, LAUREN J.

Dr. Moss is an Assistant Professor at Kutztown University in the Counseling and Student Affairs Department. She has extensive experience in the public school setting at the middle school level, both as a professional school counselor and special educator. Her professional experiences working with diverse populations have led her to research interests which include: group work, bullying prevention, social justice, and advocacy. Dr. Moss prides herself in working as a change agent for the field of counseling, particularly in the school setting, to best support and advocate for/with all clients.

NAGARAJAN, SUDHA

Sudha Nagarajan is currently a doctoral candidate at Montclair State University in the Ph.D. program in Counseling. She is a Licensed Professional Counselor in New Jersey, as well as a National Certified Counselor, Approved Clinical Supervisor, and Certified Diversity Professional. Her clinical experience pertains to working with adults with chronic mental illness and related challenges affecting physical, emotional and social wellbeing. She is actively involved with volunteerism and community outreach efforts to educate and advocate for mental health among the South Asian community through her affiliation with NAMI-NJ. Besides her dedication to the development of cultural competency among the professional community, her research interests extend to diversity and inclusion in the workplace, and acculturation experiences of globally mobile employees.

POMPEO-FARGNOLI, ALYSON, PH.D., LPC, SAC, NCC

Dr. Alyson Pompeo-Fargnoli is an Assistant Professor in the School of Education, Department of Speech Pathology, Educational Counseling and Leadership, at Monmouth University in West Long Branch, NJ. She earned her Ph.D. in Counselor Education, specializing in College Counseling Directorship and Substance Abuse/Addictions Counseling, from Montclair State University. She holds an MA in Counselor Education and a BA in Psychology from The College of NJ. She is a Licensed Professional Counselor (LPC), a National Certified Counselor (NCC), and holds a Substance Abuse/Addictions Counselor certificate. She has presented and published on topics including mental health stigma, college students and substance use, counseling college women, ecotherapy, and counselor ethics.

SANGGANJANAVANICH, VARUNEE FAII

Dr. Varunee Faii Sangganjanavanich is an Associate Professor in the School of Counseling at The University of Akron where she currently serves as a Coordinator of the Counselor Education and Supervision doctoral program. As a counselor educator, Sangganjanavanich has mentored graduate students with diverse backgrounds to facilitate their professional growth and development. Sangganjanavanich is also a Licensed Professional Clinical Counselor with supervisor endorsement in the state of Ohio. Sangganjanavanich has authored and coauthored numerous peer-reviewed journal articles, book chapters, and encyclopedia entries on counseling, supervision, and counselor preparation.

SMITH, ANGIE

Dr. Angie Smith is a Teaching Assistant Professor, Licensed Professional Counselor (LPC) and Supervisor (LPC-S) in Raleigh, North Carolina. Angie has spent the past 6 years as a Teaching Assistant Professor at North Carolina State University (NCSU). Her experience as well as research and teaching interests include career counseling and development, online teaching and learning modalities, supervision in counseling, and college counseling. Currently, she teaches courses for the Graduate Certificate in Counselor Education (GCCE) online program and master and doctoral level courses on-campus within the Counselor Education program at NCSU.

THOMPSON, LAURA

Laura Thompson, Ph.D., LPC, NCC, has worked with students in university settings, both nationally and internationally, since 1994. She earned her Master's Degree in Counseling and Educational Psychology with an emphasis in College Student Development from the University of Nevada, Reno, and her Doctorate in Counseling and Counselor Education from Syracuse University. While at Syracuse, Laura also completed a Certificate of Advanced Studies in Addiction Studies. Laura is currently working as a Counselor at Regis University in Denver. Prior to coming to Denver, she spent three years working part-time in the Counseling Center at Syracuse University. Laura's clinical and research interests include college student mental health, addiction and recovery, mindfulness, and intercultural adjustment.

WARREN, JANE, PH.D., LPC, LMFT, LAT

Jane Warren is an Associate Professor in Counselor Education. From 1985 through 2007, she was employed as a counselor, supervisor, and agency director for a Wyoming community mental health center working with both mental health and substance abuse challenges. From 2000 through 2008, she also served in the Wyoming State Legislature as a member of the House. In that role, she was successful with such legislation as changes in the ethics codes for practitioners, DUI assessments, voting rights for persons with felonies, and enhanced funding for mental health services. In 2007 she became a full time faculty member at the University of Wyoming.

WOLF, CHERYL P.

Cheryl P. Wolf, Ph.D., NCC, LPCA, GCDF, PHR, CHT is an Assistant Professor at Western Kentucky University where she teaches and coordinates the clinical practicum and internship programs. She also supervises graduate counseling students in working with international refugees who are adapting to their new communities through several funded grant projects. Her research interests revolve around overall wellness including career meaning, counselor self-care, and diversity issues like multicultural spirituality and working with refugees. Select publications on diversity include co-authorship of several book chapters: "Exploring the Intersections of Religion and Spirituality with Race-Ethnicity" and "Gender in Counseling and Religion and Spirituality" and peer-reviewed journal articles: "Integrating Religion and Spirituality into Counselor Education: Barriers and Strategies."

YASENCHAK, JOHN

John Yasenchak, Ed.D., LCPC, is Associate Professor in the Graduate Counseling and Human Relations Program, Husson University, Bangor Maine. He is also a Maine Licensed Clinical Counselor, Licensed Substance Abuse Counselor, and Certified Clinical Supervisor. For twenty years John served as clinical supervisor for the Penobscot Indian Nation Counseling Services and was Adjunct Assistant Professor in Counselor Education at the University of Maine. In addition to his doctorate in counselor education, John also holds an MA in Philosophy from Fordham University. He taught philosophy at Loyola University in Baltimore for several years and trained in both pastoral ministry. John is Past-President of the Maine Counseling Association and Chair for the North Atlantic Region of the American Counseling Association.